AMERICAN HISTORY BY ERA

The Cold War Period: 1945–1992

VOLUME 8

Other titles in the
American History by Era series:

AMERICAN HISTORY BY ERA

The Cold War Period: 1945–1992

VOLUME 8

Leora Maltz, *Book Editor*

Daniel Leone, *President*
Bonnie Szumski, *Publisher*
Scott Barbour, *Managing Editor*

GREENHAVEN
PRESS®

THOMSON
™
GALE

San Diego • Detroit • New York • San Francisco • Cleveland
New Haven, Conn. • Waterville, Maine • London • Munich

THOMSON
———✦——— ™
GALE

Cover credit: © David Turnley/CORBIS

Library of Congress, 33, 78, 152
National Aeronautics and Space Administration, 106
National Archives, 99
U.S. Department of Agriculture, 186

Cover inset photo credits (from left): Planet Art; Corel; Digital Stock; Corel; Library of
Congress; Library of Congress; Digital Stock; Painet/Garry Rissman

LIBRARY OF CONGRESS CATALOGING-IN-PUBLICATION DATA
The Cold War period: 1945–1992 / Leora Maltz, book editor.
p. cm. — (American history by era; vol. 8)
Includes bibliographical references and index.
ISBN 0-7377-1146-9 (lib. : alk. paper) — ISBN 0-7377-1145-0 (pbk. : alk. paper)
1. United States—History—1945– . 2. Cold War. I. Maltz, Leora. II. Series.
E742 .C7 2003
973.92—dc21   2002066465

Printed in the United States of America

CONTENTS

satellite elicited widespread panic among many Americans and contributed to cold war tensions.

Chapter 2: Cold War Culture: The 1950s

Chapter 3: The Cold War Heats Up: 1960–1969

ented administration, which began the 1960s on a
note of hope and promise.

Chapter 4: Resistance, Reactions, and Riots: The 1960s

tween the environmental movement and the emergent movement in consumer consciousness.

Chapter 6: Reagan, Gorbachev, and the End of the Cold War: 1980–1992

The official congressional report reveals that President Reagan and his advisers repeatedly concealed information and ignored congressional procedures.

During the sixteenth century, events occurred in North America that would change the course of American history. In 1512, Spanish explorer Juan Ponce de León led the first European expedition to Florida. French navigator Jean Ribault established the first French colony in America at Fort Caroline in 1564. Over a decade later, in 1579, English pirate Francis Drake landed near San Francisco and claimed the country for England.

These three seemingly random events happened in different decades, occurred in various regions of America, and involved three different European nations. However, each discrete occurrence was part of a larger movement for European dominance over the New World. During the sixteenth century, Spain, France, and England vied for control of what was later to become the United States. Each nation was to leave behind a legacy that would shape the political structure, language, culture, and customs of the American people.

Examining such seemingly disparate events in tandem can help to emphasize the connections between them and generate an appreciation for the larger global forces of which they were a part. Greenhaven Press's American History by Era series provides students with a unique tool for examining American history in a way that allows them to see such connections. This series divides American history—from the time that the first people arrived in the New World from Asia to the September 11 terrorist attacks—into nine discrete periods. Each volume then presents a collection of both primary and secondary documents that describe the major events of the period in chronological order. This structure provides students with a snapshot of events occurring simultaneously in all parts of America. The reader can then gain an appreciation for the political, social, and cultural movements and trends that shaped the nation. Students reading about the adventures of individual European explorers, for instance, are invited to consider how such expeditions compared in purpose and consequence to earlier and later expeditions. Rather than simply learning that Ponce de León was the first Spaniard to try to colonize Florida, for example, students can begin to understand his expedition in a larger context. Indeed, Ponce's voyage was an extension of Spain's desire to conquer the Caribbean and Mexico, and his expedition was to inspire other Spanish explorers to head north from Hispaniola and New Spain in search of rich empires to conquer.

Another benefit of studying eras is that students can view a "snapshot" of America at any given moment of time and see the various social, cultural, and political events that occurred simultaneously. For example, during the period between 1920 and 1945, Charles Lindbergh became the first to make a solo transatlantic flight, Babe Ruth broke the record for the most home runs in one season, and the United States dropped the atomic bomb on Hiroshima. Random events occurring in post–Cold War America included the torching of the Branch Davidian compound in Waco, Texas, the emergence of the World Wide Web, and the 2000 presidential election debacle in which ballot miscounts in Florida held up election results for weeks.

Each volume in this series offers features to enhance students' understanding of the era of American history under discussion. An introductory essay provides an overview of the period, supplying essential context for the readings that follow. An annotated table of contents highlights the main point of each selection. A more in-depth introduction precedes each document, placing it in its particular historical context and offering biographical information about the author. A thorough chronology and index allow students to quickly reference specific events and dates. Finally, a bibliography opens up additional avenues of research. These features help to make the American History by Era series an extremely valuable tool for students researching the political upheavals, wars, cultural movements, scientific and technological advancements, and other events that mark the unfolding of American history.

INTRODUCTION

Historians agree that the era of American history known as the cold war period came into being with the conclusion of World War II in 1945 and lasted until about 1990. These were tumultuous years for America. The nation was engaged in two wars—in Korea and Vietnam—as well as several relatively minor military engagements. American society underwent profound transformations brought about by the movements for civil rights for blacks and other minorities, women, and gays and lesbians. One decade in particular—the 1960s—brought social change on an unprecedented scale as young people challenged society's sexual mores, economic system, and social values. Hippies flocked to San Francisco, formed a counterculture, and experimented with psychedelic drugs, while African Americans rioted in the streets of Newark and Detroit. Among other events, the 1970s brought an oil crisis; the 1980s produced a conservative political administration and a social ethos favoring the accumulation of wealth and the "yuppie" lifestyle. All of these events—spanning four and a half decades—took place against the backdrop of a political and ideological conflict that divided the globe into two camps, a cold war between the Communist Soviet Union and the capitalist, democratic West.

The cold war was created partly from the power vacuum that ensued after the defeat and disarmament of once-mighty Germany and Japan. It was then, in the aftermath of World War II, that the United States and the Soviet Union emerged as the two unrivaled powers in the international arena, or as they soon became known, the "superpowers." For the next forty-five years, these two nations engaged in a high-stakes game of diplomacy, armament, proxy wars, and brinkmanship that brought the world to the verge of nuclear holocaust. The United States avoided outright military conflict with the Soviet Union. However, in an attempt to check the spread of communism in Europe and South Asia, America became heavily involved in the domestic policies, political leadership, and military campaigns of various countries and regions around the world. This interventionist foreign policy was one of the chief characteristics of America during the cold war period.

The interventionist policy of the cold war contrasted markedly with the traditional American foreign policy of isolationism that had been adhered to for most of its history. This policy was first outlined by George Washington in his farewell speech in 1796 when he argued that the United States should not involve itself in the affairs of other countries: "Europe has a set of primary interests which to us have none, or very remote, relation. . . . It is our true policy to steer clear of permanent alliances with any portion of the foreign world."[1]

Of course, the United States had not followed Washington's advice religiously, as illustrated by U.S. involvement in the Spanish-American War of 1898 and the two world wars of the twentieth century. However, Washington's caution not to get caught up in the affairs of other countries remained an important touchstone of foreign policy. It was only after 1945 that mainstream U.S. foreign policy shifted dramatically, embracing the idea of active involvement in the affairs of other states.

This new policy of interventionism generally took the form of economic and/or military assistance, leading many to feel that the United States had become the self-appointed protector of the free world. To many Americans, this was a source of great pride. It seemed that, as one of the largest and most prosperous nations in the world, perhaps the United States had a duty to aid and assist struggling democratic regimes. But increasingly during the course of the cold war, both Americans and non-Americans began to resent the U.S. interference in affairs beyond the nation's own borders for a variety of different reasons; many perceived such interventions as a form of neoimperialism.

Thus, some of America's cold war programs of international assistance were highly praised as magnanimous, laudatory gestures, while others provoked both international and domestic condemnation as needlessly meddling in the affairs of other states. The Marshall Plan and the Vietnam War were two such contrasting examples of cold war American involvement. The Marshall Plan, an economic assistance program initiated in the aftermath of World War II, is generally considered to have been a unilateral success, showing the positive results that American assistance could bring. The Vietnam War, on the other hand, has often been perceived as a national failure that deeply scarred the American people and provoked waves of angry reaction.

WORLD WAR II AND THE ROOTS OF THE COLD WAR

Although the United States and the Soviet Union (along with Great Britain and France) had been allies during World War II and had conducted a united military effort, by the end of the war, relations between the two countries were beginning to sour. Initial tensions arose out of the power vacuum that was created in Eastern Europe, which Germany had occupied during the war. In 1945, Soviet tanks pulled into Hungary, Poland, and Romania to liberate these countries from Nazi occupation, but by late 1945, it became clear that the German occupation of Eastern Europe and the Baltic States was being replaced by a Soviet presence. Having been invaded twice in a generation by Germany—through Eastern Europe—the Soviets wanted to build a line of "buffer states" between the USSR and Germany. Relations became increasingly tense: The Americans began to feel that the Soviets were acting aggressively and seemed intent on expanding their sphere of influence. In February 1946, the tension between the superpowers was articulated publicly when Soviet leader Joseph Stalin claimed that communism and capitalism were incompatible. This declaration prompted former British prime minister Winston Churchill, in a speech in Missouri in March 1946, to coin the term *iron curtain* to describe the boundary that divided the capitalist democracies of Western Europe from the Communist, Soviet-controlled regimes of Eastern Europe.

THE POLICY OF CONTAINMENT

By 1947, Poland, Romania, and Bulgaria had been taken over by Communist governments, and power struggles between Communist and capitalist parties dominated local politics in many parts of Western Europe. The Americans became alarmed, for they wanted the debilitated countries of Europe to return to, or adopt, democracy and free trade and align themselves with the West. In fact, the United States began to fear that all of Europe might "fall" to communism, an idea that became known as the "domino theory," the theory that if one or two pivotal countries in Europe embraced communism, then the whole region might adopt the Soviet system.

Meanwhile, in Greece, Communist factions were seeking to overtake the government, and in Turkey, the government was being pressured by the USSR for control of the Bosporus—the strategic waterway connecting the Black Sea to the Sea of Marmara (and leading to the Mediterranean). When a poverty-stricken Britain withdrew its troops from Greece and Turkey, President Harry S. Truman decided that America must abandon its traditional isolationism and assist the countries of Europe in fighting communism. To this end he requested $400 million from Congress to "contain" communism, arguing that "at the present moment in world history nearly every nation must choose between alternative ways of life. . . . I believe that it must be the policy of the United States to support free peoples who are resisting attempted subjugation by armed minorities or by outside pressures."[2]

By July 1947, Congress had approved the aid, and George Kennan, a brilliant and influential diplomat who had recently been appointed the head of the policy planning staff in Truman's State Department, had published a famous, anonymous article in *Foreign Affairs*. In the article, he argued that the policy of containment might need to be applied worldwide because Moscow seemed intent on capitalizing on weak governments in order to seize power. Kennan argued that "the main element of any United States policy towards Soviet Russia must be that of a long-term, patient but firm and vigilant containment of Russian expansionist policies."[3] This policy of containment, with America's pledge "to support free peoples," became the cornerstone of cold war era foreign policy and formally established the United States as the protector of democracy.

CONTAINING COMMUNISM THROUGH THE MARSHALL PLAN

After Congress's decision to help the Greek government establish a democratic regime, the first major U.S. undertaking of international assistance was a program of economic aid that was offered to all the countries of Europe to help them recover from the war. The idea of economic assistance as a political strategy was first proposed by George Kennan in a private report for

Secretary of State George Marshall in which he suggested that the United States focus on containing communism in Western Europe. Kennan argued that the best means of doing so was by strengthening the ability of the countries to fight Communist influence themselves. Marshall supported the plan, for Europe had been virtually destroyed by the war and had been further enfeebled by a crippling winter that had reduced many countries to near poverty. Remembering how fascism had spread through Europe during the economic depression of the 1930s, the United States firmly believed that economic hardships and unemployment would contribute to the spread of undemocratic regimes. In order to withstand communism, Truman and his administration felt that poverty-stricken Europe needed financial support.

In June 1947 Marshall proposed, and Congress approved, billions of dollars in loans, goods, and services to resuscitate the flailing European economies. The proposal, officially called the European Recovery Program but more commonly referred to as the Marshall Plan, was also offered to the Soviet Union and its Eastern bloc satellites. However, as expected, the Soviets refused the offer. (The program contained a clause that called for cooperation and the sharing of information between the United States and recipients of Marshall aid, which the USSR found unacceptable.) Western Europe, however, gratefully accepted the aid. The United States disbursed more than $13 billion between 1948 and 1951. In addition to its humanitarian impulse to aid people who were reportedly near starving, the United States was motivated by economic interests; it viewed Europe as its main trading partner, so it was in America's best interest for Europe to be fiscally strong. The United States thus had strategic economic and political goals in mind—but most important, the White House maintained that economic stability was essential in order to prevent the rise of communism.

The Marshall Plan was deemed highly successful. Not only were the recipient countries of Europe deeply appreciative of the U.S. assistance (which came with very few strings attached), but the funds were quickly deployed to rebuild roads and bridges, to construct new factories, and to assist small businesses. Within several years, Western Europe had substantially recovered from World War II, and the United States enjoyed both a close political alliance and a profitable trade relationship with the region.

U.S. INVOLVEMENT IN VIETNAM

The Marshall Plan was a program of material support aimed at replenishing the ravages of World War II, but later forms of U.S. intervention were military as well as economic. By the 1960s, America's role as a regulator of world politics had taken a different turn, and American troops became engaged in various international conflicts, which were seen as local theaters where the larger cold war conflict between communism and capitalist democracy were played out. The largest scale and most drawn out of these involvements was the Vietnam War.

U.S. involvement in Vietnam initially began in the form of financial aid to France in its effort to retain Vietnam as its colonial possession. This early involvement, along with the subsequent refusal to ignore the situation in Vietnam, resulted from the fear that a Communist flag flying over Vietnam would cause communism to spread through the entire region. Once again, the domino theory was invoked to justify a massive U.S. intervention.

In May 1954, the French were finally defeated at the Battle of Dien Bien Phu. At the peace conference that followed in Geneva, Vietnam was divided into northern and southern states. Ho Chi Minh, the popular nationalist leader who was being aided by the Soviets and China, presided over the north, and by 1955 a pro-Western government under Ngo Dinh Diem had taken power in the south.

However, Diem did not enjoy popular support in South Vietnam. As part of the Catholic minority, he persecuted Buddhists and ran a corrupt and undemocratic government. When President John F. Kennedy took over the White House from President Dwight D. Eisenhower in 1961, he shared his predecessor's view that Vietnam was pivotal in preventing the spread of communism in Southeast Asia, famously describing Vietnam as the "cornerstone of the Free World in Southeast Asia."[4] Moreover, Kennedy sought to use Vietnam to demonstrate to the Soviets that Communist regimes could not use aggression to take over pro-Western ones.

The Kennedy administration's initial involvement in Vietnam took the form of clandestine CIA activities to encourage the South Vietnamese to engage in counterinsurgence against the North Vietnamese. In November 1961, despite warnings from French prime minister Charles de Gaulle, who had predicted that the United States would "sink step by step into a bottomless military and political quagmire,"[5] Kennedy sent the first seven thousand troops to assist the pro-West Vietnamese leader, Diem. These "advisers," as they were called, aided their South Vietnamese counterparts with military planning and strategy, technical advice, and operations. They also played an important role by flying combat helicopters. In the next two years, the number of troops sent over steadily increased; by the middle of 1963, there were sixteen thousand U.S. military advisers in Vietnam.

By this point, it was clear that the Vietcong—the South Vietnamese who supported the northern Communist leader Ho Chi Minh—were the enemy as much as the northern troops. The situation became more complex, and the question as to who the United States was fighting became more confusing as Diem began to publicly criticize and distance himself from the Americans. In November 1963, Diem was killed in a military coup that was backed by the United States. Mere weeks later, John F. Kennedy himself was shot dead in Dallas, Texas.

Some members of Kennedy's cabinet believe that, had he lived, Kennedy would have pulled out of Vietnam. But as events transpired, Lyndon Johnson was left to pick up the reins and proceed with the policies initiated by his predecessor. President Johnson was insistent that Vietnam must not be united into a Communist state under Ho, publicly declaring his fears that if Vietnam became Communist, all of Southeast Asia would surely follow the road to communism.

THE GULF OF TONKIN RESOLUTION

Many of the men that advised both President Kennedy and President Johnson, such as General Maxwell Taylor, Secretary of State Dean Rusk, and Defense Secretary Robert S. McNamara, had been lobbying for an increase in troops to Vietnam since the initial dispatches of 1961. By 1963, they felt that the situation was at a stalemate and that decisive U.S. action was called for. In December 1963, soon after Johnson assumed power, McNamara issued a warning to the president that, unless there was a dramatic increase in U.S. troops and a shift in military strategy, South Vietnam would probably be taken over by Communist factions. McNamara and others advocated a more aggressive strategy: namely, the bombing of North Vietnam and the introduction of U.S. land combat troops. By July 1964, Johnson had authorized a 30 percent increase in U.S.

forces in Vietnam, raising the amount from sixteen thousand to twenty-one thousand.

In August 1964, the crucial turning point came: The North Vietnamese had reportedly attacked an American vessel, the *Maddox*, stationed in nearby waters. Johnson used this attack to procure the go-ahead from Congress to conduct a full-scale war. Congress authorized this request in the Gulf of Tonkin Resolution. (Johnson failed to mention to Congress that the destroyer had been in south Asian waters for espionage purposes.) The day after the attack, August 4, 1964, Johnson informed the American public of the resolution in a national television address, describing the U.S. government's "determination to take all necessary measures in support of freedom and in defense of peace in Southeast Asia."[6] Soon after, Johnson authorized further increases in the number of American troops, and in February 1965, the United States began bombing North Vietnam. By 1966, 190,000 American soldiers were stationed in Vietnam. From 1965 to 1969, the military and the Johnson administration reported that progress was being made in Vietnam. However, by the late 1960s, opposition to the war in the United States had grown into a mass movement of draft evasion and widespread condemnation of the government.

THE ANTI-VIETNAM REACTION AT HOME

Many historians feel that the Vietnam War shaped American culture in fundamental ways. Vietnam, as a manifestation of U.S. cold war policies, came to be seen as an objectionable, even immoral enterprise that caused young Americans to question their country's policies and ideals. Much of the early opposition to the war came from students—the would-be draftees—who had united to form various loose-knit groups in the early 1960s. In 1962, a group called Students for a Democratic Society (SDS) wrote the Port Huron Statement, a document critiquing many elements of cold war America, including the conglomeration of power in the hands of the military-industrial complex. They perceived this concentration of power as intrinsically undemocratic, and they increasingly blamed the corporate-political elite for the Vietnam War. By the mid-1960s, SDS and other student groups were firmly opposed to the war, arguing that the America's cold war policy of interventionism was an attempt to spread American influence throughout the world and to make "the world free for capitalism," as one student poster from an antiwar rally put it.

Although the antiwar movement was confined to a relatively minor portion of the American population, by the late 1960s, these small but vocal pockets of students were protesting the war in many corners of the country. They were also condeming the university system itself for being part of the military-corporate structure, arguing that by fulfilling government contracts for arms research, the universities were implicated in the war effort. In April 1965, the "March on Washington" drew twenty-five thousand people in a public representation of the antiwar movement. Amid the occasional burning of draft cards and the signs calling for peace and denouncing arms and chemical manufacturers, rally speeches questioned the existing political structure, accusing the U.S. government of waging an imperialist war to protect its Asian markets.

THE TET OFFENSIVE

On January 30, 1968, the North Vietnamese launched a massive attack, known as the Tet Offensive, on the American strongholds in the south. The U.S. troops and their South Vietnamese allies repelled Ho's troops within a week, making the battle a military victory of sorts for the United States. However, the Tet Offensive exposed the lies that the Johnson administration had been telling to the American people; it revealed that the North Vietnamese were not weak and demoralized, as Johnson had averred, and that America was not as close to victory as the military had reported. Therefore, despite being a military victory, the Tet Offensive was a defeat on the home front because it turned public opinion firmly against the war.

In 1969 Johnson announced that he would not run for a second term so that he could devote his attention to the withdrawal of American forces from Vietnam. Despite his legislative successes and civil rights advances, he had been broken by his mishandling of the war. Five hundred and fifty thousand troops were still stationed in Vietnam when he left the White House.

THE END OF VIETNAM

When Richard Nixon became U.S. president in 1969, he scaled down the involvement in Vietnam considerably and announced the Nixon Doctrine, which declared that in the future the United States would limit its aid to Asia to economic rather than military assistance. For years, Nixon tried unsuccessfully to hammer out a peace agreement that would secure the survival of a pro-Western regime in South Vietnam, but he met with little success. In 1970 he began bombing Cambodia because it was harboring North Vietnamese troops.

Congress withdrew American troops from Vietnam gradually throughout the early 1970s, although bombing still continued. Finally, in January 1973, a peace treaty was signed: The North Vietnamese were to leave their bases in Laos and Cambodia, but were allowed to remain in South Vietnam, where it was assumed they would take over upon the complete withdrawal of American troops. After Nixon was replaced by Gerald Ford, the end of the American commitment to Vietnam was officially announced on April 23, 1975. Saigon was captured by the North Vietnamese within a week.

THE COLD WAR AFTER VIETNAM

After Vietnam, America restricted its cold war engagements to financial aid to democratic regimes in various outposts of the Third World. U.S. troops were rarely deployed to fight in these local conflicts unless they directly threatened U.S. security. Africa, the Middle East, and Latin America remained local stages of cold war tensions, with each superpower funding various regimes, often leading to interminable civil wars.

When Ronald Reagan assumed the presidency in 1980 and famously called the Soviet Union an "evil empire," there seemed to be little hope for a cessation of hostilities. Reagan was a classic cold warrior who increased federal arms spending, cut social programs, and initiated the costly Strategic Defense Initiative (SDI), an effort to design a space-based shield that could intercept nuclear missiles. The first meeting between Reagan and Soviet leader Mikhail Gorbachev in Reykjavik, Iceland, was strained and broke down over disagreements in arms reductions. In addition, Reagan heightened U.S. involvement in Third World struggles between communism and capitalism by announcing via the Reagan Doctrine that the United States would use force to combat and undermine Communist outposts. Soon thereafter the United States became involved in combat situations in Grenada and Nicaragua.

But then, suddenly, in the mid-1980s, the cold war seemed to be winding down. Gorbachev began to enact a wide range of social, political, and economic reforms aimed at revitalizing the calcified Communist infrastructure. Reagan and Gorbachev had a successful meeting in Geneva in 1985 that led to major arms reductions. Indeed, Reagan pleasantly surprised his critics by proving to be a flexible leader who was capable of adapting quickly to a radically changing political climate.

In January 1986, Gorbachev rejected Stalin's hostile assertion of 1946 that capitalist and Communist regimes were fundamentally incompatible and suggested that the two countries must learn to coexist. A second important summit meeting took place in Reykjavik in October 1986 in which further advances were made in arms reduction and even the destruction of intermediate range missiles. By May 1988, when Reagan visited Moscow, the two men could embrace each other in front of Lenin's tomb, and later that year Gorbachev announced that he would be withdrawing all Soviet troops from Eastern Europe. In February 1989, the Soviets withdrew their troops from Afghanistan, Hungary, Romania, Czechoslovakia, and the other Eastern satellite states, and each of these countries declared their independence. The Baltic States of Lithuania, Latvia, and Estonia followed soon after.

The Berlin Wall was opened as the East German government collapsed in November 1989, and soon most of it was reduced to a pile of rubble. In October 1990, Germany was reunified and admitted to NATO. In November 1990, the official end to the cold war was written into history when the United States, the USSR, and thirty other states signed the Charter of Paris, which outlined a new course of international relations for the post–cold war period. Afterward, President George Bush officially announced that the cold war was over. By late 1991, the Soviet Union itself had collapsed into the many small republics that had made up the diverse complex of the USSR. Russia, led by Boris Yeltsin, remained a central power in the region, and the transformed society threw open its doors to tourists, scholars, and free market capitalists.

THE END OF AN ERA

By 1992, little remained of the Berlin Wall. For thirty years the wall had stood as a physical representation of a world divided into opposing ideological camps—the Communist East and the democratic West. The fall of the wall thus signaled the end of an era of friction, tension, and danger in which the two superpowers played out their game of global chess. During those years of cold war hostilities, America experienced dramatic events and transformations, some of which were related to the cold war rivalry and some of which were not. The nation sent a man to the moon and made great strides in bringing the ideal of equality closer to reality at home. Wars were fought and nuclear disaster was narrowly averted. The economy went from "stagflation" in the 1970s to prosperity, at least for some, in the 1980s. In the following chapters, authors explore the political, social, and cultural developments that occurred as America fought its cold war with the Soviet Union.

NOTES

1. Quoted in *The World's Famous Orations*, vol. 8, ed. William Jennings Bryan. New York: Funk & Wagnalls, 1906, p. 156.

2. Quoted in John Gaddis, *Russia, the Soviet Union, and the United States*. New York: McGraw-Hill, 1990, p. 186.

3. Quoted in Melvyn Dubofsky, *Imperial Democracy: America Since 1945*. Englewood Cliffs, NJ: Prentice-Hall, 1983, p. 21.

4. Quoted in Robert McMahon, ed., *Major Problems in the History of the Vietnam War*. Lexington, MA: D.C. Heath, 1995, p. 159.

5. Quoted in Paul Johnson, *A History of the American People*. New York: HarperCollins, 1997, p. 879.

6. Quoted in George McTurnan Kahin and John W. Lewis, *The United States in Vietnam*. New York: Dell, 1967, p. 158.

The Cold War Sets In: 1945–1960

CHAPTER 1

Harry S. Truman and the Origins of the Truman Doctrine

Alonzo L. Hamby

Hostility between the Soviet Union and the Western powers increased steadily following the end of World War II. By 1946, the Soviets had taken over Poland, Romania, and Bulgaria and were occupying northern Iran. In February, Stalin justified a Soviet military build-up on the basis that the two countries (the Soviet Union and the United States) were "incompatible." In response, the former British prime minister Winston Churchill issued his famous "Iron Curtain" speech in March 1946, entrenching the mutual suspicion between the two superpower blocs. Some historians date the beginning of the cold war to Churchill's declaration that "an iron curtain has descended across the continent." However, others argue that the cold war began with the first official U.S. policy announcement—the Truman Doctrine—in which the U.S. president officially committed his country to helping the democratic nations of Europe fight against communism.

In 1947, the Greek government, which was corrupt and not especially popular, was under attack by Communist rebel factions. Meanwhile, nearby Turkey, which lay on the southwestern border of the Soviet Union, was being pressured to grant control of the straits that bridged the Black Sea and the Mediterranean to the USSR. The United States feared Stalinist aggression and suspected that the Soviets were behind the Communist insurrections (although in fact more recent evidence has revealed that they were not). Thus, when the British announced in February 1947 that they could no longer afford to support democracy in Greece and Turkey singlehandedly and that they were withdrawing their aid, Truman was persuaded to abandon the traditional American policy of peacetime isolation. Confident that it was the moral responsibility of the United States to uphold democracy and that it was also politically and economically expedient, Truman requested $400 million in aid from Congress for the Greek and Turkish governments. This aid, along with "the policy of the United States to support free peoples who are resisting attempted subjugation" came to be known as the Truman Doctrine. Initially this policy was intended exclusively for Europe; however, in the course of time, it was extended to encompass almost any area of the world where democracy was perceived to be under threat from communism.

In the following article, Alonzo L. Hamby, one of the foremost historians on the Truman era, analyzes the motivations behind the Truman Doctrine by way of a biographical investigation of Truman's life. Hamby suggests that the Truman Doctrine is frequently seen as an example of an Anglo-American patrician elite seeking to protect Western culture. Here, Hamby refutes this explanation by reevaluating Truman's working-class roots and examining his lifelong commitment to an ideal of American leadership in world affairs.

On March 12, 1947, President Harry S. Truman appeared before a joint session of Congress to request a major program of aid to Greece, struggling against a Communist-led insurgency, and Turkey, under direct pressure from the Soviet Union. The president called for $400 million, a sum that if adjusted for inflation would be equivalent to perhaps half of today's entire foreign aid budget. His speech, however, had more to it than this limited, if important purpose. It declared: "It must be the foreign policy of the United States to support free peoples who are resisting attempted subjugation by armed minorities or by outside pressure."

The March 12 speech was not the first U.S.-Soviet clash of the Cold War. A number of events in the previous year had presaged it: George F. Kennan's advocacy of a policy of "containment" of Soviet expansionism; the clash over Soviet reluctance to withdraw from Iran; belligerent statements by Soviet dictator Josef Stalin; Winston Churchill's "iron curtain" speech (delivered with Truman's apparent approval); the U.S.-Soviet deadlock over United Nations control of atomic energy; the dispatch of a U.S. naval fleet to the eastern Mediterranean; Secretary of State James Byrnes's pledge of support to anticommunist Germans at Stuttgart. Truman's dismissal of Secretary of Commerce Henry A. Wallace from the administration in September 1946, had confirmed a hardening anti-Soviet line.

What Truman did on March 12, 1947, was to deliver an open confirmation of an American policy that already had taken shape in the previous year. Most importantly, he stated a broad and unequivocal rationale for it. The speech is justly remembered as a landmark event in the history of American foreign policy for two reasons: (1) It called for the first substantial commitment of funds to the containment of the Soviet Union; (2) It delivered in public for the first time the general statement of principle that I have just quoted—a "doctrine" that would drive U.S. foreign policy, the Truman Doctrine.

This essay attempts to explain how Truman came to the consciousness behind his speech of March 12. The declaration was important not simply as a U.S. commitment to Greece, nor even as a declaration of a vital U.S. interest in that area of the world we might call the Eastern Mediterranean/Middle East. It asserted an American mission in leading the world toward an international system built around liberal ideals. It was, of course, a group project, but one that required the assent and the voice of the president of the United States. Truman supplied both, readily and naturally. My question is how did he arrive at that disposition?

There is a well-developed cultural interpretation of Cold War foreign policymaking and of twentieth-century American international involvement. It holds that American foreign policy was the product of a White-Anglo-Saxon-Protestant patrician elite, mainly from the northeastern part of the United States, educated at exclusive private preparatory schools and universities, taught to envision the United States as an extension of what was beginning to be called "Western culture," dedicated to the defense of that culture, and Anglophilic to the core. There is much to be said for this argument; it is an especially good description of many of the men who made Truman's foreign policy: Dean Acheson, Robert Lovett, George Kennan, Paul Nitze, Averell Harriman, among others.

But it does not describe Truman—the offspring of a modest provincial family, educated in the Independence, Missouri, public schools, bereft of any kind of a liberal arts college experience, trained in the hard knocks of machine politics, possessing almost nothing in the way of a basis of common experience with the men I have just named. Yet nothing was foisted on him. His declaration was a heartfelt expression of deeply internalized values. What I want to do is follow the road that brought him to March 12, 1947.

EDUCATION AND CHILDHOOD IDENTITY

Let us begin by trying to visualize a fifteen- or sixteen-year-old boy, a little pudgy, terribly nearsighted, altogether just a bit of a sissy, reading a history book through very thick and heavy eyeglasses in the local library or in a high school classroom around 1900 in Independence, Missouri. Young Harry Truman was a small-town boy, a rustic by the standards of the sophisticated Northeast, but none-the-less at the end of a cultural chain that stretched from Oxford and London through Boston and New York into the American heartland. Unknown to him another boy, somewhat less bookish but with at least as keen an intelligence, Franklin Roosevelt, was imbibing a similar education at one of America's elite preparatory schools, Groton.

Independence high school and Groton were worlds apart; yet they delivered to their students similar worldviews. Both Roosevelt and Truman received an education built around the classics, English literature, and history. Many educators today would disapprovingly call it Eurocentric. Young Harry seems to have learned little, if anything at all, about the Indians who less than a century earlier had been the inhabitants of what became Jackson county, Missouri. He learned much about the Greeks of two thousand years ago, both as philosophers and warriors.

He developed a tempered admiration for Alexander the Great as a military leader of unparalleled courage and resourcefulness, who nevertheless exemplified the weakness of human nature by drinking himself into an early grave. He read Plato in translation and returned periodically to him later in life. He also took Latin, learned about Rome, and admired Hannibal and Caesar. More in Sunday school than in public school, he learned about the ancient Hebrews and the Biblical saga of Israel. He learned more ancient history in high school than most college graduates know today. The world of the eastern Mediterranean was alive and vivid for him as a child. . . .

It was equally fundamental that his education was infused with the optimistic outlook of Anglo-American liberalism that dominated the end of the Victorian age: history was the story of the expansion of liberty; moral and material progress was the overriding trend of human experience, whatever the bumps and interruptions along the way. He was taught to revere Lord Tennyson, who provided a glimpse of the end of history in his epic *Lockesley Hall:* an end to war, "the Parliament of Man, the Federation of the World," where "the common sense of most shall hold a fretful realm in awe / And the kindly earth shall slumber, lapt in universal law." By his own account, Truman carried those lines, copied and recopied, with him for a half-century.

For many twentieth-century intellectuals, World War I irrevocably destroyed the Victorian vision, and World War II obliterated the last vestiges of hope for its reestablishment. But, perhaps because he was not an intellectual, Harry Truman was an optimist to the last; he believed to his dying day that the best eras of human history were in the future, not in the past. And as the United States displaced England as the leader of the Anglo-American world, he came to believe that America had a special responsibility for moving the world in that direction, for promoting the spread of liberty and material progress.

WORLD WAR I

Far from dampening his hopes for progress, Truman's experience in World War I left them essentially untouched. First of all, the war drove home a lesson that already had been ingrained in him—power was the ultimate arbiter in relations among nations and indeed in most areas of life. From a very early age, he had known that his family was on the wrong side in the Civil War and that in some relatively benign ways, history had *happened* to them. To be a boy in Independence, Missouri, in the 1890s was to understand that the very fact one was a citizen of the United States had been decided by a contest of arms in which the strongest prevailed. Moreover, Truman was to absorb this lesson at a time of national reconciliation that mixed nostalgia for the lost cause with a fervent sense of American patriotism and destiny. . . .

Truman thus grew up with a strong sense of patriotism de-

spite his parents' Confederate antecedents. He dreamed of going to West Point and becoming a professional soldier. Instead,
he became a bank clerk who found it a natural step to join the
National Guard on his twenty-first birthday. He took pride in
his affiliation even if his grandmother loathed his dress-blue
uniform. As a young man in his twenties and thirties, he more
consciously than ever fused American patriotism with American destiny. The agent who made that mix an enduring part of
his outlook was Woodrow Wilson. . . .

THE COMING OF WORLD WAR II, 1937–1941

It was as a U.S. senator that Truman again came face to face
with foreign policy issues. He was elected in 1934 by an electorate fixated on the enormous problems of the Great Depression. There seems to have been no discussion whatsoever of foreign policy in either his primary or general election campaigns.
He took his seat in January 1935, one of thirteen freshman senators (all Democrats) who had been elected primarily by pledging unquestioning support for President Franklin Roosevelt and
his New Deal. Caught up in the currents of the isolationist thirties, he pretty much followed a weaving administration foreign
policy line. Roosevelt, an interventionist by every instinct, gave
himself political cover by refusing to oppose the Neutrality Acts
of 1935, 1936, and 1937; all of them embodied the premise that
the United States could avoid involvement in a possible European war by avoiding the policies (or "mistakes") that had led
to World War I. Truman voted for each of them. Roosevelt also
pushed cautiously but persistently for increased military expenditures. Truman equally took up this theme, more forcefully
than his chief.

On April 20, 1937, Truman delivered a speech at Larchmont,
New York, that was the first shot in a sustained campaign for
the revival of American power and the resumption of the American mission. It deserves close attention because it places him in
the vanguard of elected officials who argued for increased international involvement, and because one can draw a straight
line from it to the speech he would make about ten years later
on March 12, 1947. By the spring of 1937, the post–World War I
international system was in the intermediate stages of disintegration. Italy was consolidating its conquest of Ethiopia. Japan
had long since swallowed up Manchuria, and most prescient
observers knew that some incursion into the rest of China was

likely. Spain was embroiled in a ghastly civil war that threatened to suck in every major European power. Germany, beginning its fifth year of Nazi rule, had occupied the Rhineland and
undertaken a large rearmament program. No clear-eyed observer could look to the future with confidence. "Conditions in
Europe," Truman declared, "have developed to a point likely to
cause an explosion at any time." Or, to be only marginally more
direct, war was likely and the United States probably would be
drawn into it, just as had been the case a generation earlier.

He began with an interpretation of recent history: "We refused to sign the Treaty of Versailles, did not accept our responsibility as a world power, and tried, by tariff walls, to reap
the benefits of world trade without giving anything in return.
It did not work." Here was the Wilsonian arguing for an American mission of leadership in the world, positing liberal capitalism as the purpose of that mission. (Let us be clear, by the
way, that in Truman's mind, liberalism [individual liberties and
self-rule] and capitalism [individual economic enterprise] were
two sides of the same coin. Both of them subject to regulation
and interpretation, to be sure, but in tandem the highest development yet of human society.)

Truman virtually dismissed the very neutrality legislation for
which he had just voted: "very laudable, and I hope it will help
to keep us at peace. But, my friends, we are living in a world of
realities. . . . In the coming struggle between Democracy and
Dictatorship, Democracy must be prepared to defend its principles and its wealth." From that point of departure, Senator
Truman went on to call for a big navy, "an air force second to
none," a well-prepared army, and an industrial mobilization
plan. "The world knows our honorable record in the World
War," he concluded. "We fought for liberty and honor, just as
we always have, and just as we always shall."

Consider all these words and the assumptions behind them.
America should not have rejected world involvement and
world leadership. American military power could serve a necessary and constructive purpose in improving the world. There
were two kinds of nations, democracies and dictatorships. Not
subtle. But not fundamentally wrong either, and stated with intense conviction more than six months before Roosevelt's much
more tentative quarantine speech. . . .

With the outbreak of war in Europe, Truman emerged as a
full-blown interventionist, supporting whatever aid Britain

needed. In the fall of 1939, he backed modification of the Neutrality Acts to allow the sale of military equipment to the British
on a cash-and-carry basis. In September 1940, as a candidate for
reelection to the Senate, he reversed an earlier position and voted
in favor of a military draft. In the spring of 1941, he backed Lend-
Lease [the provision of military supplies to Britain with repayment decisions deferred to the end
of the war]. He asserted that all these
stances were matters of self-interest
for the United States. He also made
no effort to conceal his sense that the
United States was directly threatened by the Axis. In a stiff rejoinder
to a constituent who was worried
about the United States becoming
embroiled in the war, he declared:
"We are facing a bunch of thugs, and
the only theory a thug understands
is a gun and a bayonet."

Harry S. Truman

In his private correspondence,
Truman also began to use a new
word—"totalitarian." It is an inter-
esting addition to his vocabulary because it betrays an underlying conception of the stakes of international politics in the
World War II era. The Senator's central concern was the threat
presented by the Axis powers, but he also perceived a larger
struggle going on in the world. The war as he saw it was not
simply a battle of the world's "progressive forces" against "fascism;" the United States represented ideals of liberalism and
democracy that gave the armed struggle its ultimate meaning
and, from the first, rendered the U.S. alliance with the Soviet
Union problematic. Historians have often repeated his initial
reaction to the surprise Nazi attack on Germany's former ally,
the U.S.S.R.: "If we see that Germany is winning, we should
help Russia and if Russia is winning we ought to help Germany and that way let them kill as many as possible. . . ." It is
dangerous to invest too much significance into an offhand
comment. The impulse was widespread—the great Nebraska
progressive George Norris said much the same thing. And Truman said at the same time, "I don't want to see Hitler victorious under any circumstances." Still, he clearly perceived an
underlying equation between Nazism and Soviet Commu-

nism. It troubled him throughout the war.

Truman's sense of the Soviet Union had numerous sources. Perhaps the most fundamental was his worldview that assumed liberal capitalism as a norm. It had room for class conflict between "the people" and "the interests" but not for the promotion of class warfare, the liquidation of the bourgeoisie, the abolition of private property, and the dictatorship of the proletariat. In his mind, dictatorship was dictatorship. Gangsters were gangsters. Writing to his wife at the end of 1941, he remarked that the Soviet leaders were "as untrustworthy as Hitler and Al Capone.". . .

THE COMING OF THE COLD WAR

The first year of the Truman presidency was among the most momentous twelve-month spans in presidential history—the surrender of Germany, the establishment of the United Nations, the Potsdam conference, the atomic bomb and the capitulation of Japan, enormous economic stresses and strains in the domestic American transition from war to peace. Perhaps the most persistent of all the issues Truman faced was that of the U.S. relationship to the Soviet Union. To this problem, he brought all the impulses of his earlier years: a distaste for Soviet totalitarianism, a belief in the superiority (and indeed the inevitability) of liberal values, a determination to make America a world leader—and a desire to preserve the wartime alliance. To these impulses, he added another conviction—agreements had to be kept. The U.S.S.R., he believed, was failing to keep the agreements it had made at Yalta for "free elections" in Eastern Europe.

Yet his policy on Eastern Europe was ultimately more bark than bite. If he dressed down Soviet Foreign Minister Molotov, if he was understandably outraged by, among many issues, the subversion of Polish independence and the blatant repression of Bulgarian democrats, he realized that there was little the United States could do about it. He needed the Soviet Union on other matters: the United Nations, the war against Japan. Faced with Soviet intransigence in Poland, Bulgaria, and other Eastern European nations, he found himself with no other option than to search for a fig leaf that might hide at least the worst Soviet indecencies. Writing in his diary on May 23, he conceded that Eastern Europe made little difference to American interests, that Stalin could hold elections as free as those Boss Pendergast might have staged in Kansas City or Boss Hague in Jersey City.

He left the Potsdam conference with considerable optimism that he could work with Stalin to achieve a decent, if imperfect, world order. Dismay over the naked extension of Soviet power into Eastern Europe and the occasionally harsh rhetoric accompanying it had a role in the beginning of the Cold War, but Truman realized that principle, however admirable, did not necessarily constitute a national interest. The clash of important interests that precipitated the Cold War would begin elsewhere.

That area was in the Eastern Mediterranean world that had existed so vividly for Truman since his childhood. Not Greece at first; that was still an area of British influence. Rather Iran and Turkey, the front and rear gateways to the Middle East. In early 1946, Truman authorized strong pressure on the Soviet Union to withdraw its troops from northwestern Iran. He exaggerated when he later claimed that he had sent an "ultimatum" to Stalin, but there can be no doubt of his emotional involvement and his determination to maintain Iranian independence. Later in the year, he used the U.S. navy to provide strong symbolic support to Turkey, which was under strong pressure to turn over control of the Black Sea straits to the Soviets. First, there was the return of the remains of the deceased Turkish ambassador aboard the U.S.S. *Missouri,* a floating hearse that just happened to have nine 16-inch guns. Then, late in the summer, the president approved a decision to station a U.S. naval task force in the region on a permanent basis. Truman had no sentimental attachment to Turkey nor much interest in its history, but he knew his geography. Turkey was a linchpin upon which the security of the Middle East and the eastern Mediterranean rested. He wanted American intentions to be clear and firm.

On August 15, meeting with national security officials, Truman approved a policy memorandum that declared a vital American interest in Turkish independence. He told Undersecretary of State Dean Acheson that he would stand by it "to the end." He remarked to Secretary of the Navy James Forrestal that we might as well find out now if the Russians were bent on world conquest. He also produced from his desk a map of the Middle East and lectured the group on its strategic importance. (Exactly how that map got there I have never learned. We know only that it does testify to Truman's sense of the region's importance.)

The commitments to Iran and Turkey led inexorably to the last piece of the puzzle—Greece.

THE DECISION TO AID GREECE AND TURKEY

Until late 1946, Greece had not loomed large in the consciousness of American policy makers. It long had been part of the
British sphere of influence in that part of the world. But by late
1946, British power and capabilities were crumbling in Egypt,
Palestine, and Greece. That fall, the Truman administration received advance notice that Britain could no longer support the
Greek government against Communist insurgents. What followed was a carefully orchestrated national security process—
an American fact-finding mission, high-level discussions in
Washington—that could lead to only one decision.

Most American policy makers, including Truman, found the
right-wing government in Athens unpalatable. Undersecretary
of State Dean Acheson described its premier, Constantine Tsal-
daris, as "a weak, pleasant, but silly man" with little practical
sense about the limits of American support. Before the war, the
royal family, which was of German origin, had been altogether
too cozy with the Nazis. Too many of the leading members of
the government appeared authoritarian, perhaps protofascist.
Truman, I have suggested, had a sense of Greek history and
some pro-Greek sentiments. But he did not think he was moving to preserve Athenian democracy; nor would he have found
any of the Greek leaders of 1947 worthy successors to Alexander the Great or Plato. He acted primarily out of a sense of
strategic imperatives. He and his aides, moreover, readily accepted the need to couple aid to Greece with aid to Turkey,
thereby making an implicit statement that the United States was
confronting a regional crisis.

There remained the need to sell the program to an economy-
minded Republican Congress. The president, Secretary of State
[George C.] Marshall, and Undersecretary Acheson met with
congressional leaders on February 27, 1947. The story of that
meeting is well known: Marshall's sober presentation of the
need to fill the regional power vacuum or face the prospect of a
series of crises "which might extend Soviet domination to Europe, the Middle East, and Asia;" congressional apprehension
about "pulling British chestnuts out of the fire;" Dean Acheson's
emotional invocation of the global struggle between totalitarianism and democracy; and Senator [Hoyt S.] Vandenberg's assertion that the president needed to use the undersecretary's
rhetoric to "scare the hell out of the American people" and
thereby sell the program. I will leave it to others to decide

whether Acheson's role was quite as pivotal as he later claimed. I have read Marshall's presentation; on paper, it looks both impressive and sufficiently scary to me.

What we can say with certainty is that Truman and his lieutenants had come to see the eastern Mediterranean crisis of 1946–47 as a situation with far larger implications. They understood that this was only one target of Soviet expansionism. They already sensed that the Greek-Turkish aid program was but the first step in a far larger design still to be worked out in the form of the Marshall Plan and the North Atlantic Treaty. The decision to justify it with a universal principle, the Truman Doctrine, was not just a tactical judgement; it reflected a realistic understanding of the Stalinist challenge to liberal democracy in the immediate postwar era. To fragment Cold War policy into a series of specific challenges and responses would have been to deprive it of intellectual coherence and to fail to inform the public of a genuine transcendent meaning.

But just what did the "Truman Doctrine" mean? Support free peoples, anywhere, anytime, with any amount of resources? One could find that implication in it. By definition, broad general statements do not hedge. It is pretty clear, however, that the Truman administration had a sense of limits and a precision that is often ignored by the Truman Doctrine's critics. Those limits were derived from the Eurocentric outlook of the president and his national security officials and from their practical sense of the resources available to their foreign policy. For these reasons, the Truman Doctrine never applied to Chiang Kai-shek's China. General principles do not have to lead to an out-of-control crusade.

The American decision to aid Greece was part of a larger response to a regional crisis that the Truman administration had addressed for over a year. It was based on broad strategic considerations, not sentiment. But it was made all the easier by Truman's sense of history and by his apparent belief that it was natural and fitting for the United States to assume Britain's role as not simply a stabilizing influence but also a carrier of liberal values in the Eastern Mediterranean.

THE MARSHALL PLAN

GEORGE C. MARSHALL

Although the contents of the Marshall Plan had been prefigured in remarks given by Undersecretary of State Dean Acheson a month before, the program was officially announced for the first time in the following speech by Secretary of State George C. Marshall at the Harvard Commencement of June 5, 1947. The European Recovery Program, as it was technically known, articulated a new interventionist policy, announcing the U.S. decision to rebuild the damaged economies of Western Europe through substantial grants of money, goods, and services. European farmlands and businesses alike had been destroyed during World War II: Many roads, bridges, harbors, and other networks of trade and transportation had similarly been damaged. The result was a severe disruption in normal trade that, combined with an especially harsh winter of 1947, had reduced parts of Europe to a state of extreme poverty and hardship.

In addition to its humanitarian aims, the Marshall Plan offered strategic advantages. In the short term, the United States was simply giving money to Europe, but in the long term, America was ensuring the survival of its largest market, for since 1945 the Europeans had been too poor to buy American products. This was a trend that would significantly damage the U.S. economy unless it was reversed. President Truman himself stated that the Marshall Plan and the Truman Doctrine were "two halves of the same walnut"; that is, they both formed part of the plan to contain Soviet influence by ensuring that the European states were economically strong and politically stable enough to resist the onslaught of communism. Remembering how totalitarian and Nazi leaders had seized control of Germany during times of depressions and unemployment in the

Excerpted from George C. Marshall's address at Harvard University on June 5, 1947.

1930s, the Truman administration was determined to prevent the rise of communism in Western Europe by boosting the European economies.

Historians generally judge the Marshall Plan to have been successful on all counts. Congress approved more than $17 billion in aid to Europe distributed over the years 1948–1950, which significantly helped to repair the economies of Europe. By 1951, Europe had resumed its lively trade with the United States. At the same time, the Communist parties in France and Italy, which had enjoyed significant power in 1947, had lost their support and had been ejected from the political scene.

I need not tell you gentlemen that the world situation is very serious. That must be apparent to all intelligent people. I think one difficulty is that the problem is one of such enormous complexity that the very mass of facts presented to the public by press and radio make it exceedingly difficult for the man in the street to reach a clear appraisement of the situation. Furthermore, the people of this country are distant from the troubled areas of the earth and it is hard for them to comprehend the plight and consequent reactions of the long-suffering peoples, and the effect of those reactions on their governments in connection with our efforts to promote peace in the world.

DEVASTATION IN EUROPE

In considering the requirements for the rehabilitation of Europe the physical loss of life, the visible destruction of cities, factories, mines, and railroads was correctly estimated, but it has become obvious during recent months that this visible destruction was probably less serious than the dislocation of the entire fabric of European economy. For the past 10 years conditions have been highly abnormal. The feverish preparation for war and the more feverish maintenance of the war effort engulfed all aspects of national economies. Machinery has fallen into disrepair or is entirely obsolete. Under the arbitrary and destructive Nazi rule, virtually every possible enterprise was geared into the German war machine. Long-standing commercial ties, private institutions, banks, insurance companies and shipping companies disappeared, through loss of capital, absorption through nationalization or by simple destruction. In many countries, confidence in the local currency has been severely shaken. The breakdown of the business structure of Europe during the war was complete. Recovery has been seriously retarded by the fact that 2 years after the close of hostilities a peace settlement with Germany and Austria has not been agreed upon. But even given a more prompt solution of these difficult problems, the rehabilitation of the economic structure of Europe quite evidently will require a much longer time and greater effort than had been foreseen.

RURAL AND URBAN PROBLEMS

There is a phase of this matter which is both interesting and serious. The farmer has always produced the foodstuffs to exchange with the city dweller for the other necessities of life. This division of labor is the basis of modern civilization. At the present time it is threatened with breakdown. The town and city industries are not producing adequate goods to exchange with the food-producing farmer. Raw materials and fuel are in short supply. Machinery is lacking or worn out. The farmer or the peasant cannot find the goods for sale which he desires to purchase. So the sale of his farm produce for money which he cannot use seems to him an unprofitable transaction. He, therefore, has withdrawn many fields from crop cultivation and is using them for grazing. He feeds more grain to stock and finds for himself and his family an ample supply of food, however short he may be on clothing and the other ordinary gadgets of civilization. Meanwhile people in the cities are short of food and fuel. So the governments are forced to use their foreign money and credits to procure these necessities abroad. This process exhausts funds which are urgently needed for reconstruction. Thus a very serious situation is rapidly developing which bodes no good for the world. The modern system of the division of labor upon which the exchange of products is based is in danger of breaking down.

WE MUST HELP EUROPE

The truth of the matter is that Europe's requirements for the next 3 or 4 years of foreign food and other essential products—principally from America—are so much greater than her present ability to pay that she must have substantial additional help, or face economic, social, and political deterioration of a very grave character.

The remedy lies in breaking the vicious circle and restoring the confidence of the European people in the economic future of their own countries and of Europe as a whole. The manufacturer and the farmer throughout wide areas must be able and willing to exchange their products for currencies the continuing value of which is not open to question.

Aside from the demoralizing effect on the world at large and the possibilities of disturbances arising as a result of the desperation of the people concerned, the consequences to the economy of the United States should be apparent to all. It is logical that the United States should do whatever it is able to do to assist in the return of normal economic health in the world, without which there can be no political stability and no assured peace. Our policy is directed not against any country or doctrine but against hunger, poverty, desperation, and chaos. Its purpose should be the revival of a working economy in the world so as to permit the emergence of political and social conditions in which free institutions can exist. Such assistance, I am convinced, must not be on a piecemeal basis as various crises develop. Any assistance that this Government may render in the future should provide a cure rather than a mere palliative. Any government that is willing to assist in the task of recovery will find full cooperation, I am sure, on the part of the United States Government. Any government which maneuvers to block the recovery of other countries cannot expect help from us. Furthermore, governments, political parties, or groups which seek to perpetuate human misery in order to profit therefrom politically or otherwise will encounter the opposition of the United States.

ORGANIZING AID

It is already evident that, before the United States Government can proceed much further in its efforts to alleviate the situation and help start the European world on its way to recovery, there must be some agreement among the countries of Europe as to the requirements of the situation and the part those countries themselves will take in order to give proper effect to whatever action might be undertaken by this Government. It would be neither fitting nor efficacious for this Government to undertake to draw up unilaterally a program designed to place Europe on its feet economically. This is the business of the Europeans. The initiative, I think, must come from Europe. The role of this country should consist of friendly aid in the drafting of a European program and of later support of such a program so far as it may be practical for us to do so. The program should be a joint one, agreed to by a number, if not all European nations.

An essential part of any successful action on the part of the United States is an understanding on the part of the people of America of the character of the problem and the remedies to be applied. Political passion and prejudice should have no part. With foresight, and a willingness on the part of our people to face up to the vast responsibility which history has clearly placed upon our country, the difficulties I have outlined can and will be overcome.

PRESIDENT TRUMAN REPORTS ON THE SITUATION IN KOREA

HARRY S. TRUMAN

In 1945, Korea was divided along the 38th parallel into a northern and a southern state after being liberated from the Japanese by Soviet troops in the north and by American forces in the south. Two separate and unfriendly governments soon emerged, headed by the Communist-backed Kim Il Sung in the North and the despotic, though anti-Communist, Syngman Rhee in the South. When North Korea invaded the South in June 1950, the United States was quick to intervene to prevent a united Korea under Communist control.

In the following message delivered to Congress less than a month after the conflict in Korea began, President Harry S. Truman outlines the current situation in Korea and describes America's response to the invasion of South Korea by North Korea. Truman explains that at the time of the attack, a United Nations (UN) delegation had been in South Korea attempting to resolve the division between the northern and southern parts of the country. By resorting to warfare, Truman says, North Korea rejected the goals of the United Nations and its peacekeeping mission. This affront to the rule of law, and to the United Nations as a hope for world peace must not be allowed to go unchecked, Truman states.

Truman and his cabinet framed the Korean War as yet another instance of Soviet aggression, arguing that Josef Stalin was supporting Kim Il Sung (which in fact he was) with the intent

Excerpted from Harry S. Truman's address to the U.S. Congress, July 19, 1950.

of extending Soviet influence into Asia. Truman also argued that if Korea, like China, became communist, it would be very difficult for smaller states in southeast Asia—such as Vietnam, Burma, and the Philippines—to maintain democratic regimes alongside aggressive Communist neighbors. Aided by the growing fear of communism within America, the Korean war was generally accepted as a justified engagement that was necessary to halt the spread of communism

Later in the speech, President Truman proposed an increase in the appropriations budget in order to pay for the effort in Korea as well as a future U.S. military peacekeeping efforts. Truman was in fact successful in convincing Congress on this count, for on July 24, 1950, the White House announced that appropriations for the Department of Defense were to be substantially raised in order to fund military expenditures in Korea.

To the Congress of the United States:
I am reporting to the Congress on the situation which has been created in Korea, and on the actions which this Nation has taken, as a member of the United Nations, to meet this situation. I am also laying before the Congress my views concerning the significance of these events for this Nation and the world, and certain recommendations for legislative action which I believe should be taken at this time.

At four o'clock in the morning, Sunday, June 25th, Korean time, armed forces from north of the thirty-eighth parallel invaded the Republic of Korea.

The Republic of Korea was established as an independent nation in August, 1948, after a free election held under the auspices of the United Nations. This election, which was originally intended to cover all of Korea, was held only in the part of the Korean peninsula south of the thirty-eighth parallel, because the Soviet Government, which occupied the peninsula north of that parallel, refused to allow the election to be held in the area under its control.

The United States, and a majority of the other members of the United Nations, have recognized the Republic of Korea. The admission of Korea to the United Nations has been blocked by the Soviet veto.

In December, 1948, the Soviet Government stated that it had withdrawn its occupation troops from northern Korea, and that a local regime had been established there. The authorities in northern Korea continued to refuse to permit United Nations observers to pass the thirty-eighth parallel to supervise or observe a free election, or to verify the withdrawal of Soviet troops.

Nevertheless, the United Nations continued its efforts to obtain a freely-elected government for all of Korea, and at the time of the attack, a United Nations Commission, made up of representatives of seven nations—Australia, China, El Salvador, France, India, the Philippines and Turkey—was in the Republic of Korea.

Just one day before the attack of June 25th, field observers attached to the United Nations Commission on Korea had completed a routine tour, lasting two weeks, of the military positions of the Republic of Korea south of the thirty-eighth parallel. The report of these international observers stated that the Army of the Republic of Korea was organized entirely for defense. The observers found the parallel guarded on the south side by small bodies of troops in scattered outposts, with roving patrols. They found no concentration of troops and no preparation to attack. The observers concluded that the absence of armor, air support, heavy artillery, and military supplies precluded any offensive action by the forces of the Republic of Korea.

On June 25th, within a few hours after the invasion was launched from the north, the Commission reported to the United Nations that the attack had come without warning and without provocation.

The reports from the Commission make it unmistakably clear that the attack was naked, deliberate, unprovoked aggression, without a shadow of justification.

This outright breach of the peace, in violation of the United Nations Charter, created a real and present danger to the security of every nation. This attack was, in addition, a demonstration of contempt for the United Nations, since it was an attempt to settle, by military aggression, a question which the United Nations had been working to settle by peaceful means.

The attack on the Republic of Korea, therefore, was a clear challenge to the basic principles of the United Nations Charter and to the specific actions taken by the United Nations in Korea. If this challenge had not been met squarely, the effectiveness of the United Nations would have been all but ended, and the hope of mankind that the United Nations would develop into an institution of world order would have been shattered.

UN REACTION TO THE ATTACK

Prompt action was imperative. The Security Council of the United Nations met, at the request of the United States, in New York at two o'clock in the afternoon, Sunday, June 25th, eastern daylight time. Since there is a 14-hour difference in time between Korea and New York, this meant that the Council convened just 24 hours after the attack began.

At this meeting, the Security Council passed a resolution which called for the immediate cessation of hostilities and for the withdrawal of the invading troops to the thirty-eighth parallel, and which requested the members of the United Nations to refrain from giving aid to the northern aggressors and to assist in the execution of this resolution. The representative of the Soviet Union to the Security Council stayed away from the meetings, and the Soviet Government has refused to support the Council's resolution.

The attack launched on June 25th moved ahead rapidly. The tactical surprise gained by the aggressors, and their superiority in planes, tanks and artillery, forced the lightly-armed defenders to retreat. The speed, the scale, and the coordination of the attack left no doubt that it had been plotted long in advance.

THE U.S. RESPONSE

When the attack came, our Ambassador to Korea, John J. Muccio, began the immediate evacuation of American women and children from the danger zone. To protect this evacuation, air cover and sea cover were provided by the Commander in Chief of United States Forces in the Far East, General of the Army Douglas MacArthur. In response to urgent appeals from the Government of Korea, General MacArthur was immediately authorized to send supplies of ammunition to the Korean defenders. These supplies were sent by air transport, with fighter protection. The United States Seventh Fleet was ordered north from the Philippines, so that it might be available in the area in case of need.

Throughout Monday, June 26th, the invaders continued their attack with no heed to the resolution of the Security Council of the United Nations. Accordingly, in order to support the resolution, and on the unanimous advice of our civil and military authorities, I ordered United States air and sea forces to give the Korean Government troops cover and support.

On Tuesday, June 27th, when the United Nations Commission in Korea had reported that the northern troops had neither ceased hostilities nor withdrawn to the thirty-eighth parallel, the United Nations Security Council met again and passed a second resolution recommending that members of the United Nations furnish to the Republic of Korea such aid as might be necessary to repel the attack and to restore international peace and security in the area. The representative of the Soviet Union to the Security Council stayed away from this meeting also, and the Soviet Government has refused to support the Council's resolution.

The vigorous and unhesitating actions of the United Nations and the United States in the face of this aggression met with an immediate and overwhelming response throughout the free world. The first blow of aggression had brought dismay and anxiety to the hearts of men the world over. The fateful events of the 1930's, when aggression unopposed bred more aggression and eventually war, were fresh in our memory.

But the free nations had learned the lesson of history. Their determined and united actions uplifted the spirit of free men everywhere. As a result, where there had been dismay there is hope; where there had been anxiety there is firm determination.

Fifty-two of the fifty-nine member nations have supported the United Nations action to restore peace in Korea.

A number of member nations have offered military support or other types of assistance for the United Nations action to repel the aggressors in Korea. In a third resolution, passed on July 7th, the Security Council requested the United States to designate a commander for all the forces of the members of the United Nations in the Korean operation, and authorized these forces to fly the United Nations flag. In response to this resolution, General MacArthur has been designated as commander of these forces. These are important steps forward in the development of a United Nations system of collective security. Already, aircraft of two nations—Australia and Great Britain—and naval vessels of five nations—Australia, Canada, Great Britain, the Netherlands and New Zealand—have been made available for operations in the Korean area, along with forces of Korea and the United States, under General MacArthur's command. The other offers of assistance that have been and will continue to be made will be coordinated by the United Nations and by the unified command, in order to support the effort in Korea to maximum advantage.

RULE OF LAW

All the members of the United Nations who have indorsed the action of the Security Council realize the significance of the step that has been taken. This united and resolute action to put down lawless aggression is a milestone toward the establishment of a rule of law among nations.

Only a few countries have failed to support the common action to restore the peace. The most important of these is the Soviet Union.

Since the Soviet representative had refused to participate in the meetings of the Security Council which took action regarding Korea, the United States brought the matter directly to the attention of the Soviet Government in Moscow. On June 27th, we requested the Soviet Government, in view of its known close relations with the north Korean regime, to use its influence to have the invaders withdraw at once.

The Soviet Government, in its reply on June 29th and in subsequent statements, has taken the position that the attack launched by the north Korean forces was provoked by the Republic of Korea, and that the actions of the United Nations Security Council were illegal.

These Soviet claims are flatly disproved by the facts.

The attitude of the Soviet Government toward the aggression against the Republic of Korea, is in direct contradiction to its often expressed intention to work with other nations to achieve peace in the world.

For our part, we shall continue to support the United Nations action to restore peace in the Korean area.

As the situation has developed, I have authorized a number of measures to be taken. Within the first week of the fighting, General MacArthur reported, after a visit to the front, that the forces from north Korea were continuing to drive south, and further support to the Republic of Korea was needed. Accordingly, General MacArthur was authorized to use United States Army troops in Korea, and to use United States aircraft of the Air Force and the Navy to conduct missions against specific military targets in Korea north of the thirty-eighth parallel, where necessary to carry out the United Nations resolution. General MacArthur was also directed to blockade the Korean coast.

The attacking forces from the north have continued to move forward, although their advance has been slowed down. The troops of the Republic of Korea, though initially overwhelmed by the tanks and artillery of the surprise attack by the invaders, have been reorganized and are fighting bravely.

United States forces, as they have arrived in the area, have fought with great valor. The Army troops have been conducting a very difficult delaying operation with skill and determination, outnumbered many times over by attacking troops, spearheaded by tanks. Despite the bad weather of the rainy season, our troops have been valiantly supported by the air and naval forces of both the United States and other members of the United Nations.

U.S. Military Action

In this connection, I think it is important that the nature of our military action in Korea be understood. It should be made perfectly clear that the action was undertaken as a matter of basic moral principle. The United States was going to the aid of a nation established and supported by the United Nations and unjustifiably attacked by an aggressor force. Consequently, we were not deterred by the relative immediate superiority of the attacking forces, by the fact that our base of supplies was 5,000 miles away, or by the further fact that we would have to supply our forces through port facilities that are far from satisfactory.

We are moving as rapidly as possible to bring to bear on the fighting front larger forces and heavier equipment, and to increase our naval and air superiority. But it will take time, men, and material to slow down the forces of aggression, bring those forces to a halt, and throw them back.

Nevertheless, our assistance to the Republic of Korea has prevented the invaders from crushing that nation in a few days— as they had evidently expected to do. We are determined to support the United Nations in its effort to restore peace and security to Korea, and its effort to assure the people of Korea an opportunity to choose their own form of government free from coercion, as expressed in the General Assembly resolutions of November 14, 1947, and December 12, 1948.

In addition to the direct military effort we and other members of the United Nations are making in Korea, the outbreak of aggression there requires us to consider its implications for peace throughout the world. The attack upon the Republic of Korea makes it plain beyond all doubt that the international communist movement is prepared to use armed invasion to conquer independent nations. We must therefore recognize the possibility that armed aggression may take place in other areas. . . .

THE COMMUNISM THREAT MAY SPREAD

The outbreak of aggression in the Far East does not, of course, lessen, but instead increases, the importance of the common strength of the free nations in other parts of the world. The attack on the Republic of Korea gives added urgency to the efforts of the free nations to increase and to unify their common strength, in order to deter a potential aggressor.

To be able to accomplish this objective, the free nations must maintain a sufficient defensive military strength in being, and, even more important, a solid basis of economic strength, capable of rapid mobilization in the event of emergency.

The strong cooperative efforts that have been made by the United States and other free nations, since the end of World War II, to restore economic vitality to Europe and other parts of the world, and the cooperative efforts we have begun in order to increase the productive capacity of underdeveloped areas, are extremely important contributions to the growing economic strength of all the free nations, and will be of even greater importance in the future.

We have been increasing our common defensive strength under the treaty of Rio de Janeiro and the North Atlantic Treaty, which are collective security arrangements within the framework of the United Nations Charter. We have also taken action to bolster the military defenses of individual free nations, such as Greece, Turkey, and Iran.

The defenses of the North Atlantic Treaty area were considered a matter of great urgency by the North Atlantic Council in London this spring. Recent events make it even more urgent than it was at that time to build and maintain these defenses.

Under all the circumstances, it is apparent that the United States is required to increase its military strength and preparedness not only to deal with the aggression in Korea but also to increase our common defense, with other free nations, against further aggression. . . .

FINANCIAL COSTS

The steps which we must take to support the United Nations action in Korea, and to increase our own strength and the common defense of the free world, will necessarily have repercussions upon our domestic economy.

Many of our young men are in battle now, or soon will be. Others must be trained. The equipment and supplies they need, and those required for adequate emergency reserves, must be produced. They must be available promptly, at reasonable cost, and without disrupting the efficient functioning of the economy.

We must continue to recognize that our strength is not to be measured in military terms alone. Our power to join in a common defense of peace rests fundamentally on the productive capacity and energies of our people. In all that we do, therefore, we must make sure that the economic strength which is at the base of our security is not impaired, but continues to grow. . . .

The potential productive power of our economy is even greater. We can achieve some immediate increase in production by employing men and facilities not now fully utilized. And we can continue to increase our total annual output each year, by putting to use the increasing skills of our growing population and the higher productive capacity which results from plant expansion, new inventions, and more efficient methods of production.

With this enormous economic strength, the new and necessary programs I am now recommending can be undertaken with confidence in the ability of our economy to bear the strains involved. Nevertheless, the magnitude of the demands for military purposes that are now foreseeable, in an economy which is already operating at a very high level, will require substantial redirection of economic resources. . . .

The increased appropriations for the Department of Defense, plus the defense-related appropriations which I have recently submitted for power development and atomic energy, and others which will be necessary for such purposes as stockpiling, will mean sharply increased Federal expenditures. For this reason, we should increase Federal revenues more sharply than I have previously recommended, in order to reduce the inflationary effect of the Government deficit. . . .

DEFENDING FREEDOM AROUND THE WORLD

We must also prepare ourselves better to fulfill our responsibilities toward the preservation of international peace and security against possible further aggression. In this effort, we will not flinch in the face of danger or difficulty.

The free world has made it clear, through the United Nations, that lawless aggression will be met with force. This is the significance of Korea—and it is a significance whose importance cannot be over-estimated.

I shall not attempt to predict the course of events. But I am sure that those who have it in their power to unleash or withhold acts of armed aggression must realize that new recourse to aggression in the world today might well strain to the breaking point the fabric of world peace.

The United States can be proud of the part it has played in the United Nations action in this crisis. We can be proud of the unhesitating support of the American people for the resolute actions taken to halt the aggression in Korea and to support the cause of world peace.

The Congress of the United States, by its strong, bi-partisan support of the steps we are taking and by repeated actions in support of international cooperation, has contributed most vitally to the cause of peace. The expressions of support which have been forthcoming from the leaders of both political parties for the actions of our Government and of the United Nations in dealing with the present crisis, have buttressed the firm morale of the entire free world in the face of this challenge.

The American people, together with other free peoples, seek a new era in world affairs. We seek a world where all men may live in peace and freedom, with steadily improving living conditions, under governments of their own free choice.

For ourselves, we seek no territory or domination over others. We are determined to maintain our democratic institutions so that Americans now and in the future can enjoy personal liberty, economic opportunity, and political equality. We are concerned with advancing our prosperity and our well-being as a Nation, but we know that our future is inseparably joined with the future of other free peoples.

We will follow the course we have chosen with courage and with faith, because we carry in our hearts the flame of freedom. We are fighting for liberty and for peace—and with God's blessing we shall succeed.

SPUTNIK AND THE ORIGINS OF THE SPACE RACE

WILLIAM L. O'NEILL

When the Soviets successfully launched an earth-orbiting satellite named *Sputnik I* on October 4, 1957, Americans were first aghast, and then disbelieving. In the following excerpt, William L. O'Neill, history professor at Rutgers University in New Jersey, describes not only the launching of *Sputnik*, but also the veritable panic that gripped the nation when it became clear that the Soviets had beaten the Americans into space. O'Neill, who specializes in social history (and has also written extensively on feminism and anti-Semitism in America between the World Wars), thus analyzes the social effects of the space race—how it affected everyday Americans.

O'Neill argues that American anxiety over the space race was worsened by the hasty and bungled first efforts of U.S. scientists to match *Sputnik,* which proved unsuccessful and were mockingly dubbed "Flopniks" by the press. He suggests that despite the U.S. having attained a far higher level of medical, nutritional, and military technology and enjoying levels of prosperity unheard of in the Soviet Union, Americans began to fear that they were lagging behind the Russians technologically. Schools began to emphasize science, and the Eisenhower administration passed the National Defense Education Act to fund science, mathematics, and foreign language study.

Ironically, for O'Neill, Americans had the technology to produce a satellite in the 1950s but had not done so simply because their funding and research had been oriented toward other objectives. The Soviets had concentrated their research efforts on a satellite largely in an attempt to address the very real nuclear missile gap between the Soviets and the United States. They had gathered a team of German rocket scientists and had actively sought to develop satellites as a military deterrent. By launching a satellite from earth, which potentially could be armed, the Soviets sought to demonstrate their capacity to launch long-range nuclear missiles. Americans were all too aware of the fundamentally military nature of *Sputnik* and the threat that was posed by the USSR's ability to launch missiles from space.

Despite the widespread anxiety *Sputnik* generated, it did have the positive effect of placing space travel on the political agenda, spurring scientists to develop more advanced space shuttles and probes and convincing politicians to fund such research. The ultimate result of *Sputnik* was the creation of the National Aeronautics and Space Administration (NASA) in 1958 and the localization of talent, energy, and funding there that ultimately put Neil Armstrong and Buzz Aldrin on the moon on July 20, 1969.

On October 4, 1957, Russia orbited Sputnik, the first artificial earth satellite, weighing 184 pounds. After it came Sputnik II, an 1,128-pound capsule that was big enough to carry a live dog. These Soviet triumphs led to waves of anxiety that dominated American political life for the rest of Eisenhower's time in office. They extended beyond space exploration itself to include defense, education, and even the national purpose, which until then had been taken for granted. Eisenhower was astonished and baffled by these reactions, since, as he often pointed out, the facts did not justify them. But, as during the loyalty crisis [Senator Joseph R. McCarthy's campaign against suspected Communist public officials] a few years earlier, the facts did not matter. People believed that Sputnik gave the lie to American declarations of superiority over Russia. Sputnik proved that the United States was smug, lazy, and second rate, also that Russia was ambitious, disciplined, and ahead in crucial areas. Nothing Eisenhower would say or do over the next three years shook this conviction, which would result in a stepped-up arms race and fabulously expensive voyages to the moon.

AMERICAN EFFORTS

Apart from disbelieving government reassurances, Americans were not impressed with the Administration's post-Sputnik feats. Vanguard, which was supposed to put the first American satellite into orbit, blew up on national television. Wernher von Braun's Army group did orbit a satellite on January 31, 1958, using the new Jupiter rocket. Though Explorer 1 was more sophisticated than Sputnik, it weighed only 10½ pounds and did not comfort those who were impressed by Russia's much larger payloads. Neither did little Vanguard 1, which orbited on March 17. It was followed in May by a Russian satellite weighing almost one and a half tons.

The press regarded every Soviet achievement as a national defeat. The first issue of *Newsweek* to appear after Sputnik contained five pages of lamentation. It was no time to be good sports about Russia's leap into space it warned. Sputnik showed that Russia had surpassed America in rocket power. *Newsweek* quoted Democratic Senator Stuart Symington of Missouri, who said that "unless our defense policies are promptly changed, the Soviets will move from superiority to supremacy. If that ever happens our position will become impossible." A scientist was even more direct, saying that unless America caught up fast "we're dead." Russia appeared to lead in science, and science education too. "The harsh fact is," *Newsweek* concluded, "whatever we're doing is not enough." In January *Newsweek* ran a sixteen-page supplement, "The Challenge," which held that the United States was behind Russia even in quality of ground weapons, as Lieutenant General James M. Gavin had recently informed the Senate Preparedness Subcommittee. It was time to put aside interservice rivalries, the magazine argued, and create a real General Staff.

PUBLIC CONCERN

Time, whose loyalty to the Administration survived all threats, was less harsh though equally concerned. It quoted Republican Senator Styles Bridges of New Hampshire who announced after Sputnik that the "time has clearly come to be less concerned with the depth of pile of the new broadloom rug or the height of the tail fin of the new car and to be more prepared to shed blood, sweat and tears." *Time* was not sure it agreed with Senator Henry Jackson, Democrat of Washington, who had referred to a week "of shame and danger," but stood firmly behind former ambassador to Italy Clare Boothe Luce, the owner's wife, who said that "the beep of Sputnik is an intercontinental outer-space raspberry to a decade of American pretensions that the American way of life was a gilt-edged guarantee of our material superiority." And it agreed too with [atomic scientist] Edward Teller, whom it quoted often and at length on the need for more scientific research and better science teaching. Both these were invariably part of any article on the Soviet menace. Overnight Sputnik had made Russian science education the envy of American journalists.

What baffled Eisenhower, and remains puzzling today, is the readiness of so many Americans to attribute to Russia a level of excellence that it simply did not possess. By concentrating its resources on weaponry Russia could compete in the arms race. In all other respects, diet, health care, education, housing, clothing, transportation, whatever, Russia lagged behind then as it still does today. For some groups American credulity served a practical purpose. Democrats hailed Russian science and technology in order to weaken the Administration politically, educators did so to gain additional funding. Others, perhaps, were swept along by pack journalism and mob psychology as happens at times of stress. Whatever the motives behind it, America's obsession with Soviet achievements, real or not, created a problem for Eisenhower that he could not solve. For him the best times were over.

THE EFFECTS OF SPUTNIK

Many changes resulted from the anxieties induced by Sputnik. A desirable one was that science and foreign language teaching became more popular, and school standards rose. Otherwise, pressing the panic button had negative effects. The GOP lost heavily in the congressional elections of 1958, Democrats ending up with huge majorities in both houses. There was general agreement that the voters had responded to a lack of presidential leadership. Even *Time*, while insisting that Eisenhower was still doing a good job, admitted that "the widespread impression remained of a dispirited, drifting administration." Eisenhower's defense policy was chiefly responsible for his troubles. Though he remained personally popular, Eisenhower found himself with virtually no support outside his own Administration for holding the line on military spending—and very little within it. By 1960 it was universally believed that America was rushing head first into Missile Gap on account of presidential stubbornness.

The truth was exactly opposite, for Eisenhower presided over a golden age of missile development. As Walter McDougall, the leading historian of space puts it, "more new starts and technical leaps occurred in the years before 1960 than in any comparable span. Every space booster and every strategic missile in the American arsenal, prior to . . . the 1970s, date from these years." Atlas, the first U.S. Inter-Continental Ballistic Missile, became operational. Titan, a more sophisticated liquid fueled rocket, was decided upon in 1955. In 1956 the Navy was authorized to develop Polaris, the first solid-fuel rocket, which, though only an intermediate range ballistic missile, was reliable and could be launched almost at once, unlike liquid fueled rockets which took hours to fire. At almost the same time work began on Minuteman, a solid-fuel ICBM that could launch in 60 seconds. During the early '60s Minuteman joined Polaris and the B-52 to give America a three-legged deterrent.

Further, Army scientists had possessed the ability to launch a satellite years before Sputnik. In 1954 the Office of Naval Research and the Redstone Arsenal, where Army missile research was centered, proposed a joint orbital project mating an Army rocket to a Navy satellite. Wernher von Braun, former Nazi rocket chief and legendary head of the Army's missile program, asked for $100,000 to put a five pound object in space. Since the existing technology was good enough for this purpose, he noted, "it is only logical to assume that other countries could do the same. It would be a blow to U.S. prestige if we did not do it first." In fact boosting a satellite into orbit was far simpler than sending an ICBM halfway round the world with no more than a one mile margin of error, which scientists were soon to accomplish.

That America did not get into space first resulted from the taking of a calculated risk. The Administration decided against sending up a military vehicle in the near future, preferring instead to orbit a civilian satellite in 1958, the International Geophysical Year. There was a sensible reason for doing so. The "freedom of space" not having been established, it seemed more likely to gain Russian acceptance if the first orbiter was scientific rather than military. So that the civilian nature of this enterprise would be undeniable, the rocket too should be non-military. That meant waiting for Viking, a complex multistage rocket which would not be ready for years. The delay, it was understood, might enable Russia to get into space first. That would be too bad. On the other hand, it would settle all doubts as to the freedom of space and enable America to develop reconnaissance satellites without fear of Soviet complaints. They promised to yield the greatest return on America's investment in rockets, so both civilian and military leaders were exceedingly anxious to have them.

AMERICANS PANIC

As a rational man Eisenhower had accepted the danger that Russia might gain prestige by beating America into space. What he had not anticipated was that so many Americans would panic and conclude that since Russia had larger boosters it was ahead not only in space research but in ICBM technology also. The Soviet lead was actually more apparent than real. Russia had nothing comparable to the mighty American Strategic Air Command. American rockets were less powerful than Russia's because they were more sophisticated. Smaller and lighter warheads were being developed, enabling relatively low-powered rockets to hit Russia with three megaton payloads, enough to destroy any target. Russia, owing to its crude technology, needed bigger engines to launch its heavier warheads. Thanks to the U-2 spy plane, which had been overflying Russia since 1956, Eisenhower knew that the Russians did not have enough ICBMs to offset the huge American lead in manned bombers. There was no missile gap, only a slight Soviet lead that would vanish in a few years when the U.S. program matured.

Eisenhower could never explain this, as his aerial espionage program was a closely guarded secret. He asked the public to trust him and was bewildered that it did not. There was poetic justice in his dilemma. Eisenhower had not minded when Harry Truman was being harassed over the loyalty issue; indeed, he profited by it and shrank from confronting McCarthy to keep on doing so. Now Eisenhower learned how it felt to be the victim of unwarranted public fears, and how damaging it was to have them manipulated by political adversaries. There is no evidence that he grasped this parallel, or, if he had done so, that it would have made things any easier.

Cold War Culture: The 1950s

CHAPTER 2

DOMESTIC FEARS AND THE RED SCARE

GARY A. DONALDSON

In the following excerpt from his book *Abundance and Anxiety*, historian Gary A. Donaldson traces the history of the anti-Communist movement in the United States from the late 1930s until its peak in the early 1950s. He argues that fears of Communist infiltration were a manifestation of the general anxieties of the cold war era caused by issues such as Soviet power and the threat of global nuclear destruction. The anti-Communist movement was thus partly motivated by the desire to ease the public's fears aroused by foreign affairs over which they had no control.

As Donaldson explains, the cold war was a time of fear in which no one dared to call oneself a Communist. Democrats and Republicans alike thus used the insult "Communist" to accuse and discredit political opponents, and neither party was prepared to criticize the activities of the overbearing House Committee on Un-American Activities (HUAC), which was created in 1938 to expose subversive individuals, for fear of being thought "soft." As both parties tried to appear even more committed to stopping communism in America, the extremist and undemocratic practices of accusing people of Communist leanings escalated. Communist fears peaked in 1950, when Senator Joseph McCarthy began an extended besmirchment campaign by claiming in a series of public addresses that he held a list with the names of dozens of Communists who held high offices in the State Department. However, after several years, McCarthy's fanciful accusations could no longer be sustained on mere hysteria in the absence of evidence. After accusing several

highly placed U.S. Army officials of being Communists, Mc-
Carthy faced the army's special counsel Joseph Welch in a series of televised hearings in April and May 1954. In these hearings, McCarthy was publicly defeated and humiliated, and his
charges were exposed as unsubstantiated lies. Soon after, the
Senate formally censured him for abusive conduct. Ultimately,
Donaldson argues, the cold war atmosphere of fear and para-
noia quashed social and political nonconformity and helped to
create a rigid, conformist society where homogenous traditional
values of family, domesticity, and religion were forcefully embraced by almost all Americans.

I t is ironic that in the early postwar years, just as anticommunism was beginning to run rampant through the nation,
membership in the American Communist Party was the
lowest it had been since the 1920s, its numbers cut in half since
the peak periods of the 1930s. As the fear of communism
grabbed at the heart and soul of America, as it threatened to tear
America apart, the threat itself was actually diminishing.
Clearly, America was insecure, anxious.

The nation's fear of communism, real or imagined, became a
hot political issue in the late 1940s and early 1950s. The entire
era is branded with the name "McCarthyism" after the Republican senator from Wisconsin, Joseph McCarthy, the man who
dragged America through the muck of anticommunism to the
climax of the movement and then, finally, to its logical conclusion. History identifies McCarthy as the nefarious link to America's dark side, the personification of the weakness in the American character and in the democratic system itself. And he
deserves much of history's treatment, but he was not the orga-
nizer of the Red Scare, nor was he the first to see Communists
in places they should not be; and the blame for McCarthyism
does not fall solely in the laps of the Republicans.

Americans succumbed to this irrationality for a number of reasons. The cold war itself and, more important, the early setbacks
in the cold war suffered by the United States fueled the distrust
and hysteria. The "loss" of China and the Soviet atomic bomb
had a great impact and led to American feelings that such events
could not have occurred without some sort of Soviet-sponsored
espionage carried on deep inside the U.S. government. A series
of sensational spy cases informed the American public that So-

viet spies did, in fact, exist, which in turn gave birth to the question that was on everyone's lips: "How many more are there?" The war in Korea added to the fear. There American boys, in an attempt to contain communism, were being killed by Communists. All of this fear and hysteria was exacerbated by the Republican Party's search for an issue to use against the Democrats in the postwar elections, and when they found it in America's fear of communism, they played it for all it was worth.

THE HUAC

The mechanisms for the postwar Red Scare were first put in place in 1938 with the establishment of the permanent House Committee on Un-American Activities. Known almost exclusively by the inaccurate acronym HUAC, the committee was designed to ferret out subversives on both the left and the right—both fascists and Communists. In fact, HUAC was established as the result of a compromise between those who wanted to investigate Communists, socialists, and leftist radicals, and those who wanted to investigate fascists. In 1940 the Smith Act (the Alien Registration Act) made it illegal to advocate the overthrow of the U.S. government by force, and in the 1940s several states established un-American activities committees in their legislatures. States also passed laws denying employment to subversives, or to anyone belonging to organizations deemed subversive or un-American.

In the spring of 1945, before the war ended, Americans got their first taste of a Communist spy scandal. In an illegal raid on the office of *Amerasia*, a radical journal of Asian affairs, agents from the Office of Strategic Services (the forerunner of the Central Intelligence Agency) uncovered a large number of classified government documents. Indictments were returned against six people, of whom only one pleaded guilty and received a small fine. Their crime was described as "journalistic zeal." But the Republicans smelled a cover-up, and the House Judiciary Committee held hearings but found nothing. The incident would have died, but as the news was breaking in the case, the federal government was trying desperately to force Jiang Jieshi and his Nationalists to form a postwar coalition government with Mao Zedong and his Communists. Americans like Henry Luce, the publisher of *Time* magazine, and other anticommunist types believed strongly that the U.S. government should try to achieve the goal of a Nationalist China under Jiang—free of communism. They began voicing their opinion that Jiang's problems were not incompetence and corruption, as liberals in the administration claimed, but the machinations of Communists in the U.S. State Department who were pushing for the unholy Communist-Nationalist coalition in China. In addition, those indicted in the *Amerasia* case had State Department connections, and the documents that were seized dealt exclusively with Far Eastern concerns. From then on, the State Department was always a target, and after Jiang's collapse in 1949 the spotlight on the State Department became even more focused.

In the fall of 1946, the first big international spy story broke, the story that would ultimately lead Americans to realize that the Soviets had been spying on the United States for some time. It would also be a major factor in destroying Soviet credibility in the American mind. The story revolved around a disgruntled and disenchanted agent at the Soviet embassy in Toronto named Igor Gouzenko. Gouzenko decided to defect to the West, taking with him secret documents that implicated the Soviet government in a spy network and identified several Soviet spies working in the United States and Canada. The roundup brought in fifteen spies in all, including Alan Nunn May, a British scientist who had worked on atomic energy research in Canada during the war. May admitted spying for the Soviets and turning over information on American and Canadian nuclear programs. May then implicated Klaus Fuchs, a German-born physicist who had worked on the Los Alamos Project; he in turn pointed to several coconspirators who led directly to several other Los Alamos alumni and eventually to Julius and Ethel Rosenberg. The Rosenbergs were Communists and probably spies (Nikita Khrushchev mentioned them in his memoirs as being of some assistance to the Soviet nuclear program).

It was the Rosenbergs who became the center of attention, and the center of the nation's anticommunist debate, at least in part because they were apprehended in the fall of 1949, just after the Soviets exploded their first atomic bomb. It quickly became the popular opinion in America (which was probably incorrect) that the Soviets could not have developed the bomb alone, that they needed some assistance from spies in the West, and that the Rosenbergs (and probably others) had provided the necessary scientific secrets. Judge Irving R. Kaufman, in sentencing the Rosenbergs, accused them of a "diabolical conspiracy to destroy a God-fearing nation." They had given the bomb to the Soviets, he added, "years before our best scientists predicted." On June 19, 1953, at the height of the anticommunist hysteria in the country, the Rosenbergs were executed.

ANTICOMMUNISM IN POLITICS

Anticommunism entered politics as a major issue for the first time in the 1946 congressional elections when the Republicans accused the Democratic Party of being riddled with Communists and sympathetic to communism—both at home and abroad. The Republican campaign slogan accused the Democrats of the "Three C's": "Confusion, Corruption, and Communism." The result was a stunning victory that placed Republicans in control of Congress for the first time since 1930. It also awakened the Democrats to the power of the issue of anticommunism. *U.S. News and World Report* characterized the Republican campaign as "accusing the Democratic Party of being one that preaches radical doctrines and engages in radical practices. The main tenor of the Republican campaign theme is that the Democratic Party is leading the country toward Communism. . . . The Republicans are . . . accusing the Administration of being pro-Russian in its policies and are accusing the Democrats of permitting men with communistic ideas to dictate the Administration policy." After the election, journalist Marquis Childs concluded that the anticommunist issue "was one of the most potent forces in the shift from the party in power to the opposition."

Truman responded to the election results by getting tough on communism. He issued Executive Order 9835, requiring loyalty tests for federal employees, and he allowed HUAC files to be used as a source of evidence tying employees to subversive groups. Truman's motives were clearly political, with an eye toward the 1948 election campaign, when he expected to be tagged by Republicans with the soft-on-communism label—a fate his advisers were telling him he must avoid at all costs. The president may also have hoped that his loyalty order would remove the anticommunist issue entirely from American politics, but instead it seemed to verify that Communists had infiltrated federal government offices and were, in fact, a real danger to the nation's security.

THE LOYALTY PROGRAM

As a result of the order, all new federal employees underwent a loyalty investigation, and government department heads were given the responsibility of firing disloyal employees. The order also established the attorney general's list of subversive organizations. Of the 16,000 federal employees who were investigated, not one was found to be disloyal to the U.S. government or a card-carrying Communist. Two government workers were, however, fired because they were deemed "security risks," and about 200 were forced to resign because they were judged "unsuitable" for such reasons as homosexuality and alcohol abuse. Another 100 or so federal employees were fired because they were suspected of possible disloyalty. At no time were any of these people allowed to face their accusers or present evidence in their own defense. Truman's order, probably more than anything except the establishment of HUAC itself in 1938, set the stage for what was to come.

Truman's loyalty order was designed to let the electorate know that he, too, was concerned about the supposedly growing threat of domestic communism. His fiery anti-Soviet Truman Doctrine speech, delivered to Congress just a few days before the executive order was signed, made it clear that he was going after Communists abroad as well. He also used the fear of communism to sell the expensive Marshall Plan to the budget-minded Republican Congress later in 1947. In 1949 he used the same tactic to promote and finance NATO. Clearly, Truman's political approach to the issue of anticommunism, along with his need to compromise with congressional Republicans, did a lot to fuel anticommunist sentiment in the nation in the postwar years.

THE HOLLYWOOD HEARINGS

In the fall of 1947 HUAC went after the motion picture industry. HUAC chairman J. Parnell Thomas had accused the industry of turning out Communist propaganda. There followed several years of sensational attacks by HUAC on Hollywood that finally revealed little, except possibly the modest intelligence of some actors. "From what I hear," Gary Cooper told the committee, "I don't like it [communism] much because it isn't on the level." As a result of the Hollywood hearings, ten writers were ultimately jailed for failure to cooperate with the committee, and over the next few years dozens more Hollywood operatives were blacklisted and banned from their professions for invoking the Fifth Amendment rather than give the members of HUAC what they wanted: the names of Communists (or former Communists) working in the film industry.

THE ALGER HISS CASE

In the spring of 1948 HUAC received word that a senior editor at *Time* magazine named Whittaker Chambers had confessed to being a top-level Communist in Washington in the 1930s. In addition, Chambers was willing to testify about his one-time Communist association, and he agreed to identify his associates—he would name names. HUAC put Chambers on the stand in August, and among those he identified as former Communists was Alger Hiss, the director of the prestigious Carnegie Endowment for International Peace. Hiss, if HUAC could prove he was a Communist, would be quite a catch. He was on the inside in the federal government, one of the many bright young Ivy League–educated intellectuals who came to Washington in the 1930s to offer their farsightedness to the workings of the New Deal. After clerking for justice Oliver Wendell Holmes, Hiss rose auspiciously through the State Department maze to the level of director of the office in charge of United Nations affairs. From there he organized the U.N. planning conferences at Dumbarton Oaks and San Francisco, and (although a minor player) he was with FDR at Yalta. It was Hiss's Yalta connection that raised the most eyebrows among the HUAC committee members; by 1948 Yalta was being portrayed by conservatives as the great betrayal. Hiss's rebuttal before HUAC was a firm denial, almost a challenge to the committee to prove any relationship between his past and any aspect of communism. The committee backed off. Chambers proved to be an unimpressive witness, an admitted ex-Communist who had nothing to offer but his dubious "word." In the face of Hiss's indelible credibility HUAC appeared gullible, ready to believe anyone who had a story. But one HUAC member, California Congressman Richard Nixon, concluded that Hiss was lying. Based on Nixon's hunch, a HUAC subcommittee, chaired by Nixon, went after Hiss—the big fish.

Chambers claimed to have known Hiss personally in the 1930s when the two men worked as part of a Soviet-sponsored Communist cell assigned to infiltrate the federal government apparatus (particularly the State Department) in an attempt to influence foreign policy. Nixon's objective was to establish the personal relationship between Chambers and Hiss through some common knowledge. He achieved this by interrogating each man separately and then comparing notes. Incredibly, the one common denominator turned out to be the prothonotary warbler, a bird rare in the Potomac area, that both Hiss and Chambers said they had observed. Chambers insisted that the two men were avid bird-watchers in the 1930s and that together they had observed the bird on a walk along the Potomac. From there, Nixon built his case.

The statute of limitations prevented Hiss from being tried for treason, leaving only the question of perjury. Had Hiss lied to HUAC during his testimony? In late August, on the television news program *Meet the Press,* Chambers openly accused Hiss of being a Communist. After some delay (*The Washington Post* insisted Hiss either "put up or shut up") Hiss sued Chambers for libel. In the trial that followed, Chambers produced a series of documents on microfilm that had been stored in a pumpkin on his farm in Maryland. These "pumpkin papers," as they came to be called, were sensitive State Department papers; some were in Hiss's own hand, others were written on a typewriter traced to Hiss. With these revelations the implications were more than just some government infiltration and the possible influence on foreign policy. This was espionage. Few seemed to notice that Chambers had denied that espionage had been a motive in his own workings in the 1930s. Nevertheless, the production of the "pumpkin papers" seemed to prove that Hiss had lied to HUAC.

Hiss was indicted on two counts of perjury. By the time the case went to trial, it had taken on a momentum all its own. For many Americans liberalism itself was on trial. It was the Republicans accusing the Democrats of the sins of the past, of cavorting with Communists and pro-Soviet subversives at the expense of the nation's foreign policy. Much of this hysteria had to do with the new medium of television, which broadcast the Hiss perjury trials to much of the east coast. The first trial ended in a hung jury. In November 1949 Hiss went on trial again and was found guilty on two counts of perjury. He was sentenced to five years in prison, the maximum sentence.

Much of the significance of the Hiss case revolves around the willingness of prominent liberal Americans and Democratic Party leaders to rally around Hiss—and even to follow him down in flames when he was found guilty. Everyone from Eleanor Roosevelt to Dean Acheson to Max Lerner insisted that Hiss was innocent and that HUAC had stepped beyond its legal limits. Even Truman called the episode a "red herring." When Hiss was found guilty, many Americans were willing to lump together Alger Hiss, the Democratic Party, and domestic communism. And of course, a question was immediately raised in the American mind: How many more Alger Hisses are there out there—in the government, in the State Department, involved in espionage, influencing American foreign policy? The incident added to the growing fears.

Hiss was convicted on January 21, 1950. Eighteen days later, on February 9, Senator Joseph McCarthy told a Republican Women's Club in Wheeling, West Virginia, that he had in his hand a list of Communist Party members serving in the State Department. "While I cannot take the time to name all the men in the State Department who have been named as members of the Communist Party and members of a spy ring," he said, "I have in my hand a list of 205 . . . a list of names that were known to the Secretary of State and who nevertheless are still working and shaping the policy of the State Department." A few days later in Reno, Nevada, and then in Salt Lake City, he claimed there were first fifty-seven, and then eighty-one, Communists in the State Department. With that, the claims and counterclaims, the revelations and accusations, came to a head. One of America's ugliest periods was about to unfold.

McCARTHYISM

Joe McCarthy was little more than a Senate Republican sideliner with a doubtful future. He entered the Senate in 1947, and by 1950 he was two years from having to stand for reelection in a state where the grassroots-style liberalism of Robert La Follette had won the day for Democratic presidential candidates in four of the last five elections. Desperately in need of an issue, he stumbled on anticommunism when he received favorable publicity after attacking a Wisconsin newspaper and its editor for what he called "Communist leanings." But McCarthy's infamous Wheeling speech, and the five years of tirades against communism in America that followed, was hardly more than jumping into the lead on an issue that was already hot on Capitol Hill, an issue that Republicans had been using against the Democrats since 1946—and that the Democrats had themselves used to destroy Henry Wallace's third-party run in 1948. By the time McCarthy spoke to the ladies of Wheeling, the topic of anticommunism was old hat.

But for McCarthy there were a few new twists and turns. First of all, McCarthy presented a sense of urgency. His boisterous character seemed to say to millions of Americans that a fifth column (something Americans had been conditioned to fear since the 1930s and Nazi infiltration of Europe) of Communists was gaining strength in the United States, directing U.S. policy, and in fact preparing to take over the nation—as it seemed Communists had taken over other countries. For impressionable Americans the evidence of McCarthy's charges was everywhere: Communist spies like Hiss and the Rosenbergs; Soviet aggressions (both covert and overt); the reformation of the Comintern in Moscow to direct international Communist activity; communism in the labor unions, in Hollywood, in government. The fear of communism had grown to an irrational level by 1950, and Americans began seeing Communists everywhere. But more important, McCarthy was specific about where they were; he said they were in the State Department, where they were directing American foreign policy.

By 1950 America's foreign policy was, to many Americans, a horrible failure because it had not delivered what was expected from the efforts and total victories of World War II. China had fallen to communism, the Soviets had taken over eastern Europe, and now they had the atomic bomb. In addition, just as McCarthy was making his accusations, North Korea invaded South Korea and the United States was in a full-scale war (even though it was being called a "police action") against the forces of communism—American soldiers were being killed by Communists. All of this coalesced around McCarthy, the man with the answers, the man with the lists, the names of the culprits, those responsible, the scapegoats.

The Senate responded to McCarthy and his accusations by appointing a committee to investigate his charges. The Tydings Committee, headed by Democratic Senator Millard Tydings of Maryland, accused McCarthy of perpetrating a "fraud and a hoax . . . on the Senate of the United States and the American people." The Tydings Committee report was endorsed by the Senate, but strictly along partisan lines and only after a few high-pitched shouting matches and at least one shoving incident on the floor of the Senate. McCarthyism, as it was quickly being called, was now a full-blown political issue; but more important, it was also an emotional issue, one that would divide America and change the nation.

Of course, McCarthy did not stand alone in making his accusations. McCarthyism was a volatile political issue that many Republicans believed could embarrass the administration and sweep them back into the seats of power in 1952. Robert Taft egged on McCarthy, telling him that "if one case [doesn't] work, bring up another." House Minority Leader Joseph Martin praised McCarthy for exposing "the tremendous infiltration of pinks and fellow-travelers into our government." And clearly, much of the Old Guard in the Republican Party jumped on the McCarthy bandwagon as their main vehicle to a 1952 victory. But moderate Republicans were apprehensive. Through all his wailings, McCarthy had produced virtually nothing except a group of outdated dossiers compiled from the State Department's loyalty files in 1947; and all of those people either were no longer at the State Department or were later cleared by the FBI. In June 1950, Republican Senator Margaret Chase Smith and several other moderates in the party issued their "Declaration of Conscience," deriding McCarthy and his supporters for exploiting "fear, bigotry, ignorance, and intolerance" for their own political gain. A group of Republicans standing somewhere between the McCarthyites and the moderates, such as Richard Nixon, feared that McCarthy's histrionics would backfire and destroy a perfectly good political issue.

All of this was not being confined to Capitol Hill. McCarthy also received the support of the Hearst, McCormick, and Scripps-Howard newspapers. Right-wing reporters, columnists, and radio commentators like Paul Harvey also sang his praises. The old Roosevelt haters who had found the New Deal to be tainted with socialism now found their place in the sun, along with anti-intellectuals, antiliberals, midwestern isolationists, and a large number of right-wing fringe groups who hoped to liken New Deal liberalism to communism. By the early years of the 1950s, divergence from the mainstream of any sort—social, economic, political, cultural—might lead to questioning of loyalty, to charges of being what McCarthy himself often called "communistically inclined." Private businesses often conducted investigations of their own employees, the FBI compiled lists of suspected "travelers," the CIO [Congress of Industrial Organizations] purged itself of Communists, and college professors lost their jobs by the hundreds for having had vague associations with liberal groups in the 1930s. In September 1950, Nixon, along with Republican Senator Karl Mundt and conservative Democratic Senator Pat McCarran, pushed through Congress the McCarran Internal Security Act requiring Communist organizations to register with the attorney general. Although the law stopped short of making it against the law to be a Communist in the United States, it made life difficult for anyone who had ever been a Communist or had been a member of a Communist organization—as defined by the newly established Subversive Activities Control Board. Anyone, for instance, could be jailed if they were considered "likely" to commit espionage. Truman's veto of the McCarran Act was overridden and the tone was set. "Communistically inclined" by someone else's definition might cost a career, upset a life. Americans slipped into conformity. They threw away their Paul Robeson records and red neckties; they stopped drinking vodka and eating Russian caviar. Many denied their pasts and did all they could to fit into the new mainstream to avoid detection for whatever reason. Scholars discovered conformity and conservatism in many university disciplines, including history, economics, and sociology. Hollywood movies now warned of the Communist threat. Dress codes were introduced in schools and businesses, and soon "standing out" became undesirable. It was the new period of conformity, the "paranoid style," as Richard Hofstader called it; the "homogenized society," according to William Leuchtenberg. But above all, it was the supreme manifestation of the cold war at home.

THE PURSUIT OF HAPPINESS: AMERICAN SOCIETY AND POPULAR CULTURE

JOHN PATRICK DIGGINS

In the following excerpt, historian John Patrick Diggins describes the 1950s as a time that some viewed as one of cultural
stagnation, but most agree was an era of unbridled economic
growth and prosperity. From shiny new kitchen appliances to
oversized cars, Americans bought furiously, spurred on by the
new plastic credit cards that served as money when cash ran
out. This was the era, explains the author, when television
moved into every household and the advertising industry was
quick to create a whole new set of needs for consumers. Happiness was equated with economic prosperity, and the thrifti-
ness of the 1930s and the war era gave way to showy displays
of wealth.

The postwar migration of African Americans from the rural
South to the cities of the North and West also initiated what
came to be known as the "white flight," as middle-class white
Americans left the cities and self-segregated in homogenous
suburban communities. These social and geographic upheavals
resulted in African Americans' increasingly being pushed into
the urban ghetto, while white Americans inhabited a ring of

suburbs surrounding the city. The major highway networks constructed in the 1950s enabled the existence of these parallel worlds, while cheap gasoline caused Americans to produce more pollution than the rest of the world. The culture of the 1950s, with its idealization of domestic stability and its refusal to upset the status quo, set the stage for the social revolutions of the 1960s, in which young people reacted vehemently against the values of materialism and conformity so insistently promoted in this era.

John Patrick Diggins is Distinguished Professor of History at the Graduate Center of the City University of New York. He has written over a half-dozen books on subjects such as the foundations of liberalism and the American left.

A lthough McCarthyism, the cold war, Korea and politics dominated front pages in the fifties, opinion polls profiled the American people as preoccupied with their own lives and largely nonpolitical. To most white, middle-class Americans the fifties meant television; bobby sox and the bunny hop; bermuda shorts and gray flannel suits; "I Love Lucy"; Marlon Brando astride a motorcycle and Elvis belting out "Hound Dog"; Lolita the nymphet; crew cut and duck's ass hairstyles; Marilyn Monroe; James Dean; cruising and panty raids; preppies and their cashmeres and two-toned saddle shoes; Willie Mays; Rocky Graziano; drive-in movies and restaurants; diners with chrome-leg tables and backless stools; suburbia; barbecued steaks; Billy Graham and the way to God without sacrifice; the Kinsey Report and the way to sex without sin. Few items in this list would strike one as serious, but many of them have proved durable. Indeed, such subjects fascinate even members of the post-fifties generation. In the seventies and eighties mass magazines like *Newsweek* and *Life* devoted special issues to the fifties as "The Good Old Days" and Hollywood produced *The Last Picture Show, American Graffiti,* and *The Way We Were.* Nostalgia even succeeded in trivializing the Korean War, as with the immensely popular "M*A*S*H."

Nostalgia is one way to ease the pain of the present. Those who survived the sixties, a decade that witnessed the turmoils of the Vietnam War and the tragedies of political assassination, looked back wistfully on the fifties as a period of peace and prosperity. Many of those who survived the fifties, however, particularly writers and professors, passed a different verdict. "Good-by to the fifties—and good riddance," wrote the historian Eric Goldman, "the dullest and dreariest in all our history." "The Eisenhower years," judged columnist William Shannon, "have been years of flabbiness and self-satisfaction and gross materialism. . . . The loudest sound in the land has been the oink-and-grunt of private hoggishness. . . . It has been the age of the slob." The socialist Michael Harrington called the decade "a moral disaster, an amusing waste of time," and the novelist Norman Mailer derided it as "one of the worst decades in the history of man." The poet Robert Lowell summed up his impatience in two lines: "These are the tranquil Fifties, and I am forty. / Ought I to regret my seedtime?"

On the other side of the political spectrum, conservative writers tended to praise the fifties as "the happiest, most stable, most rational period the western world has ever known since 1914." They point to the seemingly pleasant fact that in the fifties, in contrast to the sixties, many nations like India and Burma achieved independence without resorting to armed force. The same era enjoyed a postwar prosperity and overcame a massive unemployment that had haunted the depression generation, and did it without raising inflation. Yet even conservatives conceded that the fifties were not a "creative time" in the realm of high culture. This was all right for many of them since "creative periods have too often a way of coinciding with periods of death and destruction."

Whatever the retrospective of writers and intellectuals, those who lived through the fifties looked upon them as a period of unbounded possibility. This was especially true of the beginning of the decade when the lure and novelty of material comforts seemed irresistible. Toward the end of the decade a barely noticeable undercurrent of dissatisfaction emerged and by the early sixties a minority of women and men would rebel against the conditions of the fifties and wonder what had gone wrong with their lives. A sweet decade for the many, it became a sour experience for the few who would go on to question not only the feminine mystique but the masculine as well. In dealing with the fifties one must deal with its contented and its discontents. . . .

THE ECONOMY

The economic context is crucial. Between 1950 and 1958, the economy expanded enormously. A steady high growth rate of

4.7 percent heralded remarkable increases in living standards and other conditions of life. This prosperity derived from a combination of factors: (a) the lingering postwar back-up demand for consumer goods together with increased purchasing power as a result of savings; (b) the expansion of plant and machine tool capacity, and other technological advances left by the war and revived by the cold war and Korean conflict; (c) the appearance of new and modernized industries ranging from electronics to plastics; (d) population growth and the expansion of large cities; (e) increases in the productivity, or output per man-hour, of the working force; and (f) the commitment to foreign aid, which made possible overseas credits and American exports.

America experienced three mild recessions in the fifties, but through them all the rate of personal income grew and reached a record high of a 3.9 percent rise in 1960. If few became rich, the great majority lived more comfortably than ever before and enjoyed shorter hours on the job, as America moved to the five-day work week. Prior to the Second World War only 25 percent of the farming population had electricity. By the end of the fifties more than 80 percent had not only lighting but telephones, refrigerators, and televisions.

THE BABY BOOM GENERATION

The generation that had borne the depression and the war was now eager to put politics behind and move into a bountiful new world. One strong indicator of confidence in the future was a sudden baby boom. Demographers had been predicting a postwar relative decline in fertility rates and no expansion of immigration quotas. Instead, population leaped from 130 million in 1940 to 165 million by the mid-fifties, the biggest increase in the history of the Republic. Population migrated as well as grew, spreading into the region that came to be called "the sun belt," states like Florida, Texas, Arizona, and California. Farms and small towns lost population. Many big cities, while still growing with lower-class and minority inhabitants, witnessed the flight of the middle class to the periphery. The massive phenomenon of suburbia would rip apart and remake the texture of social life in America.

THE RISE OF SUBURBIA

Suburbia met a need and fulfilled a dream. During the depression and the war most Americans lived in apartments, flats, or

small houses within an inner city. After the war, with GIs returning and the marriage rate doubling, as many as two million
young couples had to share a dwelling with their relatives.
Some settled for a cot in the living room, while married college
students often had to live in off-campus quonset huts. Their immediate need for space in which to raise a family was answered
by the almost overnight appearance of tracts, subdivisions, and
other developments that sprawled across the landscape. Ironically, while suburban growth cut into the natural environment,
felling trees and turning fields into asphalt streets, the emotional
appeal of suburbia lay in a desire to recapture the greenness and
calm of rural life. Thus eastern tracts featured such names as
"Crystal Stream," "Robin Meadows," and "Stonybrook," while
in the West the Spanish motif of "Villa Serena" and "Tierra
Vista" conveyed the ambience of old, preindustrial California.
In California the tracts were developed by Henry J. Kaiser and
Henry Doelger, who drew on their war-time skills for mass production to provide ranch-style homes complete with backyards
and front lawns. In the Northeast William Levitt offered New
Yorkers and Pennsylvanians houses with shuttered windows
and steep pitched roofs to mimic the cozy Cape Cod look. Levitt
had never liked cities. Having no patience with people who did,
he saw his opportunity after the war when the government
agreed to guarantee to banks the entire amount of a veteran's
mortgage, making it possible for him to move in with no down
payment, depending on the Veteran Administration's assessment of the value of the specific property. To keep building costs
down, Levitt transformed the housing industry by using prefabricated walls and frames assembled on the site. In an effort
to foster community spirit, he and other builders added schools,
swimming pools, tennis courts, and athletic fields with Little
League diamonds. For young members of the aspiring middle
class, suburbia was a paradise of comfort and convenience.

Others were not so sure. "Is this the American dream, or is it
a nightmare?" asked *House Beautiful*. Architectural and cultural
critics complained of the monotony of house after house with
the same facade, paint, and lawn inhabited by people willing to
sign an agreement to keep them the same. One song writer
would call them "little boxes made of ticky-tacky." Some children who grew up in them would agree, rebelling in the following decade against all that was sterile and standardized. The
most angry critic was the cultural historian Lewis Mumford, au-

thor of *The City in History*. Mumford feared that Levitt was doing more to destroy the modern city than did the World War II aerial bombings. He also feared that suburbia was transforming the American character, rendering it dreary and conformist when it should be daring and courageous. "In the mass movement into suburban areas a new kind of community was produced, which caricatured both the historic city and the archetypal suburban refuge, a multitude of uniform, unidentifiable houses, lined up inflexibly at uniform distances, on uniform roads, in a treeless communal waste, inhabited by people in the same class, the same income, the same age group, witnessing the same television performances, eating the same tasteless prefabricated foods from the same freezers, conforming in every outward and inward respect to a common mold."

Admonishments aside, Americans were falling in love with suburbia—at least at first; some would have second thoughts and later wonder what they had bought, the theme of the cheerless film *No Down Payment* (1957). By the end of the fifties one-fourth of the population had moved to such areas. If not beautiful, suburbia was affordable, and thousands of homeless veterans were grateful to have their place in the sun for $65 per month on a full purchase price of $6,990 that included separate bedrooms for the children and a kitchen full of glittering gadgets. Such amenities also enabled housewives to be free of some domestic chores as they became involved in community affairs while their husbands commuted to work in the cities. A frequent event was the Tupperware party, arranged by wives ostensibly to sell household conveniences but also to overcome isolation and boredom. The most serious drawback of suburbia was that its planners envisaged no need for public transportation. As a result, suburbanites became forever dependent upon the automobile. When their children reached driving age, some households became three- or even four-car families. But in the fifties, when gasoline was relatively cheap and the promising new freeways wide and uncongested, the car was seen as a solution, not a problem. Indeed, for proud teenagers it was the supreme status symbol, the one possession that with its "souped-up" carburetors and lowered chassis and various metallic colors, answered the need for freedom and diversity in a community of flatness and conformity.

In the fifties, car was king. Freeways, multilevel parking lots, shopping centers, motels, and drive-in restaurants and theaters

New cars roll off the assembly line at a General Motors plant. By the 1950s, cars had become an essential part of American life.

all catered to the person behind the wheel. By 1956 an estimated seventy-five million cars and trucks were on American roads. One out of every seven workers held a job connected to the automobile industry. In suburbia the station wagon became a common sight. But really to fulfill the American dream one needed a Cadillac, or so advertisers informed the arriviste of new wealth with such effectiveness that one had to wait a year for delivery. Almost all American automobiles grew longer and wider. Their supersize and horsepower, together with more chrome and bigger tailfins, served no useful transportation purpose but were powerful enhancers of self-esteem. At the end of the decade, when many rich Texans, some country-western singers, salesmen, and even gangsters and pimps owned a Cadillac, it became what it always was, gauche, and its image declined from the sublime to the ridiculous.

CONSPICUOUS CONSUMPTION

In the fifties the spectacle of waste, once regarded by the older morality as a sign of sin, had become a sign of status. It was no coincidence that Americans junked almost as many cars as Detroit manufactured, thereby fulfilling Thorstein Veblen's earlier prediction that modern man would be more interested in displaying and destroying goods than in producing them. Veblen's insight into "conspicuous consumption" also took on real meaning in this era as Americans rushed out to buy the latest novelty, whether it was a convertible, TV set, deep-freeze, electric carving knife, or the "New Look" Christian Dior evening dress. The postwar splurge of consumption had been made possible by the $100 billion of savings Americans had banked during the war. Immediately after the war, household appliances were in demand, then luxuries like fashionable clothes and imported wines. For those who bought homes for $8,000 or more, luxuries were seen as necessities. The middle-class suburbanite looked out his window and "needed" what his neighbor had—a white Corvette or a swimming pool. Travel to Europe, once regarded as the "Grand Tour" only for the rich and famous, became accessible to millions of Americans in the fifties. For the masses who remained at home and took to the road, new tourist attractions sprang up, like Disneyland. Mass recreational mobility changed the nation's eating habits. In 1954 in San Bernardino, California, Ray Kroc, a high-school dropout, devised a precision stand for turning out french fries, beverages, and fifteen-cent hamburgers that grew rapidly into a fast-food empire: McDonald's.

Spending less time cooking and eating, Americans had more time for shopping. Discount houses such as Korvette's and Grant's opened up for the lower-middle class while the prestigious Neiman-Marcus catered to the needs of oil-rich Texans. Parents raised in the depression naturally felt that more was better, not only for themselves but particularly for their children. Teenagers splurged on phonograph records, bedroom decorations, cashmere sweaters, trips to Hawaii, motor scooters, and hot rods. The seemingly infinite indulgence of the young worried many parents even as they contributed to it. In a survey 94 percent of the mothers interviewed reported that their children had asked them to buy various goods they had seen on television.

TELEVISION AND CREDIT CARDS

Television in America, unlike in England and much of Western Europe, was supported by the advertising industry, which did more than any other institution to fill the viewer's eyes with images of abundance. Advertisers spent $10 billion a year to persuade, not to say manipulate, the people into buying products that promised to improve their lives, whether frozen peas or French perfume. Professional football, the prime target for beer ads, invented the "two-minute warning" in the last quarter to accommodate commercials. Confronted by a medical report linking smoking to lung cancer, tobacco companies increased their ad campaigns with jingles like "Be Happy Go Lucky!" Television bloomed with romantic scenes of a dashing young man offering a cigarette to a seductively beautiful woman under a full moon. As violins rose, the match was lit, and her face turned into that of a goddess—young, eager, divine. Partial take-offs from the Bogart-Bacall films of the early forties, Madison Avenue could readily exploit such scenes, perhaps realizing that desire can always be tempted precisely because it can never be completely fulfilled.

What facilitated the illusion of fulfillment was a little rectangle of plastic dubbed the credit card. In 1950 Diner's Club distributed credit cards to select wealthy New Yorkers to give them the privilege of eating at swank restaurants without fumbling for money. By the end of the decade Sears Roebuck alone had more than ten million accounts for those who chose to live on credit or, more bluntly, to be in debt. Installment buying shot consumer indebtedness up to $196 billion, so high that certain department stores offered "debt counselors" for worried customers. One soothing nostrum was a good stiff martini, the favorite drink of suburbia and the commuters' circle. Drinking rose sharply in the fifties. So did prescription-drugs use. Sales of "tranquilizers" soared; by 1959, 1,159,000 pounds had been consumed. The following decade the Food and Drug Administration discovered that the once-popular pill "miltown" had no medicinal value. But for the fifties generation, coping with the boss's demands at work and the children's at home, popping tranquilizing drugs became a respectable adult addiction. That mental anxiety should accompany material abundance is no surprise. For centuries moralists had warned that people become unhappy when they get what they want—or think they want. Suburbia offered Americans the cleanliness and safety of a planned community, but nothing is more hopeless than planned happiness.

THE STRUGGLE FOR BLACK EQUALITY: *BROWN V. BOARD OF EDUCATION*

HARVARD SITKOFF

Historians often suggest that World War II ushered in a new era in civil rights. In the preceding decades, African Americans had lived mostly in rural pockets of the South, often isolated from one another and subject to virulent racism that prevented them from voting or participating in civil life. School attendance figures for black children were much lower than for whites. In addition, the quality of education for black children was inferior to that provided to whites; in the South in 1916 the segregated school system spent an average of $10.32 for each white child, but only $2.89 for each black child. Gradually black people began to leave the South and congregate in urban communities where they could develop a sense of collective identity. In the 1930s, President Franklin D. Roosevelt initiated some cautious advances in civil rights by appointing blacks to administrative positions in the civil service, by extending the social welfare of the New Deal to all races, and by initiating the desegregation of facilities in federal offices.

During the Second World War, as the United States fought against the racist, anti-Semitic Nazis, it became clear that the American government needed to wage its own battles against racism. The war brought some changes: The marines and navy began to admit African Americans, and in 1948 Harry S. Truman officially desegregated the armed services. In addition, the war initiated waves of emigration from the repressive South, and a young generation of black men, having served their country, began to demand their civil rights under the law. By the late 1940s, civil rights had finally been forced onto the national agenda, and the ranks of the National Association for the Advancement of Colored People (NAACP), which primarily fought for equality by means of litigation, had swelled ten times, to nearly 10 million members.

In the following article, Harvard Sitkoff discusses the NAACP and the long struggle to desegregate education. The Supreme Court's famous *Brown v. Board of Education* decision of 1954, declaring segregated schools to be unlawful, represented a major milestone in the fight for equality. However, the struggle certainly did not end with this legal victory. The Supreme Court ruling was met with staunch resistance in the South that culminated in violent opposition as nine African American students went to enroll at Little Rock's Central High School. Sitkoff examines the legal, political, and social dimensions of the *Brown* decision, noting both the hopes and frustrations that characterized the black struggle for civil rights during the first decade of the cold war.

Harvard Sitkoff has been a professor at the University of New Hampshire since 1976. A highly respected and prolific author, as well as the recipient of numerous prestigious grants, Sitkoff's current research interests include the 1960s race riots, African Americans in World War II, and the "Hollywoodization" of history.

D uring World War II, millions of Americans became aware for the first time of the danger of racism to national security. Japan focused on the United States' racist treatment of nonwhites as the core of its propaganda campaign to win the loyalty of the colored peoples of China, India, and Latin America. Each lynching and race riot was publicized by the Axis as proof of the hypocrisy of President Franklin Roosevelt's Four Freedoms. The costs of racism went even higher during the Cold War. The Soviet Union undercut American appeals to the nations of Africa and Asia by highlighting the ill treatment of blacks in the United States. Rarely in the first two decades after the Second World War did a plea for civil rights before the Supreme Court, on the floor of Congress, or emanating from the White House, fail to emphasize the point that white racism adversely affected American relations with the nonwhite majority of the world. The rapid growth of independence movements among the world's colored peoples had special significance for African-Americans. They proved the feasibility of change and the vulnerability of white supremacy, while at the same time aiding African-Americans to see themselves as members of a world majority rather than as a hopelessly outnumbered American minority.

The further decline in intellectual respectability of racist ideas also convinced blacks that the winds of change blew their way. The excesses of Nazism and the decline of Western imperialism combined with internal developments in various academic disciplines to discredit the pseudo-scientific rationalizations once popularly accepted as the basis for white supremacy. Books and essays attacking racial injustice and inequality, epitomized by Gunnar Myrdal's *An American Dilemma,* dominated discourse on the subject.

These fundamental transpositions made it easy to believe that continued progress would be automatic, that just a bit more legal action or political pressure would suffice to usher in a new era in race relations. The demise of Jim Crow would necessitate neither struggle nor sacrifice, neither radical strategies nor disruptive tactics. This faith, obviating the need for mass black direct action, also reflected the conservative American mood after World War II. After more than a decade of rapid, bewildering change, and exhausting battles against the Great Depression and the Axis, the vast majority wanted surcease. Most Americans yearned for stability. They desired harmony. The fear of increasingly rapid social change hampered support for anything thought extremist, even reformist.

White supremacists, moreover, played on the obsessive American fear of Communism to discredit the civil-rights cause. They equated challenges to the racial status quo with un-Americanism, and missed no opportunity to link the black struggle with Communist ideology and subversion. In the heyday of red-baiting after World War II, these tactics worked. Most civil-rights groups avoided direct action. Their leadership opted for a conservative posture to avoid even a hint of radicalism. When a small interracial band of pacifists and socialists from the Congress of Racial Equality and the Fellowship of Recon-

ciliation journeyed throughout the upper South to test compliance of a Supreme Court ruling against segregation in interstate
travel, the Negro press barely reported the news, and other
civil-rights organizations shunned the 1947 Journey of Reconciliation. The following year they opposed A. Philip Randolph's
call for civil disobedience to protest Jim Crow in the armed
forces. With undue haste, the civil-rights leadership condemned
the pro-Soviet remarks of Paul Robeson, a controversial black
singer and actor, and disassociated themselves from the Marxist stance of W.E.B. Du Bois. The fear of McCarthyism so inhib-
ited blacks that they failed to use the Korean War as a lever for
racial reform, as they had World War II. At mid-century, direct
action had ceased being a tactic in the quest for racial justice.

THE NAACP

That suited the NAACP [National Association for the Advancement of Colored People] hierarchy. Never entirely at ease with
the black mass actions during the New Deal and early war
years, the NAACP became less a protest organization and more
an agency of litigation and lobbying after World War II. No
longer fearing that competition from more combative black
groups would overshadow the NAACP, its branches in the
South concentrated on voter registration, while those in the
North endeavored to secure fair-employment and fair-housing
ordinances. By 1953, twelve states and thirty cities had adopted
fair-employment laws of varying effectiveness. Median black-
family income rose from $1,614 to $2,338 between 1947 and 1952.
As a percentage of median white-family income, black earnings
jumped from 41 percent in 1940 to 51 percent in 1949, and to 57
percent in 1952. That year, nearly 40 percent of blacks were engaged in professional, white-collar, skilled, and semi-skilled
work, double the proportion of 1940. The life expectancy of
blacks increased from 53.1 years in 1940 to 61.7 years in 1953,
compared to 64.2 and 69.6 for whites, and the proportion of
black families owning their homes went from 25 percent to 30
percent in the forties. Meanwhile, the proportion of blacks aged
five to nineteen enrolled in school leaped from 60 percent in 1930
to 68.4 percent in 1940, to 74.8 percent in 1950. That figure still
lagged behind the 79.3 percent of whites in school, but the gap
had narrowed dramatically. And the number of blacks in college
had soared from about 27,000 in 1930 to over 113,000 in 1950.

Such gains apparently justified the NAACP's approach and

secured its hegemony in race relations. The national office and legal staff at midcentury marshaled all their resources for a courtroom assault on de jure school segregation. Many blacks believed integrated education to be the main route to racial equality. No other African-American protest group put forth an alternative strategy of social change. By 1954, all the hopes of blacks rested on the success of the NAACP litigation. It had become an article of faith that a Supreme Court decision ruling school segregation unconstitutional would cause the quick death of Jim Crow in America.

The first major crack in the edifice of school segregation had come in 1938, when the NAACP won a Supreme Court ruling which held that an out-of-state scholarship to a black Missourian wishing to study law at the University of Missouri denied that student the equal protection of the laws guaranteed by the constitution. The Court declared that Missouri could not exclude blacks from its law school when it offered African-Americans only out-of-state tuition grants as an alternative. Hoping to make segregation so prohibitively expensive that the South would dismantle its biracial system because of the financial burden, the NAACP launched a series of suits seeking complete equality in facilities governed by the separate-but-equal rule. Then, emboldened by the strides made by blacks during the Second World War, the NAACP's Legal Defense and Education Fund, led by Thurgood Marshall and based on a foundation of scores of courageous African-American plaintiffs, shifted from skirmishes on the inequality of separate facilities to a direct attack on segregation itself. Marshall hoped his strategy would force the Court to overrule *Plessy*, the 1896 opinion that declared segregation no infringement on civil rights if the states provided blacks with separate accommodations equal to those given to whites. Marshall's work resulted first in three unanimous decisions on a single day in 1950 which demolished the separate-but-equal façade. The high court struck down Jim Crow on railway dining cars in the South; it ruled that if a state chose not to establish an equal and separate school for blacks, then it could not segregate blacks within the white school; and, lastly, the tribunal so emphasized the importance of "intangible factors" in determining the equality of separate schools that separate-but-equal no longer seemed possible. Although the Supreme Court held that it was not necessary to reexamine *Plessy* to grant relief to the three black plaintiffs, the 1950 decisions made the end of segregated schooling for students at all levels a near-certainty.

THE *BROWN* SUIT

Working closely with the grassroots leadership of the local chapters, Marshall began to coordinate a series of lawsuits in 1951 charging segregated education with being discriminatory per se, even if the facilities were equal. In Clarendon County, South Carolina, the NAACP sued in the name of several black schoolchildren, and in Prince Edward County, Virginia, they represented black high-school students. In New Castle County, Delaware, and in the District of Columbia, Marshall filed suits on behalf of both elementary and high-school black students. And in Topeka, Kansas, the NAACP argued the case of Oliver Brown, who sought to enjoin enforcement of a state law that permitted cities to maintain segregated schools, which forced his eight-year-old daughter, Linda, to travel a mile by bus to reach a black school even though she lived only three blocks from an all-white elementary school. Risking their jobs and lives, the plaintiffs persisted, and on December 9, 1952, the Supreme Court heard oral argument on all five cases, combined and docketed under the name of the petitioner listed first—Oliver Brown. Unexpectedly, the NAACP was aided by the Truman Administration, which, in its last days, filed a brief as a friend of the Court arguing against the constitutionality of segregation.

The Supreme Court initially divided on the question of overturning *Plessy*. After several months of discussion, two justices changed their mind, creating a slim majority in favor of the NAACP's contention. Now the question became whether the justices in the minority could be likewise persuaded. To that end, the Court voted for a reargument. It asked the litigants to prepare answers to questions pertaining to the intentions of the framers of the Fourteenth Amendment, the power of the Court to abolish segregation in the schools, and, if the tribunal did have such a right and chose to exercise it, whether the Supreme Court could permit gradual desegregation or did it have to order an instant end to segregation. While the lawyers revised their briefs, Chief Justice Fred Vinson died suddenly in the summer of 1953. The new President, Dwight D. Eisenhower, appointed California Governor Earl Warren to fill the vacant post. Vinson had sought to avoid ruling on *Plessy*, and in all likelihood, two other justices would have voted with him, resulting in either a further postponement on the constitutionality of school segregation or a seriously split decision.

Following the reargument, which began on December 7 and lasted for three days, the nation waited for what commentators predicted would be a historic decision. But for half a year the Court remained silent. Behind closed doors, the bickering and bargaining continued. A clear majority of the justices wanted to void segregation in the schools and to reverse *Plessy*. Two justices held out, and Warren kept postponing the decision, hoping he could gain their concurrence. Above all, the Chief Justice wanted the Court's ruling to be unanimous. Anything less on a social issue so sensitive, on a political question so explosive, would destroy the chance for full compliance by Southern whites. So, patiently, Warren beseeched and compromised. Finally, early in May, the two dissenters gave the Chief Justice their assent.

THE *BROWN* RULING

By Monday, May 17, 1954, the Supreme Court ruling on school segregation had been so overdue that many forgot its imminence. The morning's newspapers gave no hint that a decision would be announced. Most journalists in Washington speculated on the consequences of a French loss of Dien Bien Phu in Vietnam, on the outcome of the Army-McCarthy hearings, and on the chances for more rain. Even those reporters seated in the ornate chamber of the Supreme Court did not anticipate that the segregation decision would be announced when the Court convened at noon.

After forty minutes of routine business, the Chief Justice leaned forward and began to read: "I have for announcement the judgment and opinion of the Court in No. 1—*Oliver Brown et al. v. Board of Education of Topeka*." Warren traced the paths that led the cases to the Supreme Court and reviewed the history of the Fourteenth Amendment, finding it "inconclusive" in relation to school segregation because public education, particularly in the South, had barely developed in the 1860s. "Today," the Chief Justice continued, "education is perhaps the most important function of state and local governments." Since it is the key to opportunity and advancement in American life, public education "is a right which must be made available to all on equal terms." On this premise, he came to the nub of the matter: "Does segregation of children in public schools solely on the basis of race, even though the physical facilities and other 'tangible' factors may be equal, deprive the children of the minority group of equal educational opportunities?"

Warren paused. "We believe that it does." Buttressed by a footnote citing several contemporary studies on the psychological effects of segregation, the former governor contended that the separation of black children "from others of similar age and qualifications solely because of their race generates a feeling of inferiority as to their status in the community that may affect their hearts and minds in a way unlikely ever to be undone." He ended in a rising voice. "We conclude that in the field of public education the doctrine of 'separate but equal' has no place. Separate educational facilities are inherently unequal. Therefore, we hold that the plaintiffs and others similarly situated for whom the actions have been brought are, by reason of the segregation complained of, deprived of the equal protection of the laws guaranteed by the Fourteenth Amendment."

Blacks shouted hosannas as they heard the news. They hailed Marshall, the black lawyer who had used the white man's laws before an all-white Supreme Court to win a verdict voiding segregation. Their jubilant leaders vied in choosing superlatives to laud the decision. *Brown* would be the precedent for declaring unconstitutional any state-imposed or enforced segregation. African-Americans in pursuit of full citizenship rights now had not only morality on their side but the law as well. Surely, most rhapsodized, a new day in race relations had dawned. *Brown* promised a truly equal education for black children in inte-

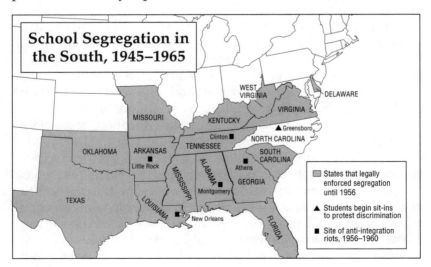

School Segregation in the South, 1945–1965

WEST VIRGINIA
DELAWARE
VIRGINIA
MISSOURI
KENTUCKY
▲ Greensboro
Clinton ■
NORTH CAROLINA
OKLAHOMA
ARKANSAS
TENNESSEE
SOUTH CAROLINA
Little Rock
ALABAMA
Athens
GEORGIA
MISSISSIPPI
Montgomery ■
TEXAS
LOUISIANA
New Orleans ■
FLORIDA

States that legally enforced segregation until 1956

▲ Students begin sit-ins to protest discrimination

■ Site of anti-integration riots, 1956–1960

grated classrooms throughout the nation. More, it offered the real beginning of a multiracial society. Robert Williams of North Carolina, who would later urge African-Americans to get guns to assert their due, remembered: "My inner emotions must have been approximate to the Negro slaves' when they first heard about the Emancipation Proclamation. . . . I felt that at last the government was willing to assert itself on behalf of first-class citizenship, even for Negroes. I experienced a sense of loyalty that I had never felt before. I was sure that this was the beginning of a new era of American democracy." *Brown* heightened the aspirations and expectations of African-Americans as nothing before had. It *proved* that the Southern segregation system could be challenged and defeated. It *proved* that change was possible. Nearly a century after their professed freedom had been stalled, compromised, and stolen, blacks confidently anticipated being free and equal at last.

IMPLEMENTING DESEGREGATION

Little in the next year shook this faith. Few Dixie politicians rushed to echo Mississippi Senator James O. Eastland that the South "will not abide by nor obey this legislative decision by a political court." Most educators foresaw scant difficulty in putting the court ruling into effect. According to a *New York Times* survey of school officials, none thought "that the threats to abandon the public school system would be carried out. . . . No one expected any violence or any real crisis to develop." Several hundred school districts in the border states (Delaware, Kentucky, Maryland, Missouri, Oklahoma, and West Virginia) and in states with local option on segregation (Arizona, Kansas, New Mexico, and Wyoming) quickly and peacefully integrated their classrooms, as did the District of Columbia at President Eisenhower's direction.

Then, on May 31, 1955, the momentum stopped. Just fifty-four weeks after the Supreme Court had taken a giant stride toward the demise of Jim Crow, it stepped backward. Its implementation decision on the *Brown* ruling rejected the NAACP's plea to order instant and total school desegregation. The justices, instead, adopted the "go slow" approach advocated by the Justice Department and by the attorneys general of the Southern states. The Court assigned the responsibility for drawing up plans for desegregation to local school authorities and left it to local federal judges to determine the pace of desegregation, requiring only that a "prompt and reasonable start toward full compliance" be made and that desegregation proceed "with all deliberate speed." Acknowledging the potential for difficulties, the Supreme Court refused to set a deadline and authorized delays when necessary. For the first time, the Supreme Court had vindicated a constitutional right and then deferred its exercise.

However much the Warren Court foresaw the endless round of further litigation and obstruction this invited, circumstances dictated the decision for gradualism. It was the price of unanimity in *Brown v. Board of Education*, the compromise needed to keep two justices from dissenting. Warren deeply believed that a divided Court on so sensitive an issue "would have been catastrophic," that only a unanimous desegregation decision stood a chance of public support.

He accepted gradualism to allay the fears of those justices who worried that the Court's inability to enforce a momentous ruling would discredit the judicial process. The compromise also reflected the unpopularity of *Brown* in the South. Public-opinion polls showed more than 80 percent of white Southerners opposed to school desegregation, and the Supreme Court hoped to head off resistance to the law of the land by permitting the change to be piecemeal. To order immediate school desegregation, the Court reckoned, would force most Southern politicians to take up the cudgels of defiance to federal authority, an action only a tiny minority had taken to date. The Justices sought to contain the rebellion, since they could not count on the other branches of the federal government.

EISENHOWER STALLS

No help would come from the White House. President Dwight D. Eisenhower refused to endorse or support the *Brown* ruling. Covetous of the votes of white Southerners and wedded to a restrictive view of Presidential authority, Eisenhower stated that he would express neither "approbation nor disapproval" of *Brown v. Board of Education*. He lumped together those who demanded compliance with the Court decision and those who obstructed it, publicly denouncing "extremists on both sides." To one of his aides, Eisenhower emphasized: "I am convinced that the Supreme Court decision set back progress in the South at least fifteen years. . . . It's all very well to talk about school integration— if you remember you may also be talking about social *dis*integration. Feelings are deep on this. . . . And the fellow who tries to tell me that you can do these things by force is just plain nuts."

Eisenhower preferred change as a result of education, rather than coercion. But he would not educate. The President rejected pleas that he tour the South seeking compliance, or call a conference of Southern moderates, or appeal on television to the nation for understanding. He simply did not favor school desegregation, much as he had never approved desegregation of the armed forces. Eisenhower regretted he had ever appointed Earl Warren to the Supreme Court, calling it "the biggest damfool mistake I ever made." And the titular head of the Democratic Party, Adlai Stevenson, barely differed on this issue from his GOP rival. Stevenson asked that the white South be "given time and patience," rejected the idea of using federal troops to enforce court-ordered desegregation, and opposed all proposals that would bar federal aid to schools maintaining segregation.

To be sure, no danger existed in the mid-fifties that Congress would legislate to speed desegregation. A conservative coalition of Midwestern Republicans and Southern Democrats controlled both the House of Representatives and the Senate, guarding against any infringement on states' rights. Not content merely to stonewall any move to support *Brown,* Southern congressmen mobilized in 1956 to fight against what Senator Richard Russell of Georgia termed "a flagrant abuse of judicial power" and what Virginia Senator Harry Byrd called "the most serious blow that has been struck against the rights of the states." On March 12, 1956, 101 members of Congress from the South signed a "Declaration of Constitutional Principles" asking their states to refuse to obey the desegregation order. Labeling *Brown* "unwarranted" and "contrary to the Constitution," the Southern manifesto proclaimed that the Supreme Court possessed no power to demand an end to segregation, that only a state, and not the federal government, can decide whether a school should be segregated or not, and that the states would be in the right in opposing the Court's order.

RESISTANCE TO THE *BROWN* DECISION

The manifesto, along with Eisenhower's silence and the Supreme Court's paradoxical "deliberate speed" ruling, ushered in an era of massive resistance to the law of the land in the eleven states of the Old Confederacy. Defiance of the Court and the Constitution became the touchstone of Southern loyalty, the necessary proof of one's concern for the security of the white race. With the overwhelming support of the South's white press and pulpit, segregationist politicians resurrected John C. Calhoun's notions of "interposition" and "nullification" to thwart federal authority.

White supremacists first resorted to stalling, doing nothing until confronted with a federal-court injunction. This forced black parents and NAACP attorneys to initiate individual desegregation suits in the more than two thousand Southern school districts. Usually, the black plaintiffs faced economic intimidation by the local white-power structure; often they risked physical harm; always, they encountered repeated postponements due to crowded court dockets and motions for delay by school authorities. After years of harassment to the plaintiffs, mounting legal costs to the NAACP, lost jobs, mortgages foreclosed, loans denied, and incalculable psychological damage to blacks due to threats and fear, school authorities would finally come up with a plan for the most limited, token desegregation.

Then black schoolchildren had to face the horrors of racist resistance. In one school district after another, segregationists forced young African-Americans to walk a gantlet of hate, fear, and ignorance, to pass by rock-throwing mobs and pickets shrieking "Nigger! Nigger! Nigger!" They pressured white teachers to ignore or persecute the black students, and encouraged white children to torment and threaten their new black classmates. "'If you come back to school, I'll cut your guts out!' could be heard in the halls," recalled a Tennessee high-school teacher. "Eggs smashed on their books, ink smeared on their clothes, in the lockers, knives flourished in their presence, nails tossed in their faces and spiked in their seats. Vulgar words constantly whispered in their ears." The harassment proved too much for some blacks. They reenrolled their children in segregated schools; they moved to other towns and states. But more and more blacks endured the hatred and persisted in their struggle for dignity and equality.

To frustrate such black courage, segregationists pressed for new laws to obstruct integration. "As long as we can legislate, we can segregate," said one white supremacist, and the Southern states rushed pell-mell to enact more than 450 laws and resolutions to prevent or limit school desegregation. Some acts required schools faced with desegregation orders to cease operation; others revoked the license of any teacher who taught mixed classes; still more amended compulsory-attendance laws, so that no child could be required to enroll in an integrated school, and provided for state payments of private-academy tuition, so that districts could abolish their public-school system rather than desegregate. . . .

Not content with legal measures of obstruction, hostile segregationists preached violent resistance. Virulent rabble-rousers, often with the approval of the South's respected spokesmen, stirred up the region's whites to attack blacks insisting on their constitutional rights. The Ku Klux Klan revived. Zealots across the South organized new klaverns, donned their white hoods and robes, and burned crosses to terrorize blacks. Too respectable to join the low-status KKK, thousands of middle-class whites rushed to enroll in the White Citizens' Councils, the National Association for the Advancement of White People, and the American States Rights Association. They wore no masks but proved just as determined as the Klan to defy *Brown* and enforce racial orthodoxy, by intimidation if possible and by insurrection if necessary. Together, the KKK, the Councils, and a host of local vigilante committees brought riots and violent demonstrations to the South at the start of the school year each September.

Their lawless behavior, often directed at young children, outraged millions of Americans who did not live in the South. Most Northerners cared little about school desegregation in Dixie and considered the NAACP too militant. Nevertheless, they were shocked at the news headlines of schools being dynamite-bombed and the televised scenes of hate-filled white mobs. Time and again in the decade ahead, such racist extremism would discredit the cause of the white South and force a majority of otherwise unconcerned citizens to demand that the federal government act to preserve order. It happened first in Little Rock.

CRISIS AT LITTLE ROCK

A New South city, Little Rock appeared an unlikely battleground in the fight over school desegregation. It had a racially moderate mayor, congressman, and newspaper, and a governor not known to be a race-baiter. Several other Arkansas communities had peacefully begun to desegregate, as had the state university, and, after a bit of stalling, Little Rock's school board acceded to a federal court order to admit nine blacks to Central High, a school with some two thousand white students, as the first step toward integration. A model of gradualism and deference to the whites of Little Rock, the desegregation process would take eight years to complete. Indeed, the only vocal opposition to it came from the local NAACP, which denounced the process as too token and too slow.

In 1957, however, the winds of resistance howled. A storm of racial demagoguery swept the South. Politicians shouted defiance of the Supreme Court and vied in pledging unyielding opposition to *Brown*. Some vowed they would go to jail rather than desegregate; some swore they would die rather than permit integration. Those who counseled moderation customarily came in second and, like George C. Wallace in Alabama, promised: "They outniggered me that time, but they'll never do it again." In Arkansas, Governor Orval Faubus believed he faced a difficult fight for reelection. But he found the answer to his ambitions in the political climate. He would campaign as the preeminent defender of white supremacy. He would "outnigger" his racist opponents. He would obstruct the federal court order in Little Rock.

On September 2, the evening before Arkansas schools were to reopen, Faubus went on television to announce that it would "not be possible to restore or to maintain order if forcible integration is carried out tomorrow," despite the fact that no Little Rock officials then anticipated trouble. He ordered a National Guard contingent to Central High School. Ostensibly, their mission was to prevent violence. But when the nine black students sought to enter the school on September 3, the guardsmen barred their way. "Governor Faubus has placed this school off limits to Negroes," announced a National Guard spokesman. The federal district court in Arkansas again insisted that desegregation begin and ordered the governor to show cause why he should not be enjoined from interfering with the school board's plan. When the black students prepared to enter Central High the following day, a milling crowd of angry whites shouted: "Niggers. Niggers. They're coming. Here they come!" The guardsmen once again barred the African-Americans seeking to enroll in Central High. The authority of the federal government and of a state had directly clashed. National attention now focused on President Eisenhower, who was constitutionally required to enforce the law of the land.

EISENHOWER ACTS

Eisenhower had no desire to do so. He had never offered leadership on racial matters. He considered *Brown* a mistake. His belief in the limits of federal power and his fondness for states' rights combined to make the President highly reluctant to intervene in Little Rock. "You cannot change people's hearts merely by laws," he told a press conference that week, adding a grave remark about the white South's concern for the "mongrelization of the race." The general believed Dixie ripe for Republicanism. He had won four Southern states in 1952, and five in 1956. Looking ahead to 1960, Eisenhower was determined to avoid any action that would reestablish the Democratic grip on the mass of white Southern voters. Purposefully, he would do nothing to rally public opinion behind desegregation. Yet he could not ignore Faubus's defiance of a federal court order, and television had made Little Rock the focus of national attention. To give the appearance of action without really acting, Eisenhower met with the governor on September 14. Both politicians talked truce and temporized.

On September 20, the federal district court repeated its order to the governor to stop interfering with school desegregation in Little Rock. Predicting bloodshed, Faubus withdrew the National Guard from Central High and left the state. However, several of the governor's henchmen, adept at mobilizing mob violence, remained in Little Rock. By early Monday morning, September 23, over a thousand shrieking white protesters surrounded the high school. Racists from across the South had flocked to the city to prevent the blacks from entering the school. While white students sang "Two, four, six, eight, we ain't gonna integrate," the mob jeered "Niggers, keep away from our school. Go back to the jungle." Over and over the crowd reassured itself: "The niggers won't get in." Suddenly someone roared: "They've gone in!" "Oh, my God!" a woman cried. "The niggers are inside!" "They're in!" others screamed. "They're in!" "The niggers are in our school." Some began a new chant: "Come on out! Come on out!" Groups of white students exited from Central High to shouts of approval, stimulating louder importuning, and more white students left the school. The mayor, fearful of violence, ordered the nine blacks withdrawn.

That evening President Eisenhower appeared on television to denounce the "disgraceful occurrence" at Little Rock. Aware that the unruly segregationist mob had riveted world attention on Little Rock, he issued a proclamation directing those who had obstructed federal law "to cease and desist." But an even larger mob milled about Central High the next morning and school board officials dreaded inflaming the howling protesters by forcing the entry of the nine blacks. Eisenhower responded by federalizing the Arkansas National Guard and dispatching a thousand troops of the 101st Airborne Division to Little Rock. The next morning, with fixed bayonets, the paratroopers dispersed the crowd and led the black students into Central High School. Armed troops remained in the school for two months, escorting the nine blacks to their classes. Then the President replaced the paratroopers with federalized Arkansas guardsmen, who continued to patrol Central High for the rest of the year.

Southern extremism had forced Eisenhower's hand. Not to have acted, he ruefully told a Southern senator, would have been "tantamount to acquiescence in anarchy and the dissolution of the union." As a last resort he dispatched federal troops to uphold national supremacy, defend Presidential authority, and enforce the law of the land. In so doing, Eisenhower became the first President since Reconstruction to use armed troops to protect African-American citizens and their constitutional rights. . . .

THE IMPACT OF THE *BROWN* DECISION

More than anything else, *Brown v. Board of Education* and its aftermath stimulated black hope and anguish. For much of the first half of the twentieth century, blacks had accepted the leadership of the NAACP in their struggle for equality and had followed the association in relying upon litigation and legislative lobbying to eradicate racism. By 1954, many African-Americans believed that the overturning of *Plessy* in the school cases would rapidly undermine the whole Jim Crow system.

But it did not happen. "Colored" and "White" signs remained over drinking fountains and rest rooms from one end of the South to the other. Southern blacks could not sit down next to a white and be served a hamburger or a cup of coffee. Drivers continued to demand that blacks stay in the back of the bus. Worse, African-Americans still attended schools that were both squalid and segregated. In 1960, only one-sixth of one percent of the black students in the South went to a desegregated school. By 1964, just two percent of the black children in the South attended integrated schools, and none at all in the two Southern counties involved in the *Brown* decision.

LIVING WITH THE BOMB

SUSAN JONAS AND MARILYN NISSENSON

During the 1950s, as the cold war intensified, Americans faced the possibility of a nuclear confrontation with the Soviets. In 1951, President Harry S. Truman established the Federal Civil Defense Administration to devise strategies for protecting Americans from the effects of a nuclear attack. The looming threat of nuclear catastrophe colored daily life in the United States. In the following selection, Susan Jonas and Marilyn Nissenson describe how the ever-present danger of nuclear war was reflected in the culture, as children were taught "duck-and-cover" drills in schools and families invested in backyard fallout shelters. Jonas and Nissenson are the authors of *Going, Going, Gone: Vanishing America*, from which this selection was excerpted.

I n 1950, the invasion of South Korea by the Communist North Korean army forced Americans to face the possibility of World War III and total nuclear annihilation. Images of the suffering inflicted five years earlier by the atomic bombs dropped on Hiroshima and Nagasaki were still vivid. The popular press pictured American cities devastated by atomic attack with transportation paralysed, power and food supplies destroyed, hundreds of thousands of casualties, and no way to get help for the sick and dying.

Acknowledging the "grim new reality," President Harry Truman created the Federal Civil Defense Administration in January 1951. Many of the materials it produced were intended to prepare schoolchildren for atomic war, to "alert, not alarm" them. Teachers and parents were urged not to become unduly emotional at the prospect of Russian attack. The national PTA urged a soothing, "positive mental health program" in response to atomic anxiety. The bomb's worst effects, such as traumatic injuries, shock, burns, radiation sickness, and death, were to be played down.

AIR-RAID DRILLS

Throughout the 1950s many cities staged regular air-raid drills. Civil defense officials tested all 741 sirens in New York City every month. A one-minute alert was followed by a warbling sound that meant "take cover." Schools, especially in target cities like New York, Los Angeles, Chicago, and Philadelphia, conducted "duck-and-cover" drills. When the teacher suddenly shouted "drop!" all the children would kneel, hands clasped behind their necks and their faces shielded.

The FCDA circulated a comic book featuring Bert the Turtle. Bert said: "You have learned to take care of yourself in many ways—to cross streets safely—and what to do in case of fire. . . . BUT the atomic bomb is a new danger . . . things will get knocked down all over town. . . . You must be ready to protect yourself." Bert warned children to "DUCK to avoid things flying through the air." With his head retracted into his shell, he urged them to "COVER to keep from getting cut or even badly burned."

Many school districts distributed special student identification, modeled after military dog tags. The tags were designed to help civil defense workers identify lost or dead children in event of nuclear attack. By 1952 New York City had issued two and a half million free dog tags to public, parochial, and private schoolchildren.

SHELTER OR EVACUATE?

In 1954 Lewis Strauss, chairman of the Atomic Energy Commission, revealed the existence of a new weapon, the H-bomb, which could incinerate an entire city. The H-bomb made obsolete all previous civil defense plans based on estimates of A-bomb damage. The only response, said one civil defense administrator in 1954, is to "die, dig, or get out." Digging bombproof shelters throughout the country would have cost more than the Eisenhower administration was willing to spend, so plans were made to evacuate cities on the basis of a four- to six-hour warning of a bomber attack.

As Americans faced the possibility of a nuclear attack by the Soviets, many families invested in backyard fallout shelters.

It was later revealed that the federal government was willing to shelter a select few. A secret concrete-and-steel bunker for members of Congress was built in 1958 into a hill adjacent to the luxurious Greenbrier resort in White Sulphur Springs, West Virginia, 250 miles southwest of Washington. The government also built quarters at Mount Weather in Virginia, where the president, members of the Supreme Court, and other top officials could ride out the emergency.

In the late 1950s, intercontinental ballistic missiles armed with nuclear warheads put an end to evacuation planning. ICBMs could cover the five thousand miles between Washington and Moscow in thirty minutes or less, which barely allowed anyone enough time to get out of town or take shelter. "Civil defense is dead, as of right now," declared a writer in the September 28, 1957, issue of the *Nation*. "To all the people who have been worrying because the stumbling procedures of the FCDA left them uncertain and unprepared, the ICBM brings a paradoxical note of cheer: you don't have to worry anymore."

FAMILY FALLOUT SHELTERS

The Rand Corporation, however, predicted that civil defense could limit carnage even in a nuclear exchange. An effective combination of military and civil defense would give half the population a good chance of survival in a thermonuclear war, which, though catastrophic, would not wipe out all life. Rand recommended that people spend one or two hundred dollars of their own money to build a family fallout shelter. . . .

"Fallout shelter fever" hit America. Sporting goods stores did a brisk business in camping equipment for use in basement shelters. The sales pitch at the Prince Georges County Shopping Plaza outside Washington, D.C., was typical. A bass voice over the loudspeaker announced, "This is condition Red." A siren wailed; a bomb exploded. A male voice screamed, "My wife, my children." Pause. "If I'd only listened to Civil Defense, I'd be in a shelter now." This commercial message was designed to attract attention to a closed-circuit TV view of a nine-by-ten-foot cinder-block basement shelter which could protect a family of four for a week before they ran out of supplies. . . .

No one knows how many shelters were sold—maybe as many as two hundred thousand. But by the end of 1962, the threat of nuclear war eased. One Detroit dealer advertised "Fallout Shelters While They Last" and slashed prices down to $100. He tried to give one away. A writer was willing to use the shelter as a study. A woman wanted it for a toolshed. A businessman in Beirut thought it would make a nice beach house. "But almost nobody wanted it as a shelter," the dealer said. A Michigan farmer finally hauled it off, because he thought it might be useful in the event of a tornado.

NOT A VIABLE SOLUTION

In December 1961 the *Washington Daily News* summed up the state of civil defense in the early 1960s: "C is for confusion; D is for Dilemma." People feared that shelter programs emphasized surviving war rather than averting it. Others complained that the government's every-man-for-himself approach brought out the worst in human nature. There were serious debates about whether or not the head of a household had the right to gun down any outsider who tried to get into the family shelter. The average person couldn't afford to build one and, in any case, thought the nation should be responsible for each citizen's personal defense.

As time passed, speculation centered on the horrors of nuclear winter: subfreezing temperatures, darkness at noon, worldwide fallout, and partial destruction of the ozone layer. As Jonathan Schell wrote in *The Fate of the Earth,* "The vulnerability of the environment is the last word in the argument against the usefulness of shelters: there is no hole big enough to hide all of nature in." Although the preoccupation with nuclear war continued, and national defense remained a major issue, civil defense ceased to be a viable solution. No one wanted to live on in a devastated and radioactive world.

The Cold War Heats Up: 1960–1969

CHAPTER 3

CAMELOT AND THE NEW FRONTIER

NORMAN L. ROSENBERG AND EMILY S. ROSENBERG

As the son of Joseph P. Kennedy, a Massachusetts millionaire whose own political career had been frustrated, John Kennedy was groomed for the political office from a young age. When his older brother died in combat during World War II, John became the focus of his father's political aspirations. Kennedy attended Choate Rosemary Hall, and then studied at Harvard. His undergraduate senior essay, *Why England Slept,* in which he analyzed the causes of Britain's failure to mobilize against fascism earlier, was published soon after he graduated. In 1946, Kennedy entered the House of Representatives, and by 1950, he had secured a seat in the Senate. While he did not sponsor any important bills during his time as a senator, in 1955 he published another book, *Profiles in Courage,* that won a 1958 Pulitzer Prize (although it later emerged that Theodore Sorenson and others had actually researched and written the book). Although he garnered a reputation as an impressive intellectual in some circles, critics felt that Kennedy had merely used his wealth and connections to secure his public success.

Kennedy defeated Richard Nixon, Dwight D. Eisenhower's vice president, by a very narrow majority in the 1960 presidential election. The recent rise of television helped elevate Kennedy's appeal, for in contrast to the rather shifty-eyed and sharp-featured Nixon, Kennedy was young, good-looking, and urbane. Coming after several older presidents—Franklin D. Roosevelt, Harry S. Truman, and Eisenhower—Kennedy's youth and vitality distinguished him; in his inaugural address, he reminded Americans that he would be the first president born in the twentieth century. People believed that his energy would infuse the country and initiate an era of hope and positive activity.

A polished orator, Kennedy succeeded in rousing a wave of idealism and patriotism. He and his attractive, aristocratic wife were seen as the closest thing to royalty that America had. After Kennedy assembled an exceptional collection of young academic and business minds to serve in his cabinet, the Kennedy White House began to be called "Camelot." In the following excerpt, historians Norman L. Rosenberg and Emily S. Rosenberg describe Camelot and Kennedy's program for social change, the "New Frontier."

Although Kennedy could hardly claim a popular mandate, his publicists quickly built an imposing image for his administration—the "New Frontier," the energetic successor to the New Deal and the Fair Deal. First, JFK assembled his version of Roosevelt's brain trust. He appointed his brother and campaign manager, Robert Kennedy, attorney general; Robert McNamara, president of Ford Motor Company, became secretary of defense; Harvard's McGeorge Bundy assumed the important role of national security adviser to the president; and Dean Rusk, head of the Ford Foundation, got the coveted position of secretary of state. Even the secondary jobs claimed top individuals. (Even Henry Kissinger found himself outgunned in such fierce competition and took over Bundy's courses at Harvard, awaiting an administration that would better appreciate his talents.) Few of these advisers had much political experience, but they had all been eminently successful in other areas. Vice-president Johnson left the first cabinet meeting dazzled by the intellect that Kennedy had assembled. "You should have seen all those men," he told his old political mentor, House Speaker Sam Rayburn. "Well, Lyndon, you may be right and they may be every bit as intelligent as you say," replied Mr. Sam, "but I'd feel a whole lot better about them if just one of them had run for sheriff once."

The Kennedy White House became celebrated as a center of art and culture. Jacqueline Kennedy, a well-educated woman who spoke several foreign languages, became the special guardian of culture: She invited artists such as cellist Pablo Casals to perform at the White House, redecorated the old mansion, and then conducted a tour of it for millions of television viewers. Kennedy parties were lavish productions in the grand style; I.F. Stone, the radical journalist, complained that the atmosphere resembled that of "a reigning monarch's court." Such a comparison probably did not disturb Kennedyphiles. Many of the president's followers reveled in the reputation of the Kennedy White House as a modern-day Camelot.

TOUGHNESS

In addition to intellect and style, the New Frontier emphasized toughness. As John Kennedy boasted in his inaugural address, he and his advisers were all young men "born in this century, tempered by war, disciplined by a hard and bitter peace." Facing the challenges of a dangerous world, they believed that they could not afford to appear soft. In defending his space program, for example, JFK bragged that Americans would accept the challenges of space "not because they are easy but because they are hard." The Kennedy team displayed its toughness during impromptu touch football games; here the president's brother Robert gained the reputation as the most hard nosed New Frontiersman, one who had no room for losers. After Floyd Patterson lost his heavyweight boxing title, the attorney general removed the ex-champ's picture from his office.

All the Kennedy people prided themselves on their ability to handle any foreign or domestic crisis, and they seemed almost anxious to find them. In 1962 Kennedy massed the full power of the national government to combat a price increase by United States Steel and several other large firms. JFK denounced the companies as unpatriotic, contrasting their actions with the sacrifices of servicemen who were already dying in Vietnam and reservists who had been called up to meet a feared confrontation with the Soviet Union in Berlin. The president coupled his verbal assaults with a massive legal offensive: The Justice Department began to seek evidence of price fixing; FBI agents started to investigate possible illegal activities by steel corporations; the Federal Trade Commission threatened to look into the same questions; and administration sources even hinted at possible antitrust actions to break up the steel giants. At the same time, the Defense Department refused to buy from companies that raised prices, and Kennedy aides pressured corporate friends to resist the lead of U.S. Steel. Confronted by this counterattack, Big Steel retreated and rolled back prices. Throughout the short skirmish the president viewed the controversy as

Americans believed that President Kennedy's youth and vitality would infuse the country and initiate an era of hope.

an extension of foreign affairs, claiming that price increases threatened national security. It was the type of problem, he believed, that required crisis management.

The president's critics viewed the situation differently. Business representatives predictably denounced Kennedy for using "police state" tactics, but even some foes of large corporations expressed concern. A young law professor, Charles Reich (who would later gain fame as author of *The Greening of America*), concluded that it was "dangerously wrong for an angry president to loose his terrible arsenal of power for the purposes of intimidation and coercing private companies and citizens." Other observers contended that Kennedy's actions reflected a dangerous crisis mentality and indicated the administration's lack of consistent domestic policies. Within a year the steel firms raised prices twice, and the Kennedy administration did nothing.

THE NEW FRONTIER

Although JFK was more interested in foreign policy than in domestic affairs, he announced general goals for his New Frontier at home. The new Democratic administration revived many of Harry Truman's old Fair Deal proposals: federal aid to education, a national health program, and expansion of other welfare-state spending programs. Kennedy never saw his education program or Medicare pass Congress, but he could take some credit for several less spectacular measures. Congress extended Social Security coverage to more American workers, covered more people by federal wage standards, raised the minimum wage to $1.25 an hour, appropriated nearly $5 billion for public housing, established the manpower training program, and passed an area-redevelopment act for West Virginia and other impoverished areas in Appalachia. These measures reflected JFK's preference for moderate, gradual reforms and his political caution.

In addition to updating the Fair Deal's gradualist social welfare programs, the Kennedy administration tried to redefine the techniques of Truman's liberal economists. In his first state-of-the-union address, JFK promised that the sluggish economy would soon show both "a prompt recovery" and "long-range growth." Kennedy, of course, blamed the country's economic problems on the Eisenhower administration: The GNP had risen slowly during the late 1950s while the unemployment rate had climbed to around 6 percent. Although Kennedy shared Eisenhower's limited background in economics—JFK had received a C in his introductory economics course at Harvard—he gathered a distinguished group of economic advisers, including John Kenneth Galbraith of Harvard and Walter Heller of the University of Minnesota. According to these advocates of the "new economics," the national government could use its power over federal expenditures and its controls over monetary policy to promote economic growth and to "fine-tune" the economy.

THE ECONOMY

The Kennedy administration adopted a number of strategies for stimulating economic growth and creating new jobs. Increased government spending pumped vital funds into the economy and brightened the general economic picture. In 1962 the White House persuaded Congress to give businesses a 7-percent tax credit for investments in new machinery and plants. At the same time, the administration granted one of business's top requests—the readjustment of depreciation schedules for corporate taxes. This action encouraged purchases of new equipment by allowing businesses to write off assets more quickly. Taken together, the investment tax credit and the revised depreciation schedules reduced business taxes and theoretically increased corporate spending by about $2.5 billion; the total tax cut amounted to almost 12 percent.

Although the economy picked up considerably, many liberal economists called for further steps to boost production and employment. John Kenneth Galbraith, who had become ambassador to India, suggested massive government expenditures for social welfare programs. Kennedy rejected this as politically impossible but did consider further tax cuts. A cut in tax revenues would increase the federal deficit; it would also, however, expand purchasing power for both consumers and businesses. Walter Heller, chairman of the Council of Economic Advisers, and Paul Samuelson, an influential economist at MIT, were among those who urged an immediate tax reduction to ward off a possible recession. But advocates of a balanced federal budget, particularly Treasury Secretary C. Douglas Dillon and Federal Reserve Chairman William McChesney Martin, rejected this example of the new economics, and Kennedy finally shelved the proposal for 1962. The following year, however, the administration unveiled a comprehensive revenue bill that did include a $10 billion tax cut and tax reforms.

Kennedy's carefully calculated approach to social and economic problems reflected his basic assumptions about the new role of liberal government in America. The "old sweeping issues have largely disappeared," he told Yale's graduating class in 1962. Basic domestic problems were now "more subtle and less simple": how to manage a complex economy; how to ensure increasing productivity and rising prosperity for all citizens. The "sophisticated and technical questions involved in keeping a great economic machinery moving ahead" required "technical answers—not political answers." Rational bureaucrats, the cool technicians who could manage complex institutions, held the keys to effective government. Although his tenure in office tempered some of his early optimism, John Kennedy died confident that his view of government remained correct and that Camelot's bright young men could solve most problems.

THE BERLIN WALL

JOHN F. KENNEDY

Berlin, the capital of defeated Germany, was a flashpoint of tension for much of the cold war. At the end of World War II, the city had been divided into zones that were controlled by the Soviets in the east, and by the Americans, French, and British in the West. The contrast between the two halves of the city was striking: West Berlin, along with most of the Federal Republic of Germany (FRG), had received large amounts of American aid during the 1950s, so its economy had recovered, industry was booming, and the population was prosperous. In the eastern German Democratic Republic (GDR), which included East Berlin, the Soviets had demanded reparations payments, preventing the economy from recovering after the war. The city of East Berlin itself was drab and gray, unemployment was high, and shortages of food had led to widespread rioting. Not surprisingly, thousands of East Germans, particularly the young and educated, had fled to the West via Berlin: nearly 150,000 in 1959 and 200,000 in 1960.

In addition to this mass exodus, Berlin became a point of intense spy activity, filled with both Soviet and CIA agents and covert operations of all kinds. The Soviets wanted the Americans out of West Berlin, and for years had been pushing for the Americans, French, and British to remove themselves so that Berlin could be a "free city." However, the Allies feared that if the Allied troops withdrew from West Berlin, the city would soon be subsumed into the Soviet bloc. In June 1961, after meeting with Kennedy in Vienna, and in defiance of the 1945 Berlin settlement, Soviet premier Nikita Khrushchev began suggesting that Berlin needed to be united (under Soviet control). Khrushchev threatened to sign a separate peace treaty with the GDR, which would include a united Berlin. President John F.

Excerpted from John F. Kennedy's speech delivered from the White House and broadcast nationally on radio and television, July 25, 1961.

Kennedy responded firmly to this pressure, confirming that the Allied troops would not abandon the city.

On July 25, 1961, Kennedy delivered the following speech, broadcast on national television, in which he reiterated America's commitment to protecting the people of West Berlin and informed the nation that he was requesting $3.25 billion in appropriations to increase the army to defend against a possible confrontation in Berlin. A couple of weeks later, on August 13, 1961, tensions were eased when the Soviets erected a twenty-nine-mile-long barbed-wire wall dividing Berlin, aimed at preventing the East German flight. Soon a solid cement wall had been built, and over the next few years Soviet guards shot those who tried to escape. Although the Allied powers and the Berliners objected strongly to the divisive wall, there was little they could do, and both Soviets and Americans recognized the absurdity of engaging in a nuclear war over the freedoms of their former enemy, the Germans. In the following months, American and Soviet tanks patrolled their respective sides of the wall, but eventually tensions dissipated without incident.

Seven weeks ago tonight I returned from Europe to report on my meeting with Premier Khrushchev and the others. His grim warnings about the future of the world, his aide memoire on Berlin, his subsequent speeches and threats which he and his agents have launched, and the increase in the Soviet military budget that he has announced have all prompted a series of decisions by the administration and a series of consultations with the members of the NATO organization. In Berlin, as you recall, he intends to bring to an end, through a stroke of the pen, first, our legal rights to be in West Berlin and, secondly, our ability to make good on our commitment to the 2 million free people of that city. That we cannot permit.

We are clear about what must be done—and we intend to do it. I want to talk frankly with you tonight about the first steps that we shall take. These actions will require sacrifice on the part of many of our citizens. More will be required in the future. They will require, from all of us, courage and perseverance in the years to come. But if we and our allies act out of strength and unity of purpose—with calm determination and steady nerves, using restraint in our words as well as our weapons—I am hopeful that both peace and freedom will be sustained.

COMMUNIST THREAT

The immediate threat to free men is in West Berlin. But that isolated outpost is not an isolated problem. The threat is worldwide. Our effort must be equally wide and strong and not be obsessed by any single manufactured crisis. We face a challenge in Berlin, but there is also a challenge in southeast Asia, where the borders are less guarded, the enemy harder to find, and the danger of communism less apparent to those who have so little. We face a challenge in our own hemisphere and indeed wherever else the freedom of human beings is at stake.

WEST BERLIN

Let me remind you that the fortunes of war and diplomacy left the free people of West Berlin in 1945 110 miles behind the Iron Curtain. This map makes very clear the problem that we face. The white is West Germany, the East is the area controlled by the Soviet Union; and as you can see from the chart, West Berlin is 110 miles within the area which the Soviets now dominate—which is immediately controlled by the so-called East German regime.

We are there as a result of our victory over Nazi Germany, and our basic rights to be there deriving from that victory include both our presence in West Berlin and the enjoyment of access across East Germany. These rights have been repeatedly confirmed and recognized in special agreements with the Soviet Union. Berlin is not a part of East Germany, but a separate territory under the control of the allied powers. Thus our rights there are clear and deep-rooted. But in addition to those rights is our commitment to sustain—and defend, if need be—the opportunity for more than 2 million people to determine their own future and choose their own way of life.

DETERMINATION TO MAINTAIN RIGHTS IN BERLIN

Thus our presence in West Berlin, and our access thereto, cannot be ended by any act of the Soviet Government. The NATO shield was long ago extended to cover West Berlin, and we have given our word that an attack in that city will be regarded as an attack upon us all.

For West Berlin, lying exposed 110 miles inside East Germany, surrounded by Soviet troops and close to Soviet supply lines, has many roles. It is more than a showcase of liberty, a symbol, an island of freedom in a Communist sea. It is even more than a link with the free world, a beacon of hope behind the Iron Curtain, an escape hatch for refugees.

West Berlin is all of that. But above all it has now become, as never before, the great testing place of Western courage and will, a focal point where our solemn commitments, stretching back over the years since 1945, and Soviet ambitions now meet in basic confrontation.

It would be a mistake for others to look upon Berlin, because of its location, as a tempting target. The United States is there, the United Kingdom and France are there, the pledge of NATO is there, and the people of Berlin are there. It is as secure, in that sense, as the rest of us, for we cannot separate its safety from our own.

I hear it said that West Berlin is militarily untenable. And so was Bastogne. And so, in fact, was Stalingrad. Any dangerous spot is tenable if men—brave men—will make it so.

We do not want to fight, but we have fought before. And others in earlier times have made the same dangerous mistake of assuming that the West was too selfish and too soft and too divided to resist invasions of freedom in other lands. Those who threaten to unleash the forces of war on a dispute over West Berlin should recall the words of the ancient philosopher: "A man who causes fear cannot be free from fear."

We cannot and will not permit the Communists to drive us out of Berlin, either gradually or by force. For the fulfillment of our pledge to that city is essential to the morale and security of Western Germany, to the unity of Western Europe, and to the faith of the entire free world. Soviet strategy has long been aimed not merely at Berlin but at dividing and neutralizing all of Europe, forcing us back to our own shores. We must meet our oft-stated pledge to the free peoples of West Berlin—and maintain our rights and their safety, even in the face of force—in order to maintain the confidence of other free peoples in our word and our resolve. The strength of the alliance on which our security depends is dependent in turn on our willingness to meet our commitments to them.

PREPARATIONS TO DEFEND THE PEACE

So long as the Communists insist that they are preparing to end by themselves unilaterally our rights in West Berlin and our commitments to its people, we must be prepared to defend those rights and those commitments. We will at all times be ready to talk, if talk will help. But we must also be ready to resist with force, if force is used upon us. Either alone would fail. Together, they can serve the cause of freedom and peace.

The new preparations that we shall make to defend the peace are part of the long-term buildup in our strength which has been under way since January. They are based on our needs to meet a worldwide threat, on a basis which stretches far beyond the present Berlin crisis. Our primary purpose is neither propaganda nor provocation—but preparation.

A first need is to hasten progress toward the military goals which the North Atlantic allies have set for themselves. In Europe today nothing less will suffice. We will put even greater resources into fulfilling those goals, and we look to our allies to do the same.

The supplementary defense buildups that I asked from the Congress in March and May have already started moving us toward these and our other defense goals. They included an increase in the size of the Marine Corps, improved readiness of our reserves, expansion of our air- and sealift, and stepped-up

Germany During the Cold War

POLAND

Hamburg

Bremen

Berlin

NETHERLANDS

Hanover

FEDERAL
REPUBLIC
OF GERMANY

EAST
GERMANY

Leipzig

Railroads
Road

0   100

Miles

CZECHOSLOVAKIA

procurement of needed weapons, ammunition, and other items. To insure a continuing invulnerable capacity to deter or destroy any aggressor, they provided for the strengthening of our missile power and for putting 50 percent of our B-52 and B-47 bombers on a ground alert which would send them on their way with 15 minutes' warning.

These measures must be speeded up, and still others must now be taken. We must have sea- and airlift capable of moving our forces quickly and in large numbers to any part of the world.

But even more importantly, we need the capability of placing in any critical area at the appropriate time a force which, combined with those of our allies, is large enough to make clear our determination and our ability to defend our rights at all costs and to meet all levels of aggressor pressure with whatever levels of force are required. We intend to have a wider choice than humiliation or all-out nuclear action.

While it is unwise at this time either to call up or send abroad excessive numbers of these troops before they are needed, let me make it clear that I intend to take, as time goes on, whatever steps are necessary to make certain that such forces can be deployed at the appropriate time without lessening our ability to meet our commitments elsewhere.

Thus, in the days and months ahead, I shall not hesitate to ask the Congress for additional measures or exercise any of the Executive powers that I possess to meet this threat to peace. Everything essential to the security of freedom must be done; and if that should require more men, or more taxes, or more controls, or other new powers, I shall not hesitate to ask them. The measures proposed today will be constantly studied, and altered as necessary. But while we will not let panic shape our policy, neither will we permit timidity to direct our program.

Accordingly I am now taking the following steps:

(1) I am tomorrow requesting of the Congress for the current fiscal year an additional $3,247,000,000 of appropriations for the Armed Forces.

(2) To fill out our present Army divisions and to make more men available for prompt deployment, I am requesting an increase in the Army's total authorized strength from 875,000 to approximately 1 million men.

(3) I am requesting an increase of 29,000 and 63,000 men, respectively, in the active-duty strength of the Navy and the Air Force.

(4) To fulfill these manpower needs, I am ordering that our draft calls be doubled and tripled in the coming months; I am asking the Congress for authority to order to active duty certain ready reserve units and individual reservists and to extend tours of duty; and, under that authority, I am planning to order to active duty a number of air transport squadrons and Air National Guard tactical air squadrons to give us the airlift capacity and protection that we need. Other reserve forces will be called up when needed.

(5) Many ships and planes once headed for retirement are to be retained or reactivated, increasing our airpower tactically and our sealift, airlift, and antisubmarine warfare capability. In addition, our strategic air power will be increased by delaying the deactivation of B-47 bombers.

(6) Finally, some $1.8 billion—about half of the total sum—is needed for the procurement of nonnuclear weapons, ammunition, and equipment.

The details on all these requests will be presented to the Congress tomorrow. Subsequent steps will be taken to suit subsequent needs. Comparable efforts for the common defense are being discussed with our NATO allies. For their commitment and interest are as precise as our own.

And let me add that I am well aware of the fact that many American families will bear the burden of these requests. Studies or careers will be interrupted; husbands and sons will be called away; incomes in some cases will be reduced. But these are burdens which must be borne if freedom is to be defended. Americans have willingly borne them before, and they will not flinch from the task now.

A NEW START ON CIVIL DEFENSE

We have another sober responsibility. To recognize the possibilities of nuclear war in the missile age without our citizens' knowing what they should do and where they should go if bombs begin to fall would be a failure of responsibility. In May I pledged a new start on civil defense. Last week I assigned, on the recommendation of the Civil Defense Director, basic responsibility for this program to the Secretary of Defense, to make certain it is administered and coordinated with our continental defense efforts at the highest civilian level. Tomorrow I am requesting of the Congress new funds for the following immediate objectives: to identify and mark space in existing structures—public and private—that could be used for fallout shelters in case of attack; to stock those shelters with food, water, first-aid kits, and other minimum essentials for survival; to increase their capacity; to improve our air-raid warning and fallout detection systems, including a new household warning system which is now under development; and to take other measures that will be effective at an early date to save millions of lives if needed.

In the event of an attack, the lives of those families which are not hit in a nuclear blast and fire can still be saved—*if* they can be warned to take shelter and *if* that shelter is available. We owe that kind of insurance to our families—and to our country. In contrast to our friends in Europe, the need for this kind of protection is new to our shores. But the time to start is now. In the coming months I hope to let every citizen know what steps he can take without delay to protect his family in case of attack. I know that you will want to do no less. . . .

SOURCE OF TENSION IS MOSCOW, NOT BERLIN

But I must emphasize again that the choice is not merely between resistance and retreat, between atomic holocaust and surrender. Our peacetime military posture is traditionally defensive; but our diplomatic posture need not be. Our response to the Berlin crisis will not be merely military or negative. It will be more than merely standing firm. For we do not intend to leave it to others to choose and monopolize the forum and the framework of discussion. We do not intend to abandon our duty to mankind to seek a peaceful solution.

As signers of the U.N. Charter we shall always be prepared to discuss international problems with any and all nations that are willing to talk—and listen—with reason. If they have proposals, not demands, we shall hear them. If they seek genuine understanding, not concessions of our rights, we shall meet with them. We have previously indicated our readiness to remove any actual irritants in West Berlin, but the freedom of that city is not negotiable. We cannot negotiate with those who say, "What's mine is mine and what's yours is negotiable." But we are willing to consider any arrangement or treaty in Germany consistent with the maintenance of peace and freedom and with the legitimate security interests of all nations.

We recognize the Soviet Union's historical concerns about their security in central and eastern Europe after a series of ravaging invasions, and we believe arrangements can be worked out which will help to meet those concerns and make it possible for both security and freedom to exist in this troubled area.

For it is not the freedom of West Berlin which is "abnormal" in Germany today but the situation in that entire divided country. If anyone doubts the legality of our rights in Berlin, we are ready to have it submitted to international adjudication. If anyone doubts the extent to which our presence is desired by the people of West Berlin, compared to East German feelings about their regime, we are ready to have that question submitted to a free vote in Berlin and, if possible, among all the German people. And let us hear at that time from the 2½ million refugees who have fled the Communist regime in East Germany—voting for Western-type freedom with their feet.

The world is not deceived by the Communist attempt to label Berlin as a hotbed of war. There is peace in Berlin today. The source of world trouble and tension is Moscow, not Berlin. And if war begins, it will have begun in Moscow and not Berlin.

For the choice of peace or war is largely theirs, not ours. It is the Soviets who have stirred up this crisis. It is they who are trying to force a change. It is they who have opposed free elections. It is they who have rejected an all-German peace treaty and the rulings of international law. And as Americans know from our history on our own old frontier, gun battles are caused by outlaws and not by officers of the peace.

In short, while we are ready to defend our interests, we shall also be ready to search for peace—in quiet exploratory talks, in formal or informal meetings. We do not want military considerations to dominate the thinking of either East or West. And Mr. Khrushchev may find that his invitation to other nations to join in a meaningless treaty may lead to *their* inviting *him* to join in the community of peaceful men, in abandoning the use of force, and in respecting the sanctity of agreements.

THE BAY OF PIGS INVASION

ADLAI E. STEVENSON

In late 1959, Cuba's Fidel Castro overthrew a tyrannical government led by Fulgencio Batista and installed himself as prime minister. Promising to eliminate inequities of wealth and land ownership, Castro's regime was embraced by many Cubans as well as by American sympathizers. However, within a short period of time, Castro had angered important U.S. investors by nationalizing millions of dollars of U.S.-owned real estate and businesses and offering no compensation. Along with these Communist economic measures, Castro embraced communism and was soon enjoying a close relationship with Russian premier Nikita Khrushchev, who was extremely pleased to have gained an ally a mere ninety miles away from the United States.

However, not all Cubans acquiesced to Castro's leadership. Rival factions fled to nearby Florida and Guatemala, where they plotted to overthrow Castro and garnered support for their cause with the CIA. In January 1961, after Castro ordered a reduction in U.S. embassy personnel, the United States officially severed diplomatic relations with Cuba. Under Dwight D. Eisenhower's administration, the CIA trained the anti-Castro rebels, supplied them with money and arms, and lent its support to an invasion of Cuba. Upon entering the White House in 1961, John F. Kennedy inherited Eisenhower's plan to invade Cuba, and he endorsed it with the provision that the planned air attack to be made by Cubans in disguised American planes would be canceled. In addition, the landing spot where U.S. ships were to drop off the rebel fighters was changed from Trinidad to the remote Bay of Pigs.

An air strike on April 15 was to wipe out Castro's air defenses,

Excerpted from Adlai E. Stevenson's statements to Committee I of the UN General Assembly, April 17 and 18, 1961.

after which the anti-Castro rebels were to land at the Bay of Pigs and then move to the nearby mountains. The assumption was that the invaders would be met with a groundswell of popular Cuban supporters wishing to overthrow Castro. This did not happen. The air strike failed to destroy Cuba's air force, and with only six planes, Castro destroyed ground troops and parachutists alike. Moreover, Castro had observed the open movements of troops in Florida and Guatemala, and on April 17, 1961, he was prepared for the invasion. He slaughtered the Cuban rebels, killing or capturing all fifteen hundred. Despite America's attempts to disguise its involvement in the embarrassing debacle, Castro knew the CIA had been behind the invasion. Fearing future attempts, he went before the United Nations to request that the United States be condemned as an aggressor.

The following selection is excerpted from the response of the U.S. ambassador to the UN, Adlai E. Stevenson, on April 17 and 18, 1961, in which he stresses that the invasion was organized and carried out by Cuban dissidents only. He attempts to distance the American government from the affair, vehemently denying charges of U.S. participation while at the same time condemning Castro's regime for its militancy.

Statement of April 17, 1961

L et me make it clear that we do not regard the Cuban problem as a problem between Cuba and the United States. The challenge is not to the United States but to the hemisphere and its duly constituted body, the Organization of American States. The Castro regime has betrayed the Cuban revolution. It is now collaborating in organized attempts by means of propaganda, agitation, and subversion to bring about the overthrow of existing governments by force and replace them with regimes subservient to an extra-continental power. These events help to explain why the Cuban Government continues to bypass the Organization of American States, even if they do not explain why Cuba, which is thus in open violation of its obligations under inter-American treaties and agreements, continues to charge the United States with violations of these same obligations.

Soon after the Castro government assumed power, it launched a program looking to the export of its system to other countries of the hemisphere, particularly in the Caribbean area. The intervention of Cuban diplomatic personnel in the internal affairs of other nations of the hemisphere has become flagrant. Cuban diplomatic and consular establishments are used as distribution points for propaganda material calling on the peoples of Latin America to follow Cuba's example. Even Cuban diplomatic pouches destined for various Latin American countries have been found to contain inflammatory and subversive propaganda directed against friendly governments.

In public support of these activities Prime Minister Castro, President [Osvaldo] Dorticós, Dr. [Raúl] Roa [Cuban representative to U.N.] himself, and many other high-ranking members of the revolutionary government have openly stated that "the peoples of Latin America should follow Cuba's example." They have frankly declared that the Cuban system is for export. On August 30, 1960, Prime Minister Castro said: "What happened in Cuba will someday happen in America, and if for saying this we are accused of being continental revolutionaries, let them accuse us." But in case that was not clear enough it was followed 2 days later by Mr. Roa's statement that the Cuban revolution "will act as a springboard for all the popular forces in Latin America following a destiny identical to Cuba."

And as late as March 4th of this year, last month, President Dorticós did not hesitate to urge a group of Latin American agricultural workers meeting in Havana to "initiate similar movements in their own countries" when they returned home. He promised them the "solidarity of a people who have already won their victory and are ready to help other people achieve theirs."

In spite of all of this, Dr. Roa now tells us that the revolutionary government wants only to live in peace, that it does not threaten its neighbors, that it has not attempted nor intends to export its revolution.

Statements of Soviet Russian and Chinese Communist leaders indicate that, by Dr. Castro's own actions, the Cuban revolution has become an instrument of the foreign policies of these extracontinental powers. The increasingly intimate relationship between Cuba and the Soviet Union, the People's Republic of China, and other countries associated with them, in conjunction with the huge shipments of arms, munitions, and other equipment from the Sino-Soviet bloc, must therefore be matters of deep concern to independent governments everywhere.

The Castro regime has mercilessly destroyed the hope of freedom the Cuban people had briefly glimpsed at the beginning of 1959. Cuba has never witnessed such political persecution as exists today. The arrests, the prisons bulging with political prisoners, and the firing squads testify to this. Since the Castro regime came to power, more than 600 persons have been executed, with a shocking disregard of the standards of due process of law and fair trial generally accepted and practiced in the civilized community of nations. The Government has even threatened to replace its slogan for this year—"the year of education"—with a new slogan—"the year of the execution wall."

There is no democratic participation of the Cuban people in the determination of their destiny. Staged rallies, at which small percentages of the population are harangued and asked to express approval of policies by shouts or show of hands, represent the procedure of a totalitarian demagog and not free and democratic expression of opinion through the secret ballot.

The Cuban farm worker who was promised his own plot of land finds that he is an employee of the state working on collective or state-run farms. The independent labor movement, once one of the strongest in the hemisphere, is today in chains. Freely elected Cuban labor leaders, who as late as the end of 1960 protested the destruction of workers' rights, were imprisoned for their pains, or took asylum in foreign embassies, or fled the country to escape imprisonment.

When in addition the people are confronted, despite aid from the Sino-Soviet bloc, with a drastic reduction in their standard of living, it is not surprising opposition to their present master grows. . . .

PROBLEM CREATED BY CUBAN REVOLUTION

The problem created in the Western Hemisphere by the Cuban revolution is not one of revolution. As President Kennedy said on March 13,

> . . . political freedom must be accompanied by social change. For unless necessary social reforms, including land and tax reform, are freely made, unless we broaden the opportunity of all of our people, unless the great mass of Americans share in increasing prosperity, then our alliance, our revolution, our dream, and our freedom will fail. But we call for social change by free men—change in the spirit of Washington and Jefferson, of Bolívar and San Martín and Martí—not change which seeks to impose on men tyrannies which we cast

out a century and a half ago. Our motto is what it has always been—progress yes, tyranny no. . . .

No, the problem is not social change, which is both inevitable and just. The problem is that every effort is being made to use Cuba as a base to force totalitarian ideology into other parts of the Americas.

The Cuban Government has disparaged the plans of the American states to pool their resources to accelerate social and economic development in the Americas. At the Bogotá meeting of the Committee of 21 in September 1960 the Cuban delegation missed few opportunities to insult the representatives of other American states and to play an obstructionist role. They refused to sign the Act of Bogotá and thereby to take part in the hemisphere-wide cooperative effort of social reform to accompany programs of economic development. The Cuban official reaction to President Kennedy's Alliance for Progress program for the Americas was in a similar vein. In a speech on March 12, 1961, Dr. Castro denounced the program, portraying it as a program of "alms" using "usurious dollars" to buy the economic independence and national dignity of the countries which participate in the program. This is insulting to the countries which participate in the program. But equally important, he chose to ignore the underlying premise of the program: a vast cooperative effort to satisfy the basic needs of the American peoples and thereby to demonstrate to the entire world that man's unsatisfied aspiration for economic progress and social justice can best be achieved by free men working within a framework of democratic institutions. The hostility of the Castro regime to these constructive efforts for social and economic progress in the Americas—and even the language—recalls the similar hostility of the U.S.S.R. to the Marshall plan in Europe.

Dr. Castro has carefully and purposely destroyed the great hope the hemisphere invested in him when he came to power 2 years ago. No one in his senses could have expected to embark on such a course as this with impunity. No sane man would suppose that he could speak Dr. Castro's words, proclaim his aggressive intentions, carry out his policies of intervention and subversion—and at the same time retain the friendship, the respect, and the confidence of Cuba's sister republics in the Americas. He sowed the wind and reaps the whirlwind.

It is not the United States which is the cause of Dr. Castro's trouble: It is Dr. Castro himself. It is not Washington which has turned so many thousands of his fellow countrymen against his regime—men who fought beside him in the Cuban hills, men who risked their lives for him in the underground movements in Cuban cities, men who lined Cuban streets to hail him as the liberator from tyranny, men who occupied the most prominent places in the first government of the Cuban revolution. It is these men who constitute the threat—if threat there is—to Dr. Castro's hope of consolidating his power and intensifying his tyranny.

It is Dr. Castro's own policy which has deprived these men of the hope of influencing his regime by democratic methods of free elections and representative government. It is Dr. Castro who, by denying Cuban citizens constitutional recourse, has driven them toward the desperate alternative of resistance—just as Batista once did.

Let us be absolutely clear in our minds who these men are. They are not supporters of Batista; they fought as passionately and bravely against Batista as Dr. Castro himself. They are not champions of the old order in Cuba; they labored day and night as long as they could to realize the promises of the Cuban revolution. They will not turn the clock back, either to the tyranny of Batista or to the tyranny of Castro. They stand for a new and brighter Cuba which will genuinely realize the pledge which Dr. Castro has so fanatically betrayed—the pledge of bread with freedom.

U.S. ATTITUDE TOWARD CASTRO REGIME

The problem which the United States confronts today is our attitude toward such men as these. Three years ago many American citizens looked with sympathy on the cause espoused by Castro and offered hospitality to his followers in their battle against the tyranny of Batista. We cannot expect Americans today to look with less sympathy on those Cubans who, out of love for their country and for liberty, now struggle against the tyranny of Castro.

If the Castro regime has hostility to fear, it is the hostility of Cubans, not of Americans. If today Castro's militia are hunting down guerrillas in the hills where Castro himself once fought, they are hunting down Cubans, not Americans. If the Castro regime is overthrown, it will be overthrown by Cubans, not by Americans.

I do not see that it is the obligation of the United States to protect Dr. Castro from the consequences of his treason to the promises of the Cuban revolution, to the hopes of the Cuban people, and to the democratic aspirations of the Western Hemisphere.

It is because Dr. Castro has turned his back on the inter-American system that this debate marks so tragic a moment for all citizens of the Western Hemisphere. It is tragic to watch the historic aspirations of the Cuban people once again thwarted by tyranny. It is tragic to see bitterness rise within a family of nations united by so many bonds of common memory and common hope. It is tragic to watch a despotic regime drive its own people toward violence and bloodshed. The United States looks with distress and anxiety on such melancholy events.

Our only hope is that the Cuban tragedy may awaken the people and governments of the Americas to a profound resolve—a resolve to concert every resource and energy to advance the cause of economic growth and social progress throughout the hemisphere, but to do so under conditions of human freedom and political democracy. This cause represents the real revolution of the Americas. To this struggle to expand freedom and abundance and education and culture for all the citizens of the New World the free states of the hemisphere summon all the peoples in nations where freedom and independence are in temporary eclipse. We confidently expect that Cuba will be restored to the American community and will take a leading role to win social reform and economic opportunity, human dignity and democratic government, not just for the people of Cuba but for all the people of the hemisphere. . . .

Statement of April 18, 1961

The current uprising in Cuba is the product of the progressively more violent opposition of the Cuban people to the policies and practices of this regime. Let us not forget that there have been hundreds of freedom fighters in the mountains of central Cuba for almost a year; that during the last 6 months skirmishes with the Castro police, attacks upon individual members of his armed forces, nightly acts of sabotage by the revolutionaries, have been increasing in number and intensity. Protest demonstrations have taken place by workers whose trade-union rights have been betrayed, by Catholics whose freedom of expression and worship has been circumscribed, by professional men whose right to free association has been violated. The response of the Castro regime has been repression, arrests without warrant, trial without constitutional guarantees, imprisonment without term and without mercy, and, finally, the execution wall.

Let me be absolutely clear: that the present events are the uprising of the Cuban people against an oppressive regime which has never given them the opportunity in peace and by democratic process to approve or to reject the domestic and foreign policies which it has followed.

For our part, our attitude is clear. Many Americans looked with sympathy, as I have said, on the cause espoused by Dr. Castro when he came to power. They look with the same sympathy on the men who today seek to bring freedom and justice to Cuba—not for foreign monopolies, not for the economic or political interests of the United States or any foreign power, but for Cuba and for the Cuban people.

It is hostility of Cubans, not Americans, that Dr. Castro has to fear. It is not our obligation to protect him from the consequences of his treason to the revolution, to the hopes of the Cuban people, and to the democratic aspirations of the hemisphere.

The United States sincerely hopes that any difficulties which we or other American countries may have with Cuba will be settled peacefully. We have committed no aggression against Cuba. We have no aggressive purposes against Cuba. We intend no military intervention in Cuba. We seek to see a restoration of the friendly relations which once prevailed between Cuba and the United States. We hope that the Cuban people will settle their own problems in their own interests and in a manner which will assure social justice, true independence, and political liberty to the Cuban people.

THE CUBAN MISSILE CRISIS

RAYMOND L. GARTHOFF

On October 15, 1962, President Kennedy was informed that nuclear missiles had been spotted and photographed by a U-2 reconnaissance plane flying over Cuba. The Kennedy administration took for granted that the missiles, which had been supplied by the Soviet Union, needed to be removed from America's doorstep; the question was simply how to achieve this objective. The government debated three options: an air strike, a land invasion of Cuba, or a blockade of the island (which would prevent further arms shipments). Deciding on the last, least confrontational course, the United States declared Cuba to be in quarantine and demanded that the Soviets remove the missiles. Yet during the next few days of negotiations, Soviet ships still proceeded toward Cuba, work on the missile launching sites continued, and tensions mounted hourly. This was brinkmanship at its most intense, with each side moving closer to the metaphorical edge of the cliff in the hope that the other would retreat in fear.

The crisis ended when the Soviets agreed to withdraw the missiles on the condition that the United States agree not to invade Cuba and to remove the quarantine. Recent evidence shows that the U.S. government also secretly agreed to dismantle its Turkish missile site, yet this aspect of the settlement was not revealed in order to enhance the American victory. (Ironically, the U.S. government had already ordered the withdrawal of the Turkish missiles, as they had taken several years to install and were inaccurate and obsolete.)

Excerpted from "The Cuban Missile Crisis: An Overview," by Raymond L. Garthoff, in *The Cuban Missile Crisis Revisited*, edited by James A. Nathan (New York: St. Martin's Press, 1992). Copyright © 1992 by James A. Nathan. Reprinted with permission.

Raymond L. Garthoff was the special assistant for Soviet affairs during the Cuban missile crisis and was involved in the decision-making process at the time. Garthoff sheds new light on the Cuban missile crisis. For example, it is commonly argued that President Kennedy insisted that the Soviets both remove their missiles from Cuba and refrain from sending organized combat forces there. In fact, Garthoff explains, the Soviets had already sent a combat force to Cuba in addition to the missiles. Moreover, unknown to the Americans at the time, Soviet ground forces possessed rocket launchers that were also equipped with nuclear warheads, and these smaller nuclear-equipped rockets were not under Khrushchev's direct command, but that of a general in Cuba.

On a spring day in 1962, Soviet Party leader Nikita Khrushchev, vacationing at a dacha in the Crimea, was visited by Defense Minister Rodion Malinovsky. As they were conversing, the marshal gestured toward the horizon to the south and remarked on the fact that medium-range nuclear missiles the United States was installing across the Black Sea in Turkey were just becoming operational. So far as we know, that is all the marshal said, and the next step was Khrushchev's reaction: Why, he mused, should the Americans have the right to put missiles on our doorstep, and we not have a comparable right? A few weeks later, while in Bulgaria, he carried the point one fateful step further: Why not station Soviet medium-range missiles in Cuba?

Khrushchev had long rankled at what he regarded as American flaunting of its political and military superiority, and successful cultivation of a double standard. Why shouldn't the Soviet Union be able to assert the prerogatives of a global power? One reason, of course, was that the United States *did* have superiority in global political, economic, and military power. Moreover, while the Soviet Union had enjoyed some spectacular successes—in particular, its primacy in space with the first earth satellite and first test of an intercontinental ballistic missile (ICBM)—in the four years or so since that time, there had been reverses. In particular, after riding an inflated world impression of Soviet missile strength during American self-flagellation over a "missile gap," improved intelligence had now persuaded the American leaders—and the world—that the *real* missile gap, and a growing one, favored the United States.

Since Khrushchev personally had overplayed the Soviet hand on missiles, he had particular reason to want to offset the new, and to him, adverse gap. Indeed, if he wanted to carry forward his still-unsuccessful campaign on West Berlin, or even to prevent American exploitation of missile superiority in other political contests, some way had to be found to overcome the growing American superiority. Available Soviet ICBMs were not satisfactory; he needed several years to await the next generation. But the Soviet Union did have plenty of medium-range missiles (a category in Soviet usage that embraced both the Western categories of "medium-range" and "intermediate range" ballistic missiles, MRBMs and IRBMs). It would certainly help deal with the problem of Soviet strategic missile weakness if the Soviet Union could create ersatz ICBMs by deploying MRBMs and IRBMs near the United States, comparable to what the United States was doing in Turkey.

The second ingredient in concocting the decision to put Soviet missiles in Cuba was the interaction of Soviet and American relations with Castro's Cuba. By the spring of 1962, Cuba had become highly dependent on the Soviet Union, economically and politically. In turn, it was a declared socialist state and Castro was in the process of merging the old-line Cuban Communist party and his own 26th of July Movement, the former providing organizing ability and a structured ideology, the latter the leaders and the popular following.

CUBAN-AMERICAN RELATIONS

Meanwhile, Cuban-American relations were precarious. The United States, frustrated by the defeat at the Bay of Pigs of the Cuban émigré invasion it had sponsored, had by no means lessened its hostility or given up its efforts to unseat Castro's regime. By the fall of 1961, the president had authorized a broad covert action program, Operation Mongoose, aimed at harassing, undermining, and optimally overthrowing the Castro regime. This effort included repeated and continuing attempts to assassinate Castro himself. While the Cuban and Soviet leaders did not (so far as it has been possible to ascertain) then know about high-level deliberations in Washington and planning papers on Operation Mongoose, they did know in considerable detail about the CIA operations in Miami sending reconnaissance and later sabotage teams into Cuba, and they knew about at least some of the assassination attempts.

Also, the United States, by February 1962, had extended its economic sanctions to a complete embargo against trade with Cuba, and had engaged in diplomatic efforts to get other countries to curtail trade. In January 1962, at Punta del Este, the United States had succeeded in getting the majority necessary to suspend Cuban participation in the Organization of American States (OAS). By the spring of 1962 the United States had also persuaded fifteen Latin American states to follow its lead and break diplomatic relations with Havana. In short, the United States was conducting a concerted political, economic, propaganda, and covert campaign against Cuba.

On the military side as well, the president had in October 1961 secretly instructed the Defense Department to prepare contingency plans for war with Cuba, with air attack and invasion alternatives. While secret, elements of these plans were tested in subsequent military exercises, and elements of the military forces needed to implement them were built up. Between April 9 and 24, when Khrushchev was brooding in the Crimea, a U.S. Marine air-ground task force carried out a major amphibious exercise, with an assault on the island of Vieques near Puerto Rico. Another exercise conducted from April 19 to May 11 on the southeastern coast of the United States involved more than 40,000 troops, 79 ships, and over 300 aircraft. While the exercise was publicly announced, the fact that it was designed to test an actual Commander in Chief, Atlantic (CINCLANT) contingency plan against Cuba was of course not disclosed. But the Cubans and Soviets assumed, correctly, that it was.

Under the circumstances, it was not surprising that Cuban and Soviet leaders feared an American attack on Cuba. There had been no decision in Washington to attack. But there were programs underway directed toward overthrowing the Cuban regime, and military contingency planning and preparation if the president decided to attack. The United States had the capabilities to attack, and its overall intentions were clearly hostile; any prudent political or military planner would have had to consider at least the threat of attack.

The Cubans sought Soviet commitments and assistance to ward off or meet an American attack. The Soviet leaders had given general, but not ironclad, public assurances of support. They were not, however, prepared to extend their own commitment so far as to take Cuba into the Warsaw Pact.

SOVIET MISSILES ARE SENT TO CUBA

Khrushchev first raised the idea of deploying Soviet missiles in Cuba with a few close colleagues in May. Khrushchev's plan was to deploy in Cuba a small force of medium-range missiles capable of striking the United States, both to bolster the sagging Soviet side of the strategic military balance, and to serve as a deterrent to American attack on Cuba. The missiles would be shipped to Cuba and installed there rapidly in secrecy. Then, the Soviet Union would suddenly confront the United States with a fait accompli and a new, more favorable status quo. The impact of the move, and perforce American acceptance of it, would bolster the Soviet stance (probably in particular in a new round of negotiation on the status of Berlin, although no concrete information is available on that point).

Anastas Mikoyan, a veteran Politburo member and close friend, expressed strong reservations on at least two points: Castro's receptivity to the idea, and the practicality of surreptitiously installing the missiles without American detection. Khrushchev readily agreed to drop the idea if Castro objected, but his sense of Castro's reaction was better than Mikoyan's. On the question of practicality, it was decided to send a small expert team headed by Marshal Sergei Biryuzov, the new commander in chief of the Strategic Missile Forces, incognito (as "Engineer Petrov"), to check out the terrain and conditions and advise on the practicality of secret deployment. The military, represented by Malinovsky and Biryuzov, favored the scheme because of what it would do to help redress Soviet strategic inferiority.

Khrushchev apparently brought the full Party Presidium (as the Politburo was then known), or rather its members available in Moscow at the time, into the decision-making process only in late May when the mission was about to depart for Havana to ascertain Castro's response and evaluate feasibility.

The military had necessarily been involved, and had been supportive, but not as decision makers. Andrei Gromyko, foreign minister but not then yet a member of the Party leadership, had also been consulted privately, and was present (though remaining silent) at the few deliberative meetings. Only recently have we learned that his private advice had been to caution Khrushchev on what he believed would be the strongly adverse American reaction, but not to oppose the whole idea directly. Similarly, the new Soviet ambassador to Havana, selected because he had the best personal rapport with Fidel Castro, Aleksandr Alekseev, initially doubted Castro's readiness to agree. But he supported anything that would strengthen Soviet-Cuban relations.

Castro readily agreed to the Soviet offer of missiles, believing that he was serving the broader interests of the socialist camp as well as enhancing Cuban security. Biryuzov, who evidently saw his task as fulfilling an assigned mission rather than providing input to evaluation of a proposal, reported that they could secretly install the missile system.

Formal orders were given to the Ministry of Defense on June 10, 1962, to proceed with the deployment, even though many details remained to be decided. In early July 1962, Cuban Defense Minister Raúl Castro visited Moscow, and he and Marshal Malinovsky drafted a five-year renewable agreement to cover the missile deployment. But despite the absence of any issue of disagreement, the draft agreement (always hand-carried, with oral instructions, as were all communications between Moscow and Havana on the matter—even encrypted messages were not trusted) went back and forth twice, and was never actually signed by Khrushchev and Castro. Khrushchev evidently held back because he feared Castro, who had wanted to make it public, would leak it once it had been signed.

THE AMERICAN FOCUS: SOVIET MISSILES IN CUBA

The "Cuban missile crisis" derives its name (in the United States; in the Soviet Union, with the accent on American hostility toward Cuba, it is called "the Caribbean Crisis") from the central role played by the Soviet missiles. As President Kennedy had warned on September 4, 1962, shortly before the first missiles actually arrived in Cuba, if such Soviet offensive missiles were introduced "the gravest issues would arise," and nine days later, he stressed that in that case "this country will do whatever must be done to protect its own security and that of its allies." It was, of course, too late to affect Soviet decisions long made and then reaching final implementation.

President Kennedy's declaration included another element, rarely recalled, to which he applied the same warning of "gravest" consequences: if, apart from missiles, the Soviet Union sent to Cuba "any organized combat force." If it had been apprehended that instead of missiles, Khrushchev had dispatched an expeditionary force of Soviet ground, air, and naval combat forces to deter an American invasion, would a crisis have emerged of similar dimensions to the one that emerged over the missiles? That question, posed as an alternative to installing missiles, is historically hypothetical. But what has not been appreciated until now is that the Soviets in fact *did* send such a combat force *in addition to* the missiles.

The Ministry of Defense in Moscow on June 10 received orders not only on the dispatch of a mixed division of Strategic Missile Force troops, comprising three regiments of R-12 (SS-4) and two regiments of R-14 (SS-5) medium-range missiles; but also a Soviet combat contingent including an integrated air defense component with a radar system, 24 surface-to-air missile battalions with 144 launchers, a regiment of 42 MiG-21 interceptors; a coastal defense component comprising 8 cruise missile launchers with 32 missiles, 12 Komar missile patrol boats, and a separate squadron as well as a regiment totalling 42 IL-28 jet light bombers for attacking any invasion force. In addition, a ground force of division size comprised four reinforced motorized rifle regiments, each with over 3,000 men, and 35 tanks. In addition, 6 short-range tactical rocket launchers, and 18 army cruise missile launchers were part of the contingent. This force was seen as a "plate glass" deterrent to U.S. invasion, and reassurance to Castro as an alternative to Cuban membership in the Warsaw Pact.

While most of the weaponry was discovered by American aerial reconnaissance during the crisis, even afterward the number of Soviet military personnel was underestimated by nearly half—22,000 instead of 42,000. The United States failed to discover that a major Soviet expeditionary contingent, under the overall command of a four-star general, General of the Army Issa Pliyev, was in Cuba in October–November 1962.

Recently, former Soviet General of the Army Anatoly Gribkov, who was responsible for planning the Soviet dispatch of forces to Cuba in 1962, has declared that 9 tactical nuclear weapons were sent for the ground force tactical rocket launchers, and with authorization for their use delegated to General Pliyev in case of an American land invasion. If true, this was one of the most dangerous aspects of the entire deployment, and this was not known in Washington.

The medium-range missiles capable of striking the United States, in contrast, were placed under strict control by Moscow: General Pliyev was not authorized to fire them under any circumstances, even an American attack, without explicit authorization by Khrushchev.

NEGOTIATING THE CRISIS

Ambassador Anatoly Dobrynin arrived at the State Department at 6:00 P.M. on October 22, 1962, at the request of Secretary of State Dean Rusk. His demeanor was relaxed and cheerful; a short time later, he was observed leaving "ashen-faced" and "visibly shaken." A few hours earlier, Foreign Minister Gromyko had departed from New York for Moscow at the end of his visit in the United States, making routine departure remarks to the press and evidently with no premonition of what the president would be saying while he was airborne. Incredibly, the Soviet leadership was caught by surprise by the American disclosure that the missiles had been discovered a week earlier and by the American "first step" action of imposing a quarantine, coupled with a demand that the missiles be removed.

Khrushchev has been reported to have initially in anger wanted to challenge the quarantine-blockade, but whether that is correct the actual Soviet response was cautious. The blockade was not challenged, and no counter-pressures were mounted elsewhere, such as Berlin (as had been feared in Washington). Even the Soviet response to the unparalleled American alert of its strategic forces and most forces worldwide was an announced, but actually hollow, Soviet and Warsaw Pact alert.

Khrushchev continued for a few days to believe that the United States might accept at least the partial Soviet missile deployment already in Cuba. But by October 26, it had become clear that the United States was determined. Moreover, the United States had rapidly prepared a substantial air attack and land invasion force. The tactical air combat force of 579 aircraft was ready, with the plan calling for 1,190 strike sorties on the first day. More than 100,000 Army and 40,000 Marine troops were ready to strike. An airborne paratroop force as large as that used on Normandy in 1944 was included in the preparation for an assault on the island. American military casualties were estimated at 18,500 in ten days of combat.

Soviet intelligence indicated on October 26 that a U.S. air attack and invasion of Cuba were expected at any time. Khrushchev then hurriedly offered a deal: An American pledge not to invade Cuba would obviate the need for Soviet missiles in Cuba and, by implication, they could be withdrawn. A truncated Soviet Presidium group (a Moscow "ExComm") had been meeting since October 23. We still know almost nothing about its deliberations, but it is clear that Khrushchev was fully in control.

Later on October 26, a new intelligence assessment in Moscow indicated that while U.S. invasion preparations continued, it was now less clear that an attack was imminent. Thus there might be some time for bargaining on terms for a settlement.

Meanwhile, Ambassador Dobrynin reported that Robert Kennedy had informed him that the United States was planning to phase out its missiles in Turkey and Italy; there might be opportunity to include that in a settlement. Moreover, the Soviet Embassy in Washington had reported that in a discussion between the KGB station chief, Aleksandr Fomin, and an American television correspondent with good State Department contacts, John Scali, the American—after checking with Secretary Rusk—had indicated that an American assurance against attacking Cuba in exchange for withdrawal of the Soviet missiles in Cuba could provide the basis for a deal, but that time was short.

A new message from Khrushchev to Kennedy was sent that night, October 26, proposing a reciprocal withdrawal of missiles from Cuba and Turkey, as well as the American assurances against invasion of Cuba. But on October 27, later called "Black Saturday" in Washington, an ominous chain of events, including the stiffened Soviet terms, intensified concern. In Moscow, Soviet intelligence again reported signs of American preparations for possible attack on Cuba on October 29 or 30. A very alarmed message was also received from Fidel Castro expressing—for the first time—Castro's belief that an attack was imminent (within 24 to 72 hours), and urging Khrushchev, in case of an invasion, to preemptively attack the United States. The effect of this call was to reinforce a decision by Khrushchev that Castro did not expect or want: prompt conclusion of a deal to remove the missiles in exchange for an American verbal assurance against attacking Cuba.

Other developments also contributed to moving Khrushchev, by October 28, to act on the basis he had first outlined on October 26. One was Castro's action on October 27 in ordering Cuban antiaircraft artillery to open fire on low-flying American reconnaissance aircraft. None were shot down, but the action clearly raised the risk of hostilities. Far more dangerous was the completely unexpected action of local *Soviet* air defense commanders in actually shooting down a U-2 with a Soviet surface-to-air missile. Khrushchev at first assumed that Cubans had shot the plane down, but at some point learned that even his own troops were not under full control. Although the much more restrictive instructions and other constraints still seemed to rule out any unauthorized firing (or even preparation for firing) of the medium-range missiles, the situation was getting out of control.

Kennedy's proposal on the evening of October 27 to exchange American assurances against invasion of Cuba for Soviet withdrawal of its missiles, coupled with a virtual ultimatum, was thus promptly accepted. Khrushchev did not risk taking the time to clarify a number of unclear issues, including what the Americans considered to be "offensive weapons." He accepted the president's terms and sent his reply openly over Radio Moscow, as well as via diplomatic communication.

LBJ AND THE VIETNAM WAR

THOMAS C. REEVES

U.S. involvement in Vietnam dates to the mid-1950s, after French colonization ended and the 1954 Geneva conference divided the country into two regions. At that point, the United States decided to provide support for the pro-Western government of President Ngo Dinh Diem in South Vietnam, which neighbored a newly Communist regime in North Vietnam. As early as 1956, Kennedy viewed Vietnam as the crucial domino in the cold war struggle for Southeast Asia, describing it as the "cornerstone of the Free World, the keystone to the arch, the finger in the dike." Kennedy believed that the United States needed to support South Vietnam in order to "save" the rest of Asia from Communist influence and demonstrate that it would not tolerate Soviet aggression.

In early 1961, President Kennedy organized an enormous, secret CIA mission to assist the South Vietnamese defend themselves against North Vietnamese guerrilla raids. In the fall of 1961, the United States sent military units euphemistically called "advisers" to South Vietnam. By fall of 1962, there were 11,000 members of the U.S. military, including Green Beret units specially trained for guerrilla combat. During the Kennedy administration, the number of U.S. troops escalated from 800 in 1960 to nearly 17,000 in 1963.

The following excerpt by Thomas C. Reeves describes the further escalation of American troops that began when Lyndon B. Johnson succeeded Kennedy in November 1963. Determined not to be known as the president who had "allowed Vietnam to fall to communism," as he put it, Johnson steadily increased ground troops in Vietnam. Johnson's term, between 1963 and

1968, marked the most intense and tragic period of the war: By 1968, there were over 500,000 American troops in Vietnam. After Richard M. Nixon took over in 1968, the new president began to withdraw ground troops, although air attacks continued. The war was finally ended by President Gerald Ford, who announced on April 23, 1975, that the U.S. commitment to Vietnam was over. Six days later, North Vietnamese Communist forces captured Saigon, the capital of South Vietnam.

Thomas C. Reeves is a professor of history at the University of Wisconsin at Parkside and a senior fellow at the Wisconsin Policy Research Institute. He has written several books on topics such as McCarthyism and the demise of the church in America as well as biographies of Presidents John F. Kennedy and Chester A. Arthur.

L ike almost all of his Washington contemporaries, Johnson was a Cold Warrior. He was firmly anticommunist and believed in the containment policy and the domino theory. Moreover, Johnson, like Kennedy, had a macho self-image and would not shrink from using force if challenged. When it seemed in early 1965 that communists were launching an effort to seize power in the Dominican Republic, LBJ sent in marines and army paratroops. The military intervention proved successful (although it violated the OAS [Organization of American States] charter and angered many Latin Americans) and democracy was restored. Action in the Dominican Republic encouraged the president to rely on the military to stop the Reds.

Johnson's assessment of the war in Vietnam was predictable. Shortly after taking office, LBJ told the American ambassador to Saigon, "I am not going to be the president who saw Southeast Asia go the way China went." This stance was supported by three top Kennedy aides who served in the Johnson administration: Secretary of State Dean Rusk, Secretary of Defense Robert McNamara, and national security adviser McGeorge Bundy.

South Vietnam was plunged into political and economic chaos after Diem's assassination. The Joint Chiefs of Staff recommended massive military intervention, but in early 1964 Johnson chose merely to increase economic and technical assistance and help South Vietnamese troops in minor covert military activities. He insisted publicly, as Kennedy had, that the war had to be won by the South Vietnamese themselves.

THE GULF OF TONKIN RESOLUTION

This approach changed dramatically on August 1 when North Vietnamese torpedo boats attacked the American destroyer *Maddox* in international waters, apparently believing that the ship had been involved in a nearby raid by South Vietnamese. In response, the navy sent in the destroyer *C. Turner Joy*, and on August 4 the Pentagon announced that both ships had come under fire in the Gulf of Tonkin.

President Johnson ordered air strikes against North Vietnam naval bases and asked Congress to give him the authority to do whatever was necessary to resist communist aggression in Southeast Asia. Congress was not told that the *Maddox* was engaged in electronic espionage or that the Gulf of Tonkin attack was shrouded in confusion and may well not have actually occurred. The "Gulf of Tonkin Resolution" passed the Senate 98 to 2 and the House 414 to 0. Johnson sought the blank check from Congress to demonstrate to the North Vietnamese, pouring men and supplies into the South, that America meant business. He also sought to deny Barry Goldwater, who had just been nominated by the GOP, the allegation that the president was "soft."

American bombing raids against North Vietnamese military bases and infiltration routes began in early February 1965. The raids were in response to a deadly attack on American military advisers by National Liberation Front forces, the Viet Cong, backed fully by Ho Chi Minh's communist regime.

In March, two marine battalions were dispatched to South Vietnam to defend an air base. In April and May Johnson made peace initiatives to Hanoi, but they were flatly rejected. In June, a month after Congress voted $400 million to back the effort in Vietnam, American troops were engaged in a ground offensive for the first time.

In July, under pressure from American military leaders, Johnson agreed to employ saturation bombing in South Vietnam and send 100,000 troops. General William Westmoreland, the U.S. commander in Vietnam, was given a free hand to direct the fighting in the South. The president and his top advisers were persuaded that without this commitment the Reds would snap up a vital part of the free world, endangering the rest of Southeast Asia. Almost all members of Congress and the vast majority of Americans agreed.

By early 1966 South Vietnam had a reasonably stable government, led by the swashbuckling pilot Nguyen Cao Ky. That

October, after an election, General Nguyen Van Thieu became president and Ky moved to vice president. Still, the prospects for military victory continued to dim. In January Americans began massive bombing raids on North Vietnam. This effort did nothing to deter the will of Ho Chi Minh to rule the whole of Vietnam (an area about the size of Missouri), and indeed led to worldwide expressions of sympathy toward him and his people. As public opinion began to shift against the American effort, the number of American troops in Vietnam increased: 385,000 by the end of 1966; 486,000 by the end of the following year. (From 1959 to 1975, North Vietnam sent 976,849 soldiers into South Vietnam and provided the great majority of weapons and supplies used in the South.)

American troops, aided by small contingents of allies from Australia, New Zealand, the Philippines, Thailand, and South Korea, employed "search and destroy" operations against the enemy. All of South Vietnam was a combat zone. This often, inadvertently and sometimes deliberately, led to the destruction of entire villages and the deaths of many innocent people.

Massive bombing and the use of indiscriminate firepower, napalm, and chemical herbicides (including the infamous Agent Orange) devastated the landscape. Thousands of peasants were uprooted from their land in the wake of attacks by both sides. Resistance to the government of Thieu and Ky as well as to the Americans increased dramatically within South Vietnam.

American troops were frustrated by savage battles in steamy jungles and swamps, long combat assignments, and the frequent inability to distinguish friend from foe in peasant villages. Many were turned off by the corruption and inefficiency of the South Vietnamese government. Some Americans became addicted to the drugs easily available in the region. Many grew increasingly uneasy about the growing resistance, at home and abroad, to the conflict. That resistance escalated as the number of American deaths mounted: almost five thousand in 1966 and some nine thousand in 1967.

ANTIWAR SENTIMENT

Antiwar forces often claimed that the Americans being sent to Vietnam were mostly draftees and more often than not black. In fact, most of those who went to Vietnam volunteered. Volunteers accounted for 77 percent of combat deaths. Defense Department statistics later showed that 86 percent of those who died in Vietnam were white and 12.5 percent were black—from an age group in which blacks comprised 13.1 percent of the population.

Large-scale antiwar demonstrations began in the spring of 1965 and became an everyday part of American life for the next decade. College students, especially in elite institutions, seized campuses, burned their draft cards, and harassed military and industrial recruiters. Returning veterans staged protests. In May 1966, ten thousand protesters marched in front of the White House. In October 1967, 50,000 people demonstrated near the Lincoln Memorial in Washington, and some tried to force their way into the Pentagon. Protesters at such gatherings chanted, "Hey, hey, LBJ, how many kids have you killed today?" Many of these angry Americans were undoubtedly influenced by scenes on the nightly television news showing the worst features of the fighting overseas.

The American people had not been so divided since the Civil War. "Hawks" sought more support for the war and victory. "Doves" wanted out of the conflict. Most citizens were no doubt somewhere in the middle of these extremes, willing to back anticommunism but increasingly worried about the cost and the value of the property in question.

Ho Chi Minh had no illusions about defeating the American fighting machine. But he was confident that if his troops could hold on long enough public opinion would force Johnson to cave in. American military leaders were also confident that they could win in Vietnam—if given enough manpower, funding, and authority. They always wanted more. General Westmoreland and the Joint Chiefs of Staff gave the president consistently positive accounts of the fighting.

THE WAR GROWS

LBJ did not want to become involved in a full-scale war in Asia. He limited military activity on numerous occasions, and he made repeated peace overtures. Still, he was not going to "chicken out" or be one of the "nervous Nellies" who "will break ranks under the strain." He told a group of U.S. servicemen in 1966, "I pray the good Lord will look over you and keep you until you can come home with that coonskin on the wall."

In early 1966, Senator William Fulbright, chairman of the Foreign Relations Committee, broke with the president and held televised hearings on the war. Secretary of Defense McNamara, a major architect of the war, became disillusioned and resigned in late 1967. (In 1995 he declared that he and other U.S. policy-makers had been "terribly wrong" in allowing the conflict to escalate.) Several others also left the administration because of the Vietnam policy. Liberals and intellectuals were now routinely opposed to the war, as were black leaders who feared that it was endangering the Great Society. Johnson's public popularity plunged, especially after he requested a tax increase to help fund the war. In November 1967, Senator Eugene McCarthy of Minnesota, a militant dove, announced his candidacy for the Democratic presidential nomination.

THE TET OFFENSIVE

In early 1968, American ground troops reached the 500,000 mark. On January 30, about 80,000 Viet Cong and North Vietnamese troops began a massive series of surprise attacks on more than one hundred cities, towns, and military bases in South Vietnam. During the attack on Saigon, the U.S. embassy was raided. The old imperial city of Hue was destroyed. Television cameras sent horror-filled pictures into the living rooms of the world. One jolting sequence featured the street corner execution of a communist rebel by South Vietnam's chief of National Police.

In all, the "Tet offensive" left 1,113 Americans and at least 3,470 South Vietnamese dead. It was the turning point in the war. While Hanoi's forces were soon driven out of the areas they attacked (the attack cost them and the Viet Cong some 30,000 lives), their daring and well-planned effort had badly damaged the credibility of American military and political leaders. Johnson and Westmoreland had been reassuring the American people that victory in Vietnam was in sight. Now, it seemed, we were losing.

On March 12, dovish Eugene McCarthy won 42 percent of the vote in the New Hampshire Democratic primary. Four days later, Senator Robert Kennedy, now also antiwar, jumped into the contest, exciting millions with memories of Camelot.

Reluctantly, sadly, and after much consultation, Johnson rejected the military's call for 205,000 more troops and decided to limit the bombing of North Vietnam in order to achieve peace talks. On March 31, in a dramatic television speech to the nation, he outlined his plan for ending the conflict and announced that he would not seek or accept his party's nomination for another term. Johnson, the supreme politician and reformer, had become another victim of the Vietnam War.

Resistance, Reactions, and Riots: The 1960s

CHAPTER 4

THE FEMININE MYSTIQUE

BETTY FRIEDAN

In her seminal 1963 book *The Feminine Mystique*, writer Betty Friedan set about describing what she called "the problem that has no name"—a certain malaise, a hopelessness, a kind of listless anxiety that so many middle-class women in the 1950s and early 1960s felt. Male psychologists of the era argued that the root of women's depression was their fundamental inability to accept their "natural" passive roles as housewives, or their "innately" neurotic natures, while Freudians insisted that their malady was a product of a negative relationship with their fathers that was manifesting itself later in life. By contrast, Friedan suggested that the problem lay not with women, but with a sexist, unjust society that prevented women from advancing in the public sphere and from having equal career opportunities. Women, she claimed, were simply bored and stifled by being contained in the "Happy Housewife Heroine" myth.

The American society of the 1950s glorified domesticity, not only idealizing the role of the child-rearing housewife, but also making deviation from this mold extremely difficult. Friedan criticized this "feminine mystique"—the social conditioning that began with four-year-old girls dressing Barbie dolls and dreaming of a matching Ken doll and was perpetuated by the male-run women's magazines, which propounded housecleaning, new hairstyles, and interior decorating as substitutes for real social and intellectual development. Friedan noted the reduction in the number of women in college since the 1920s, along with the failure of college-educated women to pursue careers. She concluded that these women's development had been stunted, and effectively prevented, by this mystique that glorified marriage and children as the only viable ways to achieve happiness. She also observed that women in the late 1930s tended to be far more independent, strong, and involved in careers than women in 1960. Women's liberation was not advancing at all, and frighteningly, it seemed to be actively receding! If women realized that they were the result of this conditioning, Friedan suggested, they would hopefully be able to break free of repressive cultural myths and develop their full potential.

Friedan's book struck a profound note of recognition among thousands of women and was pivotal in advancing female self-consciousness. In 1966, Friedan and other feminists founded the National Organization for Women (NOW), whose members concentrated primarily on political lobbying efforts to change laws that discriminated against women. They boycotted organizations that had unjust hiring practices and salary differentials and lobbied for the creation of child-care centers and the institution of pregnancy leave that would enable young mothers to continue their careers.

In the following excerpt from chapter two of her book, Friedan lists the typical contents of a 1960s magazine and describes the idealized image of the housewife created by such publications.

W hy have so many American wives suffered this nameless aching dissatisfaction for so many years, each one thinking she was alone? "I've got tears in my eyes with sheer relief that my own inner turmoil is shared with other women," a young Connecticut mother wrote me when I first began to put this problem into words. A woman from a town in Ohio wrote: "The times when I felt that the only answer was to consult a psychiatrist, times of anger, bitterness and general frustration too numerous to even mention, I had no idea that hundreds of other women were feeling the same way. I felt so completely alone." A Houston, Texas, housewife wrote: "It has been the feeling of being almost alone with my problem that has made it so hard. I thank God for my family, home and the chance to care for them, but my life couldn't stop there. It is an awakening to know that I'm not an oddity and can stop being ashamed of wanting something more."

That painful guilty silence, and that tremendous relief when a feeling is finally out in the open, are familiar psychological signs. What need, what part of themselves, could so many women today be repressing? In this age after [Sigmund] Freud, sex is immediately suspect. But this new stirring in women does not seem to be sex; it is, in fact, much harder for women to talk about than sex. Could there be another need, a part of themselves they have buried as deeply as the Victorian women buried sex?

THE PROBLEM THAT HAS NO NAME

If there is, a woman might not know what it was, any more than the Victorian woman knew she had sexual needs. The image of a good woman by which Victorian ladies lived simply left out sex. Does the image by which modern American women live also leave something out, the proud and public image of the high-school girl going steady, the college girl in love, the suburban housewife with an up-and-coming husband and a station wagon full of children? This image—created by the women's magazines, by advertisements, television, movies, novels, columns and books by experts on marriage and the family, child psychology, sexual adjustment and by the popularizers of sociology and psychoanalysis—shapes women's lives today and mirrors their dreams. It may give a clue to the problem that has no name, as a dream gives a clue to a wish unnamed by the dreamer. In the mind's ear, a geiger counter clicks when the image shows too sharp a discrepancy from reality. A geiger counter clicked in my own inner ear when I could not fit the quiet desperation of so many women into the picture of the modern American housewife that I myself was helping to create, writing for the women's magazines. What is missing from the image which shapes the American woman's pursuit of fulfillment as a wife and mother? What is missing from the image that mirrors and creates the identity of women in America today?

HOW MAGAZINES DEFINE WOMEN

In the early 1960's *McCall's* has been the fastest growing of the women's magazines. Its contents are a fairly accurate representation of the image of the American woman presented, and in part created, by the large-circulation magazines. Here are the complete editorial contents of a typical issue of *McCall's* (July, 1960):

1. A lead article on "increasing baldness in women," caused by too much brushing and dyeing.

2. A long poem in primer-size type about a child, called "A Boy Is A Boy."

3. A short story about how a teenager who doesn't go to college gets a man away from a bright college girl.

4. A short story about the minute sensations of a baby throwing his bottle out of the crib.

5. The first of a two-part intimate "up-to-date" account by the Duke of Windsor on "How the Duchess and I now live and spend our time. The influence of clothes on me and vice versa."

6. A short story about a nineteen-year-old girl sent to a charm school to learn how to bat her eyelashes and lose at tennis. ("You're nineteen, and by normal American standards, I now am entitled to have you taken off my hands, legally and financially, by some beardless youth who will spirit you away to a one-and-a-half-room apartment in the Village while he learns the chicanery of selling bonds. And no beardless youth is going to do that as long as you volley to his backhand.")

7. The story of a honeymoon couple commuting between separate bedrooms after an argument over gambling at Las Vegas.

8. An article on "how to overcome an inferiority complex."

9. A story called "Wedding Day."

10. The story of a teenager's mother who learns how to dance rock-and-roll.

11. Six pages of glamorous pictures of models in maternity clothes.

12. Four glamorous pages on "reduce the way the models do."

13. An article on airline delays.

14. Patterns for home sewing.

15. Patterns with which to make "Folding Screens—Bewitching Magic."

16. An article called "An Encyclopedic Approach to Finding a Second Husband."

17. A "barbecue bonanza," dedicated "to the Great American Mister who stands, chef's cap on head, fork in hand, on terrace or back porch, in patio or backyard anywhere in the land, watching his roast turning on the spit. And to his wife, without whom (sometimes) the barbecue could never be the smashing summer success it undoubtedly is . . ."

There were also the regular front-of-the-book "service" columns on new drug and medicine developments, child-care facts, columns by Clare Luce [ambassador to Italy and wife of

Time magazine founder Henry Luce] and by Eleanor Roosevelt [wife of President Franklin D. Roosevelt, U.S. delegate to the UN, and chairman of the Human Rights Commission], and "Pats and Pans," a column of readers' letters.

THE TINY WORLD OF THE HOME

The image of woman that emerges from this big, pretty magazine is young and frivolous, almost childlike; fluffy and feminine; passive; gaily content in a world of bedroom and kitchen, sex, babies, and home. The magazine surely does not leave out sex; the only passion, the only pursuit, the only goal a woman is permitted is the pursuit of a man. It is crammed full of food, clothing, cosmetics, furniture, and the physical bodies of young women, but where is the world of thought and ideas, the life of the mind and spirit? In the magazine image, women do no work except housework and work to keep their bodies beautiful and to get and keep a man.

This was the image of the American woman in the year [Fidel] Castro led a revolution in Cuba and men were trained to travel into outer space; the year that the African continent brought forth new nations, and a plane whose speed is greater than the speed of sound broke up a Summit Conference; the year artists picketed a great museum in protest against the hegemony of abstract art; physicists explored the concept of anti-matter; astronomers, because of new radio telescopes, had to alter their concepts of the expanding universe; biologists made a breakthrough in the fundamental chemistry of life; and Negro youth in Southern schools forced the United States, for the first time since the Civil War, to face a moment of democratic truth. But this magazine, published for over 5,000,000 American women, almost all of whom have been through high school and nearly half to college, contained almost no mention of the world beyond the home. In the second half of the twentieth century in America, woman's world was confined to her own body and beauty, the charming of man, the bearing of babies, and the physical care and serving of husband, children, and home. And this was no anomaly of a single issue of a single women's magazine.

WHAT READERS "WANT"

I sat one night at a meeting of magazine writers, mostly men, who work for all kinds of magazines, including women's mag-

azines. The main speaker was a leader of the desegregation battle. Before he spoke, another man outlined the needs of the large
women's magazine he edited:

> Our readers are housewives, full time. They're not in-
> terested in the broad public issues of the day. They are
> not interested in national or international affairs. They
> are only interested in the family and the home. They
> aren't interested in politics, unless it's related to an im-
> mediate need in the home, like the price of coffee. Hu-
> mor? Has to be gentle, they don't get satire. Travel? We
> have almost completely dropped it. Education? That's
> a problem. Their own education level is going up.
> They've generally all had a high-school education and
> many, college. They're tremendously interested in ed-
> ucation for their children—fourth-grade arithmetic.
> You just can't write about ideas or broad issues of the
> day for women. That's why we're publishing 90 per
> cent service now and 10 per cent general interest.

Another editor agreed, adding plaintively: "Can't you give
us something else besides 'there's death in your medicine cabinet'? Can't any of you dream up a new crisis for women? We're
always interested in sex, of course."

At this point, the writers and editors spent an hour listening
to Thurgood Marshall [first African American Supreme Court
judge] on the inside story of the desegregation battle, and its possible effect on the presidential election. "Too bad I can't run that
story," one editor said. "But you just can't link it to woman's
world."

As I listened to them, a German phrase echoed in my mind—
"Kinder, Kuche, Kirche," [children, cooking, kitchen] the slogan
by which the Nazis decreed that women must once again be
confined to their biological role. But this was not Nazi Germany.
This was America. The whole world lies open to American
women. Why, then, does the image deny the world? Why does
it limit women to "one passion, one role, one occupation?" Not
long ago, women dreamed and fought for equality, their own
place in the world. What happened to their dreams; when did
women decide to give up the world and go back home?

UC BERKELEY AND THE FREE SPEECH MOVEMENT

MARIO SAVIO

At first, the student movement that began in the early 1960s was predominantly comprised of middle-class white students from elite universities. Such a group gathered at Port Huron, Michigan, in the spring of 1962, where the newly founded organization Students for a Democratic Society (SDS) drafted a moderate manifesto that called for the increased participation of all members of society in the democratic process. In the following two years, SDS spread to over a hundred and twenty-five college campuses, including both private northeastern colleges and large western and midwestern state schools. SDS increasingly began to challenge the Vietnam War, to support civil rights, and to oppose the growing "technocracy" of America—that is, the mechanized facelessness of corporate America. SDS believed that power elites such as those in charge of the military-industrial complex effectively controlled politics and made a mockery of the concept of democracy.

It was particularly this technocracy that helped spur protests in 1964 on the University of California–Berkeley campus, an extremely large state campus, which was the first university to number and register their students by computer. Students disliked the IBM cards, the huge faceless lectures, the Puritanlike curfews, and the restrictions on students. Most of all, they developed the growing conviction that the university was not a free institution of learning and development, but instead a

Excerpted from "An End to History," by Mario Savio, in *"Takin' It to the Streets": A Sixties Reader*, edited by Alexander Bloom and Wini Breines (New York: Oxford University Press, 1995). Copyright © 1964 by Mario Savio. Reprinted with permission.

government-controlled academic corporation simply aimed at producing fact-filled automatons to staff the ranks of corporate America.

Events in Berkeley came to a head when the administration banned student organizations from distributing leaflets on campus. In September 1964, police attempted to arrest a group of students who were illegally handing out pamphlets. After putting the first student, Jack Weinberg, in the patrol car, police suddenly found the car mobbed by hundreds of students, who surrounded the car for thirty-two hours and passed time by climbing atop the vehicle and making speeches. This incident, in which students actually had an opportunity to voice their concerns, was later hailed as an instance of a participatory democracy, and it initiated the formation of the Free Speech Movement (FSM).

The Berkeley campus was racked by student protests, such as the November 1964 sit-in at Sproul Hall to protest lack of free speech and political freedom, which led to the arrest of 778 students. In the following essay, written in 1964, Mario Savio, a leader of the Berkeley FSM writes about the issues that sparked these student protests. He compares the fight against repressive campus officials to the struggle for civil rights in Mississippi that Savio had participated in with the Student Nonviolent Coordinating Committee (SNCC). A student-run civil rights organization that had been formed in 1961 in the wake of Greensboro and other sit-ins, the SNCC had organized a famous and daring voter registration drive in Mississippi.

In comparing student activism to the civil rights movement, Savio appears to see in them both the hope of changing the ills of America. He also speaks of the alienation that many Berkeley students feel, questioning the university's commitment to the ideals of critical thinking, and arguing that without the freedom to discuss the issues that matter, real intellectual growth and self-examination are impossible.

L ast summer I went to Mississippi to join the struggle there for civil rights. This fall I am engaged in another phase of the same struggle, this time in Berkeley. The two battlefields may seem quite different to some observers, but this is not the case. The same rights are at stake in both places—the right to participate as citizens in democratic society and the right to due process of law. Further, it is a struggle against the same enemy. In Mississippi an autocratic and powerful minority rules, through organized violence, to suppress the vast, virtually powerless, majority. In California, the privileged minority manipulates the University bureaucracy to suppress the students' political expression. That "respectable" bureaucracy masks the financial plutocrats; that impersonal bureaucracy is the efficient enemy in a "Brave New World."

BUREAUCRACY

In our free speech fight at the University of California, we have come up against what may emerge as the greatest problem of our nation—depersonalized, unresponsive bureaucracy. We have encountered the organized status quo in Mississippi, but it is the same in Berkeley. Here we find it impossible usually to meet with anyone but secretaries. Beyond that, we find functionaries who cannot make policy but can only hide behind the rules. We have discovered total lack of response on the part of the policy makers. To grasp a situation which is truly Kafkaesque, it is necessary to understand the bureaucratic mentality. And we have learned quite a bit about it this fall, more outside the classroom than in.

As bureaucrat, an administrator believes that nothing new happens. He occupies an ahistorical point of view. In September, to get the attention of this bureaucracy which had issued arbitrary edicts suppressing student political expression and refused to discuss its action, we held a sit-in on the campus. We sat around a police car and kept it immobilized for over thirty-two hours. At last, the administrative bureaucracy agreed to negotiate. But instead, on the following Monday, we discovered that a committee had been appointed, in accordance with usual regulations, to resolve the dispute. Our attempt to convince any of the administrators that an event had occurred, that something new had happened, failed. They saw this simply as something to be handled by normal University procedures.

The same is true of all bureaucracies. They begin as tools, means to certain legitimate goals, and they end up feeding their own existence. The conception that bureaucrats have is that history has in fact come to an end. No events can occur now that the Second World War is over which can change American society substantially. We proceed by standard procedures as we are.

The most crucial problems facing the United States today are the problem of automation and the problem of racial injustice. Most people who will be put out of jobs by machines will not accept an end to events, this historical plateau, as the point beyond which no change occurs. Negroes will not accept an end to history here. All of us must refuse to accept history's final judgment that in America there is no place in society for people whose skins are dark. On campus students are not about to accept it as fact that the university has ceased evolving and is in its final state of perfection, that students and faculty are respectively raw material and employees, or that the university is to be autocratically run by unresponsive bureaucrats.

Here is the real contradiction: the bureaucrats hold history as ended. As a result significant parts of the population both on campus and off are dispossessed, and these dispossessed are not about to accept this ahistorical point of view. It is out of this that the conflict has occurred with the university bureaucracy and will continue to occur until that bureaucracy becomes responsive or until it is clear the university can not function.

The things we are asking for in our civil rights protests have a deceptively quaint ring. We are asking for the due process of law. We are asking for our actions to be judged by committees of our peers. We are asking that regulations ought to be con-

In 1964 hundreds of students staged a sit-in at UC Berkeley to protest the lack of free speech and political freedom on campus.

sidered as arrived at legitimately only from the consensus of the governed. These phrases are all pretty old, but they are not being taken seriously in America today, nor are they being taken seriously on the Berkeley campus.

I have just come from a meeting with the dean of students. She notified us that she was aware of certain violations of University regulations by certain organizations. University friends of SNCC, which I represent, was one of these. We tried to draw from her some statement on these great principles, consent of the governed, jury of one's peers, due process. The best she could do was to evade or to present the administration party line. It is very hard to make any contact with the human being who is behind these organizations.

THE UNIVERSITY

The university is the place where people begin seriously to question the conditions of their existence and raise the issue of whether they can be committed to the society they have been born into. After a long period of apathy during the fifties, students have begun not only to question but, having arrived at answers, to act on those answers. This is part of a growing understanding among many people in America that history has not ended, that a better society is possible, and that it is worth dying for.

This free speech fight points up a fascinating aspect of contemporary campus life. Students are permitted to talk all they want so long as their speech has no consequences.

One conception of the university, suggested by a classical Christian formulation, is that it be in the world but not of the world. The conception of Clark Kerr, by contrast, is that the university is part and parcel of this particular stage in the history of American society; it stands to serve the need of American industry; it is a factory that turns out a certain product needed by industry or government. Because speech does often have consequences which might alter this perversion of higher education, the university must put itself in a position of censorship. It can permit two kinds of speech, speech which encourages continuation of the status quo, and speech which advocates changes in it so radical as to be irrelevant in the foreseeable future. Someone may advocate radical change in all aspects of American society, and this I am sure he can do with impunity. But if someone advocates sit-ins to bring about changes in dis-

criminatory hiring practices, this cannot be permitted because
it goes against the status quo of which the university is a part.
And that is how the fight began here.

The administration of the Berkeley campus has admitted that
external, extra-legal groups have pressured the University not
to permit students on campus to organize picket lines, not to
permit on campus any speech with consequences. And the bureaucracy went along. Speech with consequences, speech in the
area of civil rights, speech which some might regard as illegal,
must stop.

Many students here at the University, many people in society,
are wandering aimlessly about. Strangers in their own lives,
there is no place for them. They are people who have not learned
to compromise, who for example have come to the University to
learn to question, to grow, to learn—all the standard things that
sound like clichés because no one takes them seriously. And they
find at one point or other that for them to become part of society, to become lawyers, ministers, businessmen, people in government, that very often they must compromise those principles
which were most dear to them. They must suppress the most
creative impulses that they have; this is a prior condition for being part of the system. The University is well structured, well
tooled, to turn out people with all the sharp edges worn off, the
well-rounded person. The University is well equipped to produce that sort of person, and this means that the best among the
people who enter must for four years wander aimlessly much of
the time questioning why they are on campus at all, doubting
whether there is any point in what they are doing, and looking
toward a very bleak existence afterward in a game in which all
of the rules have been made up, which one cannot really amend.

It is a bleak scene, but it is all a lot of us have to look forward
to. Society provides no challenge. American society in the standard conception it has of itself is simply no longer exciting. The
most exciting things going on in America today are movements
to change America. America is becoming ever more the Utopia
of sterilized, automated contentment. The "futures" and "careers" for which American students now prepare are for the
most part intellectual and moral wastelands. This chrome-
plated consumers paradise would have us grow up to be well-
behaved children. But an important minority of men and
women coming to the front today have shown that they will die
rather than be standardized, replaceable and irrelevant.

THE HIPPIE REVOLUTION

Lewis Yablonsky

In some ways, the hippie revolution was a reaction to the conformity and conservatism of mainstream American culture in the 1950s. The hippies rejected Christianity and its values and turned to Buddhism and the religions of the East. They rejected the widespread American materialism and the nine-to-five routine that financial security demanded and dressed in old clothes, slept outside, and challenged traditional aesthetics of cleanliness, neatness, and order. They opposed stability and glorified the life of travel and adventure. Drugs and music were both central to this new vision of life, broadening the narrow confines of suburbia.

Mass anger at the Johnson administration for the war in Vietnam produced a generation that rejected war, nationalism, and materialism and embraced ideas of peace, harmony, and free love. Yet despite these aspirations, the hippie movement was largely hedonistic and chemically dependent. The movement was also predominantly white and middle-class, comprised of people such as Sonny, the young man interviewed in the following excerpt, who had grown frustrated with the repressed confines of upper-middle-class society and its competitive, materialistic mores. In response, Sonny had rejected college and the material comforts of his parents' home and had moved to New York's East Village to get stoned and to get in touch with love and beauty.

In this excerpt, sociology professor Lewis Yablonsky interviews Sonny as part of his larger project for his 1968 book *The*

Hippie Trip. Yablonsky traveled to various hippie communes and centers to conduct research about the counterculture, interested not only in the views and beliefs which hippies like Sonny articulated, but also in what such an outlook revealed about American society in the 1960s.

I n the crevices of the hippie movement are many unsung heroes. Stars who are not yet as glamorous and famous as Tim Leary has become in the popular mass media or Gridley Wright [a hippie who became a hero to many while on trial for marijuana possession] in the underground press. These lesser-known hippie high priests influence the novitiates and teenyboppers enormously. Their "rap" is delivered at all hours and in all hippie locales to youths seeking "the way" that they have found.

One young man of twenty-two who represents this significant role in the hippie movement was Sonny. . . . Sonny was introduced to me by my hippie guide Chuck as "a truly beautiful religious cat." After a brief discussion with him, I decided it would be important for me to get his "rap."

Sonny grew up in a wealthy eastern suburban town. His father was a $50,000-a-year executive. "My father is a proper super-straight cat who belongs to the right country club, drinks his share of the liquor on Saturday night, and is very taciturn, particularly when it comes to talking with his wife." His mother was "a standard hysterically square broad who pampered me to death." (Sonny, I later found out, prior to turning on to LSD and his hippie way of life, had attempted suicide around twenty times.)

Sonny seemed older than his twenty-two years, and was handsome by classic Hollywood standards in the image of Marlon Brando. He had a brilliant smile that he flashed on me many times during our brief but intense encounter. He had long black hair, wore a walrus mustache, and was properly festooned with beads, bells, and rough leather boots.

I interviewed Sonny in the Village pad of one of his disciples. He was enormously turned-on by some "great pot" he had recently smoked. Sonny's "rap" was for me a remarkably good summary of the hip philosophical sounds I had heard in many corners of [New York City's] East Village. Although some of what he says is a "repeat," the totality of his dialogue is a coherent statement of the hip life style and viewpoint in the East Village and other urban centers of the hippie world.

THE INTERVIEW

S: I was a super-straight young man from respectable parents in a middle-class Roman Catholic home. We, of course, belonged to the country club. My eyes were on the commercial stars of America. I had a nice little sports car—the whole scene. Well, for a good period of time, I thought I'd be a marine biologist and I always had an interest in writing. It was kind of a toss-up between the two. I was going to be something very earth-shattering, very noble, very respected.

LY: What kind of hangups did you have? What things bugged you?

S: Oh, I had the typical hangups caused by psycho-repression and everything that every young person in America has—religious hangups, family hangups. I guess it would be easier to list the hangups I didn't have. I had the whole gamut of frustrations and indecisions that most young people in this country face. Most young people go through a period of indecision, doubt, rebellion, etc., and then figure, "Okay, fuck it. I'll accept everything."

LY: Did you ever get tangled up with any psychiatry?

S: Oh yeah, I had an out-of-sight psychiatrist! After the second time I quit college. My psychiatrist was probably the most neurotic man I ever met in my life. If you can picture a psychiatrist's office with a cross and crossed American flags underneath it, you get some idea of this man. To me he seemed very sick. I was fine when I came in, but he convinced me that I was out of my mind. I guess at the time I was going through a rather traumatic period where I still had the kind of held-over guilt feelings that are fostered from having a rather dogmatic world view pushed upon you. I still had emotional ties to that world view that had been drummed into me ever since I could begin to understand and comprehend. There was a very real conflict going on between, you know, my mind, my conscious mind and my subconscious mind . . . if you want to call it something like that. I'd get extremely uptight. I could see nothing but the hostility and anger that the people I cared for, my parents, were experiencing.

I had a very dark view of the world. I had already dropped out of college. My principal interest at that time had been philosophy and I traced Western philosophy to the point where I had absolutely smashed any positive view of the religious thing that I could have. I became wrapped up in despair and I suppose it became a kind of despair I liked. It became sort of an ever-present thing. It got to be too much and, you know, I slashed my arms and wrists. (I noticed around twenty slash-mark scars on his arms.)

LY: How many times did you try suicide?

S: Oh, I have absolutely no idea. I had the main hassle of our time. My refusal to accept the life that my parents picked for me. Most parents within the society are doing something they don't really want to do. You know, there's always some dream that they always wanted, yet they can't do it. And they're caught up in a very materialized sort of game structure. And they excuse this or they rationalize that by saying, "Well, we're going through this so our children can have a better life." That's the excuse that every parent uses, you know, when he isn't leading the type of life that he'd like. And so, when a child grows up and decides that he doesn't want what they've had in their mind for him for all these years, they kind of forget that perhaps he has the right to decide his own form of life. And so you get into a real conflict with them and yourself at that point.

The whole society's based on a very egocentric form of game structure. All the games within the society are ego games. Of prime importance within this society is the self-image and the image presented to others. It just becomes a very paramount thing in everybody's life. It's influenced by movies. People try and be a movie star like John Wayne or somebody like that. They stroll down the street looking tough. They grab onto certain concepts of masculinity and femininity which have nothing to do with what's masculine at all . . . it's just a facade. This allows the self, or ego, to dominate feelings and true expressions. So you become not really yourself, but just kind of a shallow mirror image of some originally false idea. The games would break down if the people became aware that they are games. . . .

LSD

LY: When did you have your first LSD experience?

S: I guess it was about a year and a half ago.

LY: What did it do for you?

S: When I first began to take acid, I wasn't really ready. I was still in a kind of depressed, masochistic stage and it intensified that quite a bit. But eventually there came a period where I began to understand what acid was about and began to use it properly. The first thing it should be used for is to go through your own mind. To look at yourself from outside of yourself to see what kind of things are working in you that are fucking you up, that are making you a manic-depressive, or whatever form your insanity takes.

LY: Did you find anything specific you could put your finger on or was it a general reaction when you began to explore your own, I guess, inner space?

S: Well, I think the most specific thing I thought was that I'd been blind all my life to what is beautiful. You're surrounded so much in this society with what is ugly that it becomes almost the only aesthetic value you can judge. You can see the ugly. You can always see the ugly. If you want to you can get upset by it. People aren't raised to be willing to see the beautiful and I began to see the beautiful. I began to know things such as good karma. I began to be able to sit in the woods and feel a part of it . . . feel a part of nature . . . feel the oneness that is possible. I began to understand what love and beauty are all about.

THE HIPPIE MOVEMENT

LY: In your opinion how did the hippie movement start?

S: The hippie movement, if you want to call it that, is a natural outgrowth of the 50's beatnik movement plus the important extra ingredient—acid.

Beat people like [Jack] Kerouac, [Henry] Miller, Gregory Corso, Allen Ginsburg are still with us. These are people who have become dissatisfied with American society and the American way of life. At that point, they were beginning to see the ridiculousness of it. That's pretty much all they were seeing. They were looking at the negative side of society and they weren't reacting really by trying to change anything positive. They were associated, of course, with the left. The beatnik movement of the 50's was basically just a commentary movement. A group of people expressing themselves principally through the arts. They said, "This is ridiculous, fuck it; we want no part of it."

Their rallying cry, if they had any, was the sexual revolution. Probably their best spokesman was Henry Miller. Their movement, if you want to judge it by the sexual revolution, was fairly successful—at least in this country. There's been a very definite change in sexual mores, particularly among young people.

That period is pretty much passed now. The junction point between what you might call the hippie world and the beatnik world of the previous generation was the introduction of LSD and other psychedelic drugs. Probably people became aware of it at first through [Aldous] Huxley's essays. LSD, mescaline, grass, have been on the scene almost forever but it's spreading now. And I would say that if the hippie movement has a rallying cry it would have to be the psychedelic-drug revolution.

Instead of people saying everything is shit and walking around with their eyes to the ground, kicking stones, mumbling curses under their breath, and adopting a very superior attitude, like "We know where it's at and nobody else does, and you people are too far gone to even approach it," you have, well, things like we just saw in Tompkins Square Park [in the East Village]—people with flowers on . . . you know, running around ringing bells. They're kind of happy.

It's been going on in small groups since the time of . . . Christ. It's nothing, I think, but people becoming aware of their humanness. People dropping off all the hangups and the frustrations that society has foisted upon them. Society exists, I think, almost as a third thing—as an entity in itself. For its own self-preservation and perpetuation it has to install certain attitudes within the people who are in it. These attitudes may be fine for maintaining *that* form of society and keeping *that* form of society alive and functioning. But it has a very real tendency to fuck up the personalities and the minds of the people within it.

The hippies or the flower people or whatever you want to call 'em are nothing but people who've dropped these hangups. People who can behave as children when they want to, unashamedly. And I don't think there is any human being alive who wouldn't want to just run and skip in the streets like a kid. Swing from light posts, climb trees. People who aren't afraid of loving each other. People who aren't suspicious.

SHARING

Friendship no longer becomes a thing of dominance, you know, where one friend dominates the other or where you're always suspicious that maybe someone's out to get you or knife you in the back. It's . . . it's just open. It's dropping all the false trappings of society.

If you need money or anything, you ask somebody for it. If

you want to, people turn you on free. I went to three different places last night. Every place I went, I got stoned. I had some grass this morning so I found some people in the park and came up here and got nicely stoned. . . .

The concept now is to try and get away from trading and bartering. I kind of feel that everybody has one thing which they like to do. Sometimes more than one thing. One function that makes them happy. And to a lot of people that are here in the Village the only reason that they got the courage to come here is because that thing is in the arts. If you're serious about art, you can't really exist in this society because there's just no way to live. This society isn't geared for serious poets, artists, painters.

The people here have their thing. But there are also other people. For example, people down on Wall Street—maybe they would really dig being farmers. Nothing would make them more happy than to till the land, till the soil. To other people, they have a thing like they keep building things. All the frustrated little fix-it shops out in suburbia. Those people would really be happy if they could make something beautiful. And although it isn't very practical in this society now, or in the very near future, it's plausible to envision a society where everybody could just go out and "do their thing." The only way that that could work, each one doing his own thing, is if you do away with the whole concept of pay.

These ideas are working now. It's working down here and it's working in the communities and tribes out in the country. When you do your thing. If you dig farming, you give the food away, except for what you need to eat. If you're making things—chairs, tables, or anything like that—you give them away to those who need it. And if you need help on something, you just ask somebody, "Hey, I'm doing this today," and so they come and help you. It's sort of a total sharing.

I don't think it's a socialistic idea at all. I think it's more a humanist idea. And it will work 'cause it works down here. If you're hungry now, I'd tell you where to go where people have food. You just walk in the door and they'd give you a plate of food. If you wanted to get stoned now, I could tell you where to go.

LY: What you're talking about now has only really come about in the last six months or a year.

S: I'd say last year. This whole thing, we'll call it a movement, has grown so much in the last year it's unbelievable.

I've been traveling through college towns. The academic atmosphere is nice to visit every once in a while. The number of college students who are turning on to dope, love, and beauty is unbelievable! I can see it in the schools. The school I went to a year ago and returned to again last year has changed. It was textbooks before, now it's flowers and love.

LY: Do you think it's a real love?

S: Oh, well, speaking on a general basis is ridiculous. I can only take you out and show you people that I know. I undoubtedly have sort of surrounded myself with friends that have the same sort of ideas and feelings that I do.

THE REACTION OF SQUARES

LY: What is it that you see? How do you think square middle-class Mr. Jones is going to react to the hip movement?

S: It's not only Mr. Jones. Puerto Rican Mr. Gonzales is carrying a knife. I think that his reaction to it right now is one of basic hostility and anger. It stems a great deal from envy. I think a great deal of the hostility is because they're seeing people who are happy doing things that they've been told all their life will never make them happy. People in this society have been told you have to work eight hours a day or you won't eat. And there are people down here who are just happy in doing their thing. People who are not working for anybody in the Establishment are staying alive and they're eating.

They've been told that promiscuous sex is bad, so they have filled themselves with sexual frustration. They have all kinds of hangups and probably the most warped sexual fantasies that you could imagine. I know from some of the chicks down here who get weird propositions from straight cats all the time.

LY: What do they come on with?

S: That whole thing is very negative and it's not really worth going into.

LY: You mean they're perverse sexual propositions?

S: Sure, perverse propositions. Their attitude of sex is basically a very sick one. Sex in this country is such a fantastically important thing. It's put on an unattainable pedestal and it has so many ties. It's a confused thing. It's almost designed to bring guilt. Most people don't enjoy it. They don't know what they're doing. They can't really have sex and be a part of it. Sex is a very human thing and it should be a very natural thing and a very beautiful thing which, for the most part in this society, it is not.

I don't mean sex in the sense of going out and getting laid—or going down to a bar, getting drunk, and then driving some chick out in your Chevrolet and, you know, screwing her in the back seat. Sex is a very beautiful thing, but in this society it isn't.

LY: Is it beautiful in hippie society?

S: For the most part, it is. It's free. It's natural. Nobody makes a big deal of it. It's not a big deal. It isn't the big, you know, all-important question. If a group of hippie males get together they really don't talk about some broad's bust size or who got laid last night. You know what locker-room conversation is like. I don't know whether you've ever played football and that, but the all-important questions are drinking and sex.

I'd like to go back to one question. You said, "What do you think the reaction of Mr. Jones will be?" And I think that's completely dependent on how the hippie attitude or the hippie movement, if you want to call it that, is expressed in the arts. It hasn't been expressed well, yet. The only way that people are going to understand what's happening is if they can understand the people who are a part of this. What they see now are bearded freaks.

They assume that all the bearded freaks take drugs. They don't differentiate between LSD, grass, cocaine, or cough medicine. They put them all in the same category and then imagine that we're all out to beat them, steal their color TV sets, and rape their daughters. So you know they're antagonistic.

A large number of people in the hippie movement are in the arts. Most of them are very bad, but most artists of any period are very bad. You only get a few very good ones. If artistically these ideas that are happening now, if the feelings that people are beginning to get now can be expressed, and expressed in such a way that not only other hippies will understand it but the straight people will understand it too, then perhaps there can be a meeting of minds. Perhaps if the harsh edge of hostility toward hippies by Mr. Jones was taken away, then when a hip person went through Ohio these people could see more than bearded freaks. If they can see people who are happy then the power of the movement is expressed to them.

The power of the movement is through artistic expression and through just being. That's what the Be-In concept is. The whole idea of a Be-In is just to have a whole bunch of hippies, or people who feel like this, in a group—happy and doing their thing. When straight people go by and see somebody else happy when they themselves aren't, maybe they'll begin to question why they aren't. . . .

LY: To go back to the community reaction thing—why do you think middle-class people are so hostile toward hippies?

S: Mr. Jones is hostile in large part because he sees joy and happiness where joy and happiness shouldn't be. He isn't so much worried about it for himself, but he's worried about it for his sons and daughters. Because Mr. Jones is basically not a happy person. Mr. Jones comes home at night, he's tired—he has a beer, he watches TV, and goes to bed. He gets up the next morning and goes through the same thing. Mr. Jones is caught up in a very depressing sort of life and he knows that his children would say that he is not basically a happy man. Mr. Jones drinks too much. He gets pissed off a lot. He grumbles and complains a lot.

And then he sees these people out there having fun. Mr. Jones doesn't believe, because he's very skeptical, that they're really happy. But he's afraid that his sons and daughters will see "the flower children" and believe that they really are happy. Perhaps his children do not want to grow up and be grumbling and mumbling like Mr. Jones. They may want to go out dancing in the streets and do what they want to do.

Right here on the East Side, if you want to speak about a very local matter, we're living in what basically is a ghetto. Predominantly Negro, Ukrainian, Puerto Rican, and hippie. Next to the hippies, the Puerto Ricans are the latest arrivals, so they're the poorest. And the ones with the most frustrations to take out on someone. They're pretty well boxed in and they don't have too much of a chance.

The hippies have been condemned by society, particularly since the [May 30, 1967] Tompkins Square incident [in which police beat hippies gathered at Tompkins Square Park]. That kind of showed the Puerto Ricans down here that the Establishment police say it's all right to hit a hippie. The hippies are bad. It's giving them a scapegoat. They can hit without getting hit back. There are no gangs of hippies walking the streets with switchblades who are going to, you know, get revenge. And now that they've seen that the police can beat hippies, they've found out that the law probably won't get after them for beating up a hippie or two—or cutting them. That's how you get this natural violent reaction.

LY: Where do you see the movement heading?

S: I see a lot of people coming to the rather obvious conclusion that cities are an unnatural place to live. Cities breed hostility. Cities as a human environment are architecturally negative. I think a lot of hip people are coming to the conclusion that the cities, for them at least, are a very unnatural way to live. And people who have the kind of ideas I've been telling you about have decided to get out into small tribes, find an open area of open land or woods somewhere, do their thing, and live in the country.

THE CIVIL RIGHTS MOVEMENT

GARY H. KOERSELMAN

In the following article, American cultural historian Gary H. Koerselman traces the history of the civil rights movement. In the early 1960s, he writes, Martin Luther King Jr.'s philosophy of nonviolent resistance permeated the movement. King was a compelling and powerful leader, respected by both black and white Americans, who preached a Christian ideal of forgiveness and love and held as an ideal a unified society in which all races would be equal and integrated. In the summer of 1963, King led the famous march on Washington, D.C., in which he delivered his riveting, visionary speech "I Have a Dream."

Koerselman relates how in the early 1960s, members of the civil rights movement embraced King's peaceful philosophy, and protesters at sit-ins, for example, were generally painfully polite and dignified as they waited hours and hours in protest of segregated facilities. In 1964, King was awarded the Nobel Peace Prize in recognition of his leadership and his ideals of nonviolence, which were inspired by Indian leader Mahatma Gandhi.

Yet by the mid-1960s, a strong white backlash emerged in reaction to civil rights. White resistance to the movement was manifested in the violence and riots that swept the country and in the Ku Klux Klan murders that continued to be ignored by both the local police and the FBI. Koerselman describes how this violence led to a black backlash within the movement as many blacks became understandably disillusioned with King's philosophy of nonviolence. There had been only modest successes achieved in civil rights legislation, and blacks were still confronted with mob brutality and police violence.

Excerpted from *The Lost Decade: The Story of America in the 1960's*, by Gary H. Koerselman (New York: Peter Lang, 1987). Copyright © 1987 by Peter Lang Publishing, Inc. Reprinted with permission.

Under the leadership of Malcolm X and the Nation of Islam, the Black Power movement emerged, celebrating African culture and rejecting King's goal of integration into mainstream white society. Koerselman explains how one of the groups to emerge from this new separatist conception of black identity was the Black Panthers, who refused to embrace nonviolence as a means of counteracting racist attacks and openly asserted their right to defend themselves. The FBI, which had relentlessly pursued the pacifist King until his assassination in 1968, soon turned its attention on the Panthers, jailing and killing several prominent leaders. This campaign, along with internal power struggles, led to the disintegration of the movement by the mid-1970s.

B y the time Lyndon Johnson entered the presidency, civil rights had become a primary national concern endorsed by liberals and widely covered by the press. America "is a country where institutions profess to be founded on equality, and which yet maintains the slavery of black men," once observed British philosopher John Stuart Mill as he contemplated the guilt Americans felt about their racial dilemmas. The Civil War had eradicated slavery but not discrimination against blacks; and in the new atmosphere of democratic liberalism, Johnson sensed the opportunity to place the full weight of the presidency behind stronger civil rights legislation. "One of the presidents (Lincoln) I admire most signed the Emancipation Proclamation 100 years ago," Johnson told members of the National Urban League, his fists clenched, "but emancipation was a proclamation and was not a fact. It shall be my purpose, and it is my duty, to make it a fact." Johnson told Congress that "should we defeat every enemy, and should we double our wealth and conquer the stars and still be unequal to this issue, then we will have failed as a people and as a nation."

Johnson's personal commitment aside, the pressures on any President for new civil rights legislation would have been strong. Public opinion had swung in favor of legislative action. In 1942, for example, only 30 percent of those sampled believed that black and white children should attend the same schools, compared to 67 percent in 1965. Supported by favorable public opinion, the modern civil rights movement had already established a history of its own and gained widespread support from other institutions. For years the NAACP [National Association for the Advancement of Colored People] had persisted before the United States Supreme Court in order to eliminate legally sanctioned segregation. Finally, in 1954, Thurgood Marshall, Special Counsel for the NAACP, persuaded the Court in *Brown* vs. *Topeka* to overturn the "separate but equal" doctrine which had been established by *Plessy* vs. *Ferguson* in 1896. . . .

FROM EISENHOWER TO KENNEDY

President Johnson understood that the Supreme Court's insistence on civil rights obliged the other branches of government to follow suit. The best model for presidential leadership came in 1957 when Eisenhower had ordered federal troops into Little Rock, Arkansas, to support the integration of Central High School. Eisenhower's initial reluctance was overshadowed during the 1960 presidential campaign when both Nixon and Kennedy campaigned for favorable civil rights planks. Kennedy captured the imagination of blacks, however—and 68% of their vote—when in October he made a special plea for the release of Dr. Martin Luther King from an Atlanta, Georgia, jail where the prominent civil rights leader had been sentenced to four months hard labor for leading a sit-in demonstration at a department store.

President Kennedy initially moved cautiously on civil rights, fearful of political recrimination from the southern Democrats. He appointed a prestigious commission on equal employment opportunity, declared an end to hiring discrimination in federally financed projects, pushed for an end to segregation in interstate transportation, placed a record number of blacks in federal offices, and ceremoniously issued an Executive Order against discrimination in federally-aided housing projects. Kennedy ordered federal troops into Mississippi in support of James Meredith's admittance to the university, but he grimaced at the activities of the Freedom Riders and shied away from recommending the legislation liberals desired.

DR. MARTIN LUTHER KING

The real impetus for stronger legislation had to come from the blacks themselves behind their own indigenous leadership. By the Sixties Dr. Martin Luther King, head of the Southern Christian Leadership Conference, had become America's most prominent black civil rights leader. Born in Atlanta and graduated from Boston University, Dr. King first rose to national fame

in 1956 when he led a yearlong boycott against the segregation
of public transportation facilities in Montgomery, Alabama.

King's non-violent protest activities at first electrified some
Americans and made most of them uncomfortable. Former
President Harry Truman called him a "first-class troublemaker,"
and FBI Director J. Edgar Hoover referred to him as a "liar" and
a "communist dupe." By 1964, however, when he received the
Nobel Peace Prize, King enjoyed widespread moral support
from both blacks and whites. Even then few Americans understood the true philosophy of this modern prophet whose message of brotherhood was rooted fundamentally in traditional
American religious and democratic principles. "Injustice anywhere is a threat to justice everywhere."

King appeared as a modern day Moses leading his people
from the bondage of second-class citizenship toward the
promised land of equal justice and opportunity. Yet King's mission involved the redemption of the entire nation not just
blacks. His promised land amounted to a truly integrated community founded on the principles of mutual love and concern
rather than the capricious principles of competition and intrigue
which he believed had come to dominate American life. According to King, segregation represented a "blatant denial of the
unity which we all have in Christ," and the nation could not be
at peace with itself until this terrible condition was removed.

King's non-violent tactics flowed from his redemptive mission. By attracting public attention to segregation, thereby forcing it into the political arena, King hoped to challenge the public's conscience to remove this incongruity and establish a more
perfect union. "Non-violent direct action seeks to create . . . a
crisis and establish such creative tension that a community that
has constantly refused to negotiate is forced to confront the issue," wrote King in his letter from the Birmingham jail. "It seeks
so to dramatize the issue that it can no longer be ignored." King
had learned much from Mahatma Gandhi, Indian liberator, and
America's 19th century spokesman of non-violent protest,
Henry David Thoreau. King believed with Thoreau that "under
a government which imprisons any unjustly, the true place for
a just man is also a prison." And King understood with Thoreau
that "a minority is powerless while it conforms to the majority;
but it is irresistible when it clogs by its whole weight. If the alternative is to keep all just men in prison, or give up war and
slavery, the State will not hesitate which to choose."

King's democratic idealism was mixed with a pragmatic notion of stimulating redeeming action. On the one hand, he believed in working through established order, never advocating overthrow of the government or special privilege for blacks. Even when nervous authorities became violent, King did not physically retaliate but turned the other cheek. "Let no man pull you so low as to make you hate him," warned King, quoting Booker T. Washington [19th-century African American educator who maintained that economic independence would need to precede social equality]. "Along the way of life, someone must have sense enough and the morality enough to cut off the chain of hate." This powerful image of persistent righteousness greatly influenced his fellow Americans, as revealed in a comment by Cleveland Browns' [fullback] rambling Jimmy Brown: "He never struck back. So he became my idol." On the other hand, King remained firm in his mission. Even though he did not ask for charity, he demanded long-withheld justice. He persisted unremittingly in his strategy without compromise or exception. "In any non-violent campaign there are four basic steps," he wrote: "collection of the facts to determine whether injustice exists; negotiations; self-purification; and direct action."

While King remained hopeful about the fulfillment of the great American dream, he harbored a few illusions concerning the enormous amount of vociferous resistance his actions would generate. The ultimate racial peace that King sought would surely rattle the very foundations of the comfortable old order and bring about bitter and often unreasoned recrimination not unlike that experienced by unpopular Biblical prophets of old. King became fond of quoting Christ: "I have not come to bring peace, but a sword." King's idealism was tinged with fatalism. "It may get me crucified. I may even die," King once speculated, "but I want it said . . . in the struggle that he died to make men free."

VIOLENCE IN ALABAMA

Hence the historical paths of the determined prophet King and the reluctant President Kennedy converged once again during the spring of 1963 when the civil rights leader brought his struggle to Birmingham, Alabama, probably the most segregated city in the country. King led a series of marches against discrimination in shops, restaurants, and in public and private employment. Once he was jailed but released on bail. The tension mounted. On May 3, 1963, a thousand demonstrators marched from the Sixteenth Street Baptist Church into the downtown area. Suddenly violence broke out as a horde of helmeted policemen, led by the indomitable police Chief Eugene "Bull" Connor and armed with electric cattle prods, high-pressure fire hoses, and growling police dogs, descended unmercifully upon the hapless black throng, injuring several. The brutal scene shocked and outraged the nation.

In Birmingham an accord soon followed which desegregated public facilities, expanded employment opportunities for blacks and established a bi-racial study group. But tension still remained, and it could spread elsewhere. Clearly, the time had come for Kennedy to exercise the moral leadership of the Presidency. "We are confronted primarily with a moral issue," announced Kennedy, "it is as old as the Scriptures and is as clear as the American Constitution."

KENNEDY ACTS

Kennedy's study of history and politics had convinced him that unabated injustice could lead to serious social disruption and even revolution. "In these moments of tragic disorder," Americans have an obligation "to reject the temptations of prejudice and violence and to reaffirm the values of freedom and law on which our free society depends," Kennedy told a Vanderbilt University audience. In June, after Alabama's pugnacious young Governor George C. Wallace had arrogantly tried to frustrate the admission of blacks to the state university, Kennedy decided to make a nationwide television appeal as he submitted a strengthened civil rights bill to Congress. "We face a moral crisis as a country and as a people," admonished Kennedy. "It cannot be met by repressive police actions. It cannot be left to increase demonstrations in the streets. It cannot be quieted by token moves or talk. It is time to act!"

Southerners balked at Kennedy's new civil rights initiative. Just hours after his television appeal Medgar Evers of the Mississippi NAACP was murdered. A few weeks later four small girls died in an Alabama church bombing. Meanwhile, Senator James O. Eastland, Chairman of the Senate Judiciary Committee, blocked Kennedy's civil rights bill in committee.

In spite of Southern intransigence, public opinion continued to mount for Kennedy's demands for strong civil rights legislation. In August of 1963, one century after the Emancipation

Proclamation, over 200,000 Americans marched in Washington, D.C., singing "We Shall Overcome": "Black and White together/Black and White together/ We shall overcome, some day." At the Lincoln Memorial Dr. King delivered, in resonant tones, what might have been the most moving sermon of the century. "Even though we face the difficulties of today and tomorrow, I still have a dream," affirmed King in his magnificent drone. "I have a dream that on the red hills of Georgia the sons of former slaves and the sons of former slave-owners will be able to sit together at the table of brotherhood. . . . I have a dream that even the state of Mississippi, a state sweltering with the heat of injustice, will be transformed into an oasis of freedom." He closed with a dramatic appeal: "Free at last! Free at last! Thank God Almighty, we are free at last!"

JOHNSON AND THE CIVIL RIGHTS ACT

The momentum created by the Washington march and Kennedy's assassination transfixed public opinion so that Johnson could make civil rights a reality. While in the Senate Johnson had been a formidable civil rights foe, but, as President, he became an unswerving supporter. He made his position clear in the 1964 State of the Union Message. "Let this session of Congress be known as the session which did more for civil rights than the last hundred sessions combined," exhorted the President. In an address at Howard University the President used the "foot-race" analogy to rationalize his position. "You do not take a person who, for years, has been hobbled by chains and liberate him, bring him up to the starting line of a race, and then say 'You are free to compete with all the others,' and still justly believe that you have been completely fair," admonished LBJ. The President demanded more than equal treatment; he demanded action which would guarantee equal opportunity, a principle as old as the American dream. In this sense Johnson appealed to a fundamental American notion of equity which emphasized individual merit as the standard of human worth and dignity.

In the U.S. Senate Minnesota's loquacious Hubert Humphrey, who personally had a hand in most of the decade's significant legislation and whose outspoken support for racial equality dated back as far as the 1948 National Democratic Convention, where he had insisted on placing a strong civil rights plank in that year's party platform, led the struggle in the Senate against one of the longest and most acrimonious southern filibusters in

history. "The Negro in the South is a happy person. He understands the members of the white race, and they understand
him," protested Arkansas Congressman Ezekiel "Look" Gath-
ings. Finally, the liberals resorted to cloture in order to secure the
most comprehensive civil rights legislation since Reconstruction.

The Civil Rights Act of 1964 prohibited the use of literacy
tests as a voting qualification, made unlawful discrimination in
public facilities, authorized the United States Attorney General
to file desegregation suits, outlawed discrimination in programs
receiving federal funds, made discrimination in employment illegal, and established an Equal Employment Opportunity Commission for enforcement purposes. In 1965 a second act guaranteed voting rights by authorizing the federal government to
perform registration procedures and suspending the use of literacy tests. Almost one million new black voters were registered
by 1970. In 1968 a third civil rights act sought to guarantee open
housing. Thus Johnson accomplished his grandiose civil rights
goals. No other president since Lincoln could match his record.
"For generations Negro Americans have prayed for a President
who would not only see their peculiar disabilities but would do
something about them. Lyndon Johnson was such a one," wrote
Roy Wilkins of the NAACP. Most Americans believed that civil
rights had now been put behind them. Dr. Martin Luther King
captured the optimism of the moment when he said, "it has
been a sea of great moments for us all."

THE RIGHT STRIKES BACK

In the midst of this apparent success, however, a series of iron-
ical, if not inevitable, events turned the civil rights movement
into directions which few Americans had anticipated. The ominous events began with Barry Goldwater's capture of the Republican Presidential nomination in 1964. Goldwater had voted
against the Civil Rights Act, ruefully citing his states' rights philosophy. His obdurate stand attracted a surprising number of
white bigots and other anti-civil rights people. The Congress on
Racial Equality (CORE) paraded a coffin outside the Republican convention in order to signify the death of the movement
should Goldwater become president.

At the Democratic National Convention a few weeks later
civil rights advocates were profoundly disappointed when the
most prominent white liberals failed to support the persistent
Fanny Lou Hamer and the Mississippi Freedom Party in their

effort to unseat the all-white regular delegation. Meanwhile, in California, Proposition No. 14, which would repeal the state's open housing laws, received overwhelming support from voters; and in other parts of the country the middle class and blue collar workers began rallying around the saucy George Wallace.

The facade of racial progress was further stripped away in 1965 when Dr. Martin Luther King brought his movement north to Chicago, where the vile reaction in the blue-collar suburb of Cicero demonstrated that racism was as insidious in the North as the South. King came to Chicago from Selma, Alabama, where he had faced the violent obstinacy of Sheriff Jim Clark, who opposed efforts to register black voters. A 50-mile march from Selma to Montgomery was interrupted by beatings and death. Selma and Cicero proved that mountains of prejudice could not be wiped away with the mere passage of legislation.

RIOTS THROUGHOUT THE COUNTRY

Meanwhile, the first of more than fifty inner big city racial explosions occurred in the Watts section of Los Angeles in 1965, when five days of rioting left 34 persons dead, 853 wounded, and 4,000 under arrest. The main business district along 103rd Street was destroyed; the area later became known as "charcoal alley." The bellows of curling black smoke and intermittent exchange of gun fire presented an uncommon and disturbing scene for millions of Americans who had grown complacently accustomed to domestic tranquility. In the next few years riots occurred in other major cities, leaving 107 dead and almost 4,000 injured.

The big city riots were largely spontaneous, the tragic result of horrid living conditions, hot summer weather, unemployment, and police oppression. Whitney Young, Jr., President of the National Urban League, called them the result of "poverty and dope, and the refusal of authorities to crack down on the Mafia, which traffics in narcotics." Many black families had only recently moved north, refugees of southern agricultural mechanization, and were suffering the consequences of being unprepared for northern industrial life, where economic opportunity remained scarce.

THE WHITE BACKLASH

The underlying causes of the riots escaped the attention of most whites, however, who preferred to blame communist agitators and irresponsible radicals rather than to grapple with the truth.

In Chicago Mayor Richard J. Daley emphatically ordered the police "to shoot to kill any arsonist or anyone with a Molotov cocktail in his hand." The Mayor received applause from poor whites, who, struck by fear, were busily arming themselves against an invasion from black ghettoes, and from the more affluent middle class, which demanded repressive governmental measures. Whites were also beginning to resent not only violence but welfare, court-ordered busing, and open housing legislation. The liberal social architects were left confused and baffled.

The growing white backlash prompted younger, more impatient blacks to advocate a more drastic course of action based on separatism and forceful confrontation. Much of the new black furor took its inspiration from Malcolm X, desperado prophet of the Black Muslim movement. Malcolm X preached racial separation, moral self-improvement, economic self-sufficiency, and pan-Africanism, which meant an ultimate black exodus "back to our own African homeland." Malcolm X showed contempt for American liberalism, calling it a mere placation of blacks. He dubbed Christianity as a White man's religion and taught that blacks "can sometime be 'with' whites, but never 'of' them."

Malcolm believed that "the Negro is better off by himself, so he can develop his character and culture in accord with his own nature." Malcolm X criticized King's non-violent tactics, claiming that "the Negro is justified to take any steps at all to achieve equality. . . . There can be no revolution without bloodshed," he insisted. "When our people are being bitten by dogs, they are within their rights to kill those dogs," claimed the embittered leader. "No man in our time aroused fear and hatred in the white man as did Malcolm," wrote Melvin S. Handler in the introduction to Malcolm's autobiography, "because in him the white man sensed an implacable foe who could not be had for any price—a man unreservedly committed to the cause of liberating the black man in American society rather than integrating the black man into the society." Malcolm's life was cut short by brutal assassination engineered by a detractor from within the Black Muslim movement in 1964, but by then he had already implanted a fierce black nationalism in the minds of many younger black leaders.

BLACK POWER

"Black Power" became the symbol of the new black nationalism; "Black is Beautiful" was its slogan. Black Power was not necessarily to be equated with black militancy. Even though it drew much of its rationale and inspiration from persons such as Malcolm X, it represented not so much a radical departure as a maturation of the black-American movement. It represented a tough-minded realistic formula for achieving practical goals. A good many moderate blacks viewed the movement as a wholesome stage in positive advancement toward equality. Responsible black opinion was well represented by Robert S. Browne, Executive Director of the Black Economic Research Center, who said that "we will never again allow ourselves to accede to 'integration' as the sole possible route." "There is nothing in the concept of community control that differs with the belief in an integrated, open society based on pluralism," wrote Urban League Director Whitney Young. "The failure of white institutions to provide equal services for the ghetto means that the black community itself must control its institutions."

Black Power in its best sense emphasized the need for blacks to acquire an indigenous Afro-American consciousness rooted in a pride for black culture and life styles not unlike that of other nationalities which had immigrated to American shores. It called for the repudiation of white majority values, morals, and ethics and for the eradication of the traditional Negro image of "the lazy stupid, crap shooter, chicken stealing idiot," as one proponent put it. Black Power involved both an affirmation and a search for identity. According to one spokesman, it represented "not so much a negation of white power as it is an affirmation of the worth and dignity of the black man without reference to the white ideal."

Black Power represented "an exploration of black culture and the realization that within this culture are those values which a black minority can, without shame, embrace," wrote activist author Addison Gayle, Jr. Gayle described it as "a creative concept aimed at destroying one hundred years of mental enslavement, distorted images and meaningless cliches." He saw it further as "a rebuke to white experts who do not realize that to be black in America is to journey through the fiery labyrinthine corridors of hell."

Black Power called upon blacks to gain control over their own affairs and institutions. At issue was the black individual's "ability to control a part of his life, the ability to control some of the economic forces that now only act on him, the ability to make them act in his own behalf," asserted Julian Bond, Georgia legislator and a founder of the Student Non-Violent Coordinating Committee (SNCC). "Every group in this country owns its own neighborhoods but us," pointed out SNCC's leader Stokely Carmichael. "If we are to proceed toward true liberation, we must cut ourselves off from white people. We must form our own institutions, credit unions, co-ops, political parties, write our own histories," stated an SNCC position paper. By banding together to insure the force of numbers, blacks, much as organized labor a generation earlier, could bargain collectively with whites in order to win their rightful share of American prosperity. "Black Power means black people coming together to form a political force," explained Carmichael. "It's an economic and physical bloc that can exercise its strength in the black community." Put more plainly, Carmichael told a group of whites: "Look, buddy, we're not laying a vote on you unless you lay so many schools, hospitals, playgrounds and jobs on us."

SELF-EMPOWERMENT

Black Power had many positive results. It resulted in the election of such politicians as Mayors Richard Hatcher of Gary, Indiana, and Carl Stokes of Cleveland, Ohio. It led to rent strikes against absentee landlords who extracted exorbitant rents without maintaining the property, supermarket boycotts against food chains which reserved the highest quality products for suburban stores without differentiating in price, and the beginnings of black capitalism and the organization of citizen police protection associations. It prepared blacks for employment opportunities. The Center for Community Action led by CORE founder James Farmer, for example, stressed remedial education, job training, and retraining. The Center operated upon the proposition that while "picket lines may pay off old scores, vocational training will pay the grocery bill." Such activities envisioned economic and neighborhood control for blacks.

"Operation Breadbasket" in Chicago, under the leadership of Jesse Jackson, sought to bring food to the inner city poor. In Detroit the East Side Voice of Independent Detroit, under the direction of the burly Frank Ditto, who called himself a responsible agitator, initiated several "black pride" projects. "Operation Bootstrap" in Watts found employment for skilled blacks. In Indianapolis black clubs removed trash in massive neighborhood clean-up efforts. "Slums are made by people, not by plaster or bricks," asserted sponsor Mattie Rice Coney proudly. "Civic re-building begins with people who care about themselves." On Broadway an all-black cast brought *Hello, Dolly* to its audience in a most refreshing style. These accomplishments gave blacks a new self-confidence and a new sense of purpose necessary for the assertion of their race and culture.

Some of the symbolism and inciting rhetoric connected with the Black Power movement, however necessary to stimulate blacks, tended to disturb whites who had not taken the time to understand the experience behind the rhetoric. Whites were offended, for example, when during the 1968 Olympics two black medal winners saluted the playing of "The Star Spangled Banner" by raising gloved fists. Allusions to violence and disruption by Carmichael and his SNCC associate H. Rap Brown proved especially disconcerting to whites. Carmichael first gained national attention in 1966 when he publicly advised blacks not to participate in Vietnam: Tell LBJ "hell no, I won't go." According to Carmichael, ghetto blacks shared more in common with such suppressed groups as the Viet Cong than with their white American compatriots; both groups existed in a colonial status, victims of white capitalistic imperialism. Dark-skinned brothers and sisters should not become instruments of white imperialism against each other.

RESORTING TO VIOLENCE

While seldom advocating outright violence, Carmichael and his followers came armed and prepared to fight back in defense of their neighborhoods. "We believe in violence," claimed Carmichael. "I am using all the money I can raise to buy arms." H. Rap Brown claimed that "violence is as American as apple pie." "If President Johnson is worried about my rifle, wait until I get my atom bomb," shouted Brown. "If you are gonna loot, brother, loot a gun store. Don't be running around here looting no liquor, cause liquor's just for celebrating," harangued Brown. "We ain't got nothing to celebrate about. You better get yourselves some guns, baby." "If America don't come around," warned Brown, "we are going to burn it down, brother. We are going to burn it down if we don't get our share of it."

From San Quentin Eldridge Cleaver, who described himself as a "full-time revolutionary in the struggle for black liberation in America," in his *Soul on Ice* justified violence by arguing that the black male had systematically been robbed of his masculinity through the years. Soledad brother George Jackson spread revolution among other black prisoners who could easily point to injustice in the legal system. At the University of California the militant Angela Davis, a brilliant young philosophy instructor, provided a Marxist rationale for black revolution.

Black Muslim world heavyweight boxing champion Muhammad Ali told the National Conference of Black Students that "by nature, blacks and whites are enemies." In New York City James Foreman, Director of the United Black Appeal, demanded $500 million in "reparations" from the nation's white churches and synagogues. "The Church is the jugular vein of the country, because wrapped up in the church is a vital system which helps perpetuate the kind of exploitation of blacks which goes on," explained Foreman.

BLACKS AND JEWS

When Black Power rejected white leadership, the movement lost the crucial support of the Jewish community. Not only had Jews sympathized with the horrors of persecution, but a strong civil rights consciousness served to protect themselves as well. In the early days of the movement Jews stood as martyrs alongside blacks. For example, the two white men who were summarily murdered in Philadelphia, Mississippi, in 1964 along with black James Chaney were Jewish.

A bitter struggle involving the community schools in the Brownsville section of Brooklyn, New York, in 1967 led to a clash between Jews and blacks for control. The dispute drew national attention when the Jewish head of the American Federation of Teachers, Albert Shanker, got involved in an ugly dispute with local blacks over the issue of black anti-Semitism. The Jews were becoming increasingly uneasy about problems of reverse discrimination. While blacks had almost no representation in high influential places such as university faculties, Jews were proportionately overrepresented. Things began to appear too much as if a gain for blacks would be a loss for Jews, hence there was less than complete agreement on a host of civil rights issues ranging from affirmative action to school desegregation. By 1968 Jews had become deeply disturbed about the violence.

The year 1968 proved to be a bad year for the civil rights movement. The Six Day War of 1967 caused further alienation. Radical blacks began to see Israel as a major perpetrator of colonialism in such places as Southern Africa, where many black brothers were falling before rifles obtained in Israel. For their part, the Jews became pre-occupied with the survival of a Jewish state in the face of growing Arab and Soviet hostility.

A group of radical blacks led by Bobby Seales and Huey Newton had organized the Black Panther Party, which actively began preparations for guerrilla warfare in the urban ghettoes. Newton charged that Cleaver had led blacks down the road to "reactionary suicide." In his book *Revolutionary Suicide*, Newton called for "a United Nations-supervised plebiscite to be held throughout the black colony in which only black colonial subjects will be allowed to participate, for the purpose of determining the will of black people as to their national destiny."

DR. KING IS ASSASSINATED

The assassination of Martin Luther King on April 4, 1968, triggered a wave of violence that left forty persons dead. The tragic death of King severely damaged any dreams of racial unity. Instead racial polarization prevailed, and the color line was laid bare. "When White America killed Dr. King, she declared war on us," snapped Stokely Carmichael. "We have to retaliate for the death of our leaders. The executions of those deaths are going to be in the streets." Blacks must "abandon the nonviolent concept used by Dr. King," urged Lincoln Q. Lynch, Chairman of the United Black Front, "and adopt a position that for every Martin Luther King that falls, ten white racists will go down with him." King left a leadership vacuum that the more radical civil rights elements quickly sought to fill, thus reducing further the tentative support previously enjoyed among whites. At the White House President Johnson could see the reflections of a burning city dancing off the Capitol buildings. The idealism had gone out of the civil rights movement. Thus made vulnerable, the movement was destined to grind slowly to a halt under the stern law-and-order policies of the upcoming Nixon Administration.

Lyndon Johnson could point to only scanty progress toward racial equality. The Supreme Court would remain firm, and the media was eliminating many of its most blatant stereotypes. In the film *Grasshopper* Jimmy Brown would embrace Jacqueline Bisset, remarking that "it couldn't have been done years ago." But in real life basketball star Lew Alcindor would have to file a lawsuit in order to rent the apartment of his choice.

Most disappointing was the fact that equal economic opportunity still eluded blacks. Family incomes for blacks increased

55 per cent during the Sixties compared to 64 per cent for whites. While blacks comprised 11 per cent of the population, only 5.1 per cent possessed an annual buying power of more than $15,000, the estimated income needed to maintain a comfortable standard of living. Only two per cent of the nation's business enterprises belonged to blacks, and only three of the 3,182 highest corporation executives and board directors were black. In the building trades, described as the "bastion of discrimination" by Roy Wilkins, Executive Director of the NAACP, only four per cent of the construction workers were black. Among plumbers, electricians, and skilled manufacturing, the percentage was even lower. Economist Sylvia Porter concluded that for blacks "giant economic strides" had simply not been made "except in the publicity handouts."

Federal assistance for the employment of blacks proved even more disappointing. A soft drinks manufacturer received $950,000 in federal contributions over two years but employed only 22 of the promised 300 blacks. Twenty-two California firms received $11.6 million from the federal poverty program for creating only 1,010 new jobs. Father Theodore M. Hesburgh, Chairman of the United States Civil Rights Commission, summarized the sorry record. "This commission has had it up to here with . . . communities that have to be dragged kicking and screaming into the U.S. Constitution," admonished Hesburgh. "People aren't serious about equality of opportunity and the government isn't serious about equality of opportunity."

In the final analysis Americans proved unwilling to face the dire implications of racial equality. Even the President's Kerner Commission, appointed to study racial affairs, declared that "our nation is moving toward two societies, one black, one white—separate and unequal." First white backlash and then black backlash brought about disenchantment, reaction, and withdrawal similar to that which had diminished the post–Civil War civil rights movement a century earlier. Not even the inimitable political antics of Lyndon Johnson could penetrate the unyielding color line, and now the President himself stood to reap the blame for all the violence and default.

THE CHICANO STORY

FRANCIS DONAHUE

In the following selection, Spanish studies professor Francis Donahue sketches the origins and development of the Chicano movement in the United States. Donahue suggests that the revolutionary fervor of the 1960s—especially the civil rights movement—inspired the Mexican American community to begin to seek fair wages and to combat racist discrimination. Mexican Americans, or Chicanos, as they became known in the 1960s, had begun to arrive in the United States in large numbers in the first decade of the twentieth century, mainly as seasonal laborers on large farms. After World War II, their numbers increased rapidly, with communities centered mostly in California and the southwest. There they lived without modern amenities, toiled in the fields for fourteen-hour days, and aged rapidly due to this hard labor. According to Donahue, most of the immigrants were afraid to protest these conditions; illegal immigrants feared deportation, while legal immigrants feared losing their jobs.

In 1962, a migrant worker named Cesar Chavez began to organize the Californian grape workers. He formed the National Farm Workers Association (NFWA) in 1963. Using traditional labor union methods of strikes, picketing, and marches, Chavez succeeded in winning labor contracts from several growers and in bringing national media attention to the plight of Chicano workers. Focusing not only on poor labor conditions, but also on racial issues, Chavez called for a national boycott of nonunion table grapes between 1967 and 1970 and gained mass support in the East. By 1972, the descendant of the NFWA, the United Farm Workers, joined the American Federation of Labor and Congress of Industrial Organizations (AFL-CIO), the most powerful American trade union organization.

Donahue discusses not only the birth of the important

Mexican American workers' unions, but also the cultural organizations that developed to seek equal rights for all Chicano people and to instill a sense of nationalist pride among Chicano Americans.

A cross the Southwest and in Chicano enclaves elsewhere in this country, an epic crusade is shaping up as Mexican Americans struggle valiantly to be considered respected and equal members of America's multi-racial society. As the nation's second disadvantaged group (after the Blacks), Chicanos formerly constituted an "invisible minority" who meekly accepted their role as a subservient mass of farmhands and unskilled or blue collar workers.

No longer. In the past seven years Chicanos have been galvanized into joining the major historical current which has swept over the United States in the last twenty-five years, the home-grown revolution of rising expectations—first the Blacks, then Students, Women, the Gays, and now the Chicanos. Sparking their crusade have been *La Huelga*, the Chicano grape strike and subsequent boycott of California grapes and other agricultural products; *La Causa*, a general term related to the overall advancement of Chicanos; and *La Raza*, a growing awareness of self-identity as an ethnic group with its own singular culture and life-style. . . .

THE FARM WORKER

The farm worker stands as the most newsworthy Chicano of all. Yet he constitutes a small minority of the Chicanos—under 400,000 in California. "Since I joined the farm workers, I've visited farm labor camps all over the state and it's horrible how these people live," explains Margie Coons, a volunteer working out of the Los Angeles office of the United Farm Workers Union. She helps organize workers and, on weekends, accosts shoppers urging them to boycott the market because it handles non-union grapes or lettuce. "Whole families crammed into tiny cardboard shacks, sometimes with no plumbing, no lights, no sanitation of any kind. And they work so hard that they look like old men and women while they're still young. The average life span of a Chicano field worker is only forty-nine years. And the average family income is only $2,300 a year."

In 1962 emerged the first charismatic Chicano leader, Cesar

Chavez, who, in that year, launched his now-famous campaign to unionize Chicano and other farm workers in California. Born in 1927 near Yuma, Arizona, on an eighty-acre farm, Chavez at an early age came to know the heat-blistered, penny-pinched existence of the migrant field hand. When the family farm failed during the Depression, Cesar's parents loaded their belongings and their children into a beat-up automobile and headed for the Golden State. From the Imperial and Coachella valleys in the south, the family worked its way—hoeing, leafing, and picking apricots, grapes, asparagus, beets, potatoes, and plums—through the San Joaquin Valley and into the northern reaches of the Napa Valley. Cesar had his share of brushes with prejudiced Anglos. Once when he refused to move to the "Mexican section" of a San Jose theater, he was ushered out and subjected to a verbal dressing-down at the police station. Cesar was sixteen.

Chavez's dawning social conscience was honed by experience with the Community Service Organization in San Jose, where he was engaged in welfare work among Chicanos for ten years. Besides reading widely, he followed the course of the Negro Civil Rights Movement and came to acquire his own stable of social saints: Emiliano Zapata, Mexican peasant leader of the 1911 Revolution; Mahatma Gandhi, Jawaharlal Nehru, and Martin Luther King, all noted for their dedication to non-violent social change.

With his $1,200 savings Chavez founded the National Farm Workers Association (now the United Farm Workers Union) and, within two years, had signed up about a thousand members. He created a credit union, issued a newspaper, and soon moved to bring pressure on grape growers in the Delano, California, area for better wages and working conditions for "his men."

Through a spectacular 1965 strike, which grabbed headlines across the country, Chavez dramatized the farm workers' cause. Within a short time, growers came up with an offer to increase wages 120 percent. Chavez had won the first round and was on his way. He trained his sights on other table grape growers, to the tune of marches by workers bearing aloft the banner of the Mexican Virgin of Guadalupe, flanked by a new Chicano symbol, a banner depicting a black Aztec eagle on a red field. *Viva la huelga* ("strike")! *Viva la causa! Viva la union!* Demonstrations staged in focal spots across the California countryside breathed life into a nascent populist movement.

Converging on Delano were newsmen, TV cameras, and interviewers from radio shows. The Chavez story was soon beamed into homes here and abroad. Behind that story, the news media uncovered the sorry specifics of Chicano existence throughout the Southwest, compounded of prejudice, discrimination, inadequate education, poverty, and second-class citizenship. Thanks to the Chavez cause and the news media, the "invisible minority" became visible. It was becoming vocal as well.

Chicanos now had a home-grown hero, as well as a positive *causa* around which they could rally. "With the poetic instinct of *La Raza*, the Delano grape strikers have made it *[huelga]* mean a dozen other things," states Luis Valdez, director of El Teatro Campesino, a Chicano dramatic aggregation based in San Juan Bautista, California. "It is a declaration, a challenge, a greeting, a feeling, a movement. We cry *huelga*. It is the most significant word in our entire Mexican American history. Under the name of *huelga* we created a Mexican American *patria* [homeland] and Cesar Chavez was our first *presidente*. We came back with an utterly raw and vibrant Mexican character. We shouted *Viva la Huelga* and that word became the word of life for us."

CHICANO POWER

Faced with the need to publicize their cause, Chicanos began to agitate in 1966 for a White House Conference on Mexican American Affairs. Washington deemed such a conference premature. Instead, it offered a Cabinet Committee Hearing on Mexican American Affairs in El Paso, Texas, in October 1968. During deliberations many Chicano delegates became convinced the hearing was geared to lining up support for the Establishment rather than coming to grips with issues which Chicanos had raised. They walked out of the hearing, which was held in a posh downtown hotel, and moved to a slum *barrio* ("neighborhood") where they held a rump session. After scoring Anglos for downgrading Chicano culture, they pointed to the pressing need to organize the *barrios* in pursuit of economic, political, and educational goals.

Showcasing this rump session was a setting befitting a political convention. Held proudly aloft by brown hands were placards proclaiming *La Huelga*, "Chicano Power," and "Adequate programs and funds for 'Our People' first, then 'Viva Johnson.'" To the still ill-defined organization, the raucous rump session gave the name *La Raza Unida*.

At a subsequent meeting in San Antonio, in January 1969, the

Raza Unida party began to define its goals. These included efforts to develop community organizations to work for Chicano civil rights, to plug for better schools and for sanctions against companies known to practice discrimination in hiring or promotion.

THE CHICANO MOVEMENT

For the Chicano Movement, the past seven years are the prologue to a wider struggle for a more rewarding tomorrow. "Change now, not *mañana,* we've waited too long already!" That is the pulsating mood of the militant new minority. In taking their battle to the Establishment, the Movement runs along today on four major monorails, whose destinations may be listed as self-identity, a pluralistic philosophy for subculture, social protest, and unity within the burgeoning Movement itself.

In their struggle for a respectable place in American society, Chicanos are striving for a clearer understanding of their own identity as members of a subculture. The latter, a variation of lower class culture, stands in marked contrast to the predominantly white, Anglo, middle-class culture which prevails throughout the United States.

Pervading that subculture is an emerging ethos, an integrated amalgam of characteristics stemming from Mexican culture,

Migrant workers are bused to the fields. Cesar Chavez helped bring media attention to the plight of the Chicano workers.

particularly its Indian elements, from American culture, and from the century-old experience of living as an exploited minority in the United States. Rankled by Anglo attitudes which have undervalued "Mexican culture" as practiced by Chicanos, the latter feel a compelling need to proclaim their life-style as an alternative way of living constructively in this country. They see no need to be assimilated into the Melting Pot in order to be considered loyal citizens.

Basic to the Chicano ethos is marked emphasis on the family. While more equalitarian than its Mexican prototype, the family does not regularly prove to be a stable unit. The father, who is the dominant force, is often absent. The mother remains the one continuing, adhesive element holding the family together. Teenage pregnancies inside and outside of marriage are frequent.

Highly prized is personal pride or dignity. This is closely associated with *machismo* ("the masculinity cult") which has various outlets: it may be the need to redress vigorously any slight to one's honor or that of the family; it may connote an exaggerated concern for sexual conquests; it may express itself in a haughty squandering of money on friends, or in gambling, usually to the financial detriment of the economically strapped family.

COMMUNITY

Concern for spiritual values (good friendship, close family ties, politeness in social relationships, reverence for the land) overrides a quest for materialistic values. Not that the Chicano does not want material goods. Still, he does not feel the driving motivation inherent in the Puritan work ethic which spurs Anglos to continue working long after their basic material needs have been provided for.

Influencing the Chicano's approach to life is a brotherhood concept, an inherited *copadrazgo* system of institutionalized social obligations forged between godparents and godchildren and between godparents and parents themselves. It is not enough for one "to make it on his own." Rather, as a member of a brotherhood, the Chicano senses an obligation to stay in the *barrio* and work for the betterment of his fellow *carnales* ("brothers"). Those who rise to professional or administrative positions are expected to continue working on behalf of the Chicano community. If, instead, they integrate with the Establishment and move to the suburbs, they are branded *Vendidos* ("traitors to the cause").

SPANISH LANGUAGE

Basic to the ethos is language—Spanish, liberally condimented with English expressions and often with "invented" words with an intonation peculiar to Northern and Central Mexico. A binary phenomenon characterizes the speech of many Chicanos, that is, a mixture of linguistic symbols of English and Spanish blended into the syntactic structure of one of the two languages: "Looking at his younger son, the *jefito se pone a pensar* .... 'I had a dream *la otra noche.'"

Besides this increased concern for self-identity, a majority of Chicanos espouse a philosophy which holds that subcultures, like the Chicano, should be allowed to maintain and develop their heritage without the need to follow the time-honored custom of "assimilation" into the WASP (White, Anglo-Saxon Protestant) mold, which has distinguished most immigrant groups. Chicanos do not consider themselves immigrants. They were here first. The Anglos came to join them, and subsequently to control them.

The Chicano aim is to be considered as equal, if unique, members in a democratic corporation of subcultures, known collectively as the United States. "Integration is an empty bag," explains Rodolfo "Corky" Gonzales, leader of the Denver-based Chicano Crusade for Justice. "It's like getting out of the small end of the funnel. One may make it, but the rest of the people stay at the bottom."

To promote this anti-Melting Pot philosophy, the major vehicle is the alternative plan of education which is being implemented at the elementary level in the Southwest. "English as a Second Language," a program pioneered in the early 1960s, channels the Chicano first grader into classes designed to teach him English the entire school day. The purpose is to prepare him for an English-dominated classroom. Yet, when the Chicano has mastered sufficient English, Anglo and Black students of his age group often have a two-year headstart on him in subject matter work. To remedy this, many public schools in California, and elsewhere in the Southwest, began in 1966 to adopt a Bilingual Bicultural Approach. Spanish is the language in which the entering Chicano learns basic subject matter. During certain class hours he is given instruction in English. Outcome of this approach is that the Chicano is now succeeding in moving from grade to grade with his Black and Anglo peers while picking up English, formally and informally, along the way. . . .

SOCIAL PROTEST

As its third major goal, the Movement regularly mounts programs and demonstrations of social protest to alert Chicanos to their plight as an exploited minority whose civil rights, economic status, and personal safety are not as secure as those of Anglos. It also strives to sensitize the community outside of the *barrio* to abuses committed against Chicanos. Spearheading the protest was Cesar Chavez's *Huelga* which has now taken the form of a lengthy boycott of many California growers. Added to this are efforts to spotlight injustices in the courts, with police and politicians, in military and business practices, to name a few. Chicanos gave wide coverage to the racist attitude of a San Jose judge who, in hearing a case involving a Chicano teenager, blurted out in anger: "Maybe Hitler was right . . . you and your kind should not be allowed to live.". . .

UNITY

A quest for unity in the Movement, the fourth goal, is being noted increasingly in Denver, Los Angeles, San Antonio, Phoenix, and Santa Fe. Fanning out across the Southwest and extending into Middle West enclaves are a plethora of organizations representing special interest groups within the Chicano community. Among groups and committees there is ample evidence of rivalry and inadequate coordination. Chicanos experience marked difficulty in developing viable, large-scale organizations.

After the sharp exchanges at the first conference of *La Raza Unida* with its rump session in 1967, a second attempt at unity grew out of the Chicano Youth Liberation Conference held in Denver in March 1970. On behalf of Aztlan, the Indian name for the ancient Aztec nation, delegates drafted a "Spiritual Plan" which reads in part:

> Aztlan belongs to those who plant the seeds, water the fields, and gather the crops . . . not to the foreign Europeans. We do not recognize capricious frontiers on the Bronze Continent. . . . With our heart in our hands and our hands in the soil, we declare the independence of our Mestizo Nation.

This ambitious statement, while carrying a strong emotional charge, did not produce a fusion of groups in the Movement.

At the First National Chicano Political Caucus, in April 1972, the issue of unity was again paramount. Purpose of the conclave was to write a platform that Chicano activists could support during the 1972 presidential year, one that would indicate to candidates what Chicanos expect in the way of reforms in exchange for their political support. In attendance at the caucus were Chicanos representing the Democratic, Republican, and *Raza Unida* parties. . . .

LOCAL POLITICAL CONTROL

In keeping with their desire for cultural pluralism, Chicanos are moving toward a policy of working for local control of areas in which they are in the majority. Such control would include city hall, the schools, the police and fire departments, and other community services. California, with its massive concentration of Chicanos, is the logical state to kick off a drive for Chicano control of *barrio* areas. While Chicanos serve as mayors and councilmen and on school boards in some Southern California towns, the three million Mexican Americans of California have no state senator out of forty, only two state assemblymen out of eighty, and only one congressman out of thirty-eight. In Los Angeles none of the fifteen city councilmen is a Mexican American. To correct this situation, Chicano activists, with some outside support, launched a campaign in 1971 to establish Chicano districts in the California State Reapportionment battle. Although they were unsuccessful—the state failed to draft a Reapportionment plan—the idea proved very attractive to many Chicano leaders.

"Gerrymandering has kept Chicanos politically impotent and has prevented the *barrios* from electing their own people," declares Francisco Sandoval, Professor of Chicano Studies at California State University (Long Beach). "But we can't wait another ten years for Republicans and Democrats to redistrict the areas. We can't wait ten years for crumbs off the table. The Chicano must take his destiny into his own hands."

Despite the lack of unity in the Movement, Chicano power is gradually being forged and wielded in a variegated process designed to assure social justice and an enriched quality of life for a minority group which, as history books will one day chronicle, came of age in the 1965–1972 period.

The Forgotten Decade: The 1970s

CHAPTER 5

Feminism, Lesbianism, and the Gay Rights Struggle

David Farber

In the following excerpt, David Farber, a history professor at the University of New Mexico who has written extensively on American history during the 1960s and 1970s, discusses feminism in the 1970s and the gay rights movement that also arose in that decade. Although women had fought for and gained rights in earlier eras (especially during the 1840s and the 1920s), Farber notes that after World War II women had been forced to leave the workforce and to retreat from the public domain. At that time the role of housewife and mother was argued to be a woman's natural calling. By the early 1960s, women were arguing that this role was restrictive. Women from all over the country banded together to form a mass movement, fighting to liberate themselves from the strictures of domesticity and child rearing and to enter the public sphere if they so chose. Through books and magazines, as well as "consciousness raising" groups, women voiced their frustrations and critiqued the rigid role defined for them by a male-dominated society.

In the second half of the excerpt, Farber notes how the women's movement was influenced by and connected to the gay rights movement of the early 1970s. He discusses the famous Stonewall Riot of 1969 in New York's West Village and the emergent gay consciousness that arose from this incident. As gay power became a prominent social and political issue, the feminist movement moved to embrace the struggle for lesbian rights as part of feminism. Moreover, both movements sought to overturn the ideal of straight, male-dominated patriarchal society as the desirable American model and to expand cultural boundaries to include gay parents, single-mother families, and other nontraditional arrangements.

B etween 1968 and 1975, dozens of articles and best-selling books spread the feminist message. Terms such as "patriarchy," "male chauvinist pig," and "sexism" entered the American vocabulary. On college campuses, in exclusive men's clubs, in women's magazines, at construction sites, anywhere where feminists detected "male supremacy," women carried their fight for equal rights and, more radically, their campaign to overthrow the social view that, when it came to the roles of men and women in a society, "biology is destiny." Radical feminists, while alienating a large majority of Americans, had also succeeded in focusing the nation's attention both on gender inequality and on the immense cultural and political forces that constructed and constrained gender roles in America.

By 1970, millions pondered the radical feminists' messages. In 1970, when Kate Millett's *Sexual Politics* was published, *Time* magazine put her on the cover. Less than two years later, *Ms.*, a feminist women's magazine, sold out all 250,000 copies of its first issue in eight days. By the early 1970s, NOW [the National Organization for Women] and dozens of small radical feminist groups were joined by the Women's Equity Action (focused on gender discrimination in universities), the National Women's Political Caucus (which aimed to elect more women to office), and Human Rights for Women (an abortion rights group). According to historian Rosalind Rosenberg, by the late 1970s, thousands of women's groups were fighting at the local and national level for social change.

Rank-and-file members of these groups, financial supporters, and other sympathizers were primarily college-educated, middle-class white women. Many had read books like Betty Friedan's *The Feminine Mystique* (1963), Robin Morgan's *Sisterhood Is Powerful* (1970), Kate Millett's *Sexual Politics* (1970), Shulamith Firestone's *The Dialectic of Sex* (1970), the Boston Health Collective's *Our Bodies, Our Selves* (1971), Germaine Greer's *The*

Female Eunuch (1972), and later Susan Brownmiller's *Against Our Will: Men, Women and Rape* (1975), a searing indictment of how the police and court systems treated rape. But many women were pulled into the women's movement by more than reading a book, no matter how eye-opening it was.

CONSCIOUSNESS-RAISING GROUPS

What came to be called "consciousness-raising groups" were integral to the rise and development of the movement. These women-only rap sessions began informally within the radical movement. Women talked to each other openly about intimate details of their lives, often for the first time. But instead of treating these things as psychological issues to be individually resolved, they considered the broader social implications of their personal feelings: why do I, and so many women, someone might ask, feel under constant sexual pressure from men; or why do I, and so many women, get so nervous about talking to large groups of people; or why am I, and so many women, unable to confront a man when wronged by him? One early participant, feminist author Susan Brownmiller, wrote that in consciousness-raising groups "a woman's experiences at the hands of men were analyzed as a *political* phenomenon." Politically radical and astute women were turning the therapeutic ideal on its head and asking not why am *I* unhappy, but what do my personal feelings and experiences say about how society is organized to make women politically, culturally, and economically subordinate to men?

By the early 1970s, these consciousness-raising groups were springing up in cities and suburbs around the country. Many of the women who participated were married and had children; many were the "discontented" housewives of the early 1960s who had been searching for years for answers to their frustrating sense of being unfulfilled by the traditional gender role they had embraced. Gloria Cohen, for example, saw a note for a women's group pinned up on the bulletin board at her daughter's elementary school. She called up her sister and they decided to go. As her sister recalled, the meetings were "just so eye-opening":

> . . . We talked about our marriages, and what we wanted and just about being women in a way I had never done before even with my closest friends. It wasn't just whining, it was trying to figure out *why*,

> why we felt things and what we could do to make our
> marriages more equal and our lives better. Mainly, it
> was just so eye-opening to realize that other women
> had the same problems as you and that it wasn't your
> fault that you felt angry and wanted more for yourself.

Many women, for the first time, shared stories about being raped or abused. They told about the illegal abortions they had endured: "I went with another woman who was also having an abortion. We didn't know each other. We met at a restaurant and then we followed a woman to a car; she blindfolded us in the car. I was fine. . . . I bled the whole next day. But I was fine. The other woman died." Such terribly private stories, when shared, moved many women to public action.

FEMINISM SPREADS

Ms. magazine publicized the consciousness-raising groups and even provided a how-to article. No organization oversaw these informal groups and no national membership rolls existed, but it is likely that throughout the 1970s millions of women participated in or had a close friend or relative who went to such groups. The groups worked to link radical feminists, NOW's reformers, and a great many previously unpoliticized women. By the early 1970s, the women's liberation movement, once composed of a few political insiders and small cadres of radicals, was becoming a mass movement.

Throughout the 1970s, the women's movement gained in power and mainstream acceptance. NOW activists and their allies won a series of sweeping court decisions that essentially ended legal discrimination against women. And while they failed to achieve passage of the Equal Rights Amendment, they succeeded in solidly enlisting the federal government in their cause.

In 1973, the Supreme Court ruled in *Roe* v. *Wade* that women had a constitutional right to control their own bodies and have an abortion. What had once been dismissed as radical nonsense, that men should not have the right to "colonize" women's bodies, had, in one critical instance, become the law of the land.

BLACK WOMEN AND ANTIFEMINISTS

Despite great legal and political victories, the women's movement remained extremely controversial and was not just opposed by "male chauvinist pigs." While some black women became feminists, many black women active in the civil rights struggle and the Black Power movement felt that matters of racial justice had a prior claim on their energies and that the women's movement hurt their cause by diverting resources and attention from it. In addition, they were suspicious of what they saw as the mainly middle-class desires of the new feminists. As one activist said wryly: "Black women . . . could not understand why these white women were so gung ho about working and being the same as men. Black women . . . had been working all of their lives. They would have been glad to sit at home and not work. . . . For the black women it was a question of liberating black men and not women."

Many women, a clear majority at least through the early 1970s, opposed the movement because they felt it did not recognize or respect their lives. They feared the economic consequences of a gender-blind society in which a man's legal and moral responsibility to support his wife and children would be weakened. They worried about seeing their daughters sent off to war or into dangerous work environments. Many women, in then Congresswoman Barbara Mikulski's words, did not want to see their daughters have to go back to the factories or rough-and-tumble times they had escaped: "They wanted to be 'ladies' . . . and they wanted their daughters to be 'ladies.'" Being "just" a housewife, many American women believed, was a whole lot better than any real-life alternative. Not surprisingly, many women were also appalled by radical feminists' well-publicized arguments that marriage, monogamy, and motherhood were all traps that essentially reduced women to men's chattel and that housewives were little more than unpaid servants. These bald arguments, regardless of their heuristic value or even their accuracy, were not likely to win most women over to the side of feminism. Finally, many men and women were horrified by the women's movement's increasingly close identification with lesbianism.

LESBIANS AND THE FEMINIST MOVEMENT

The women's movement had long wrangled over that issue. In part, radical feminists' political analysis and support of lesbianism stemmed from their overall concerns about how sex and sexuality were used by men to oppose women. Much of what made the women's liberation movement radical was its analysis of how men reduced women to sexual objects and the ways in which women cooperated in their own objectification. Women could not achieve real equality, many feminists argued, until they could stop men from seeing them primarily as sex objects. Provocatively, and not unreasonably, radical feminists argued that until women took more responsibility for their own sexual fulfillment—in part by focusing their sexual partners' attention on clitoral rather than vaginal stimulation—they could not expect to achieve sexual parity, let alone gender equality with men. Lesbianism offered a profound response to the intertwining problems of sex and sexuality. As one radical argued: "The lesbian rejects male sexual/political domination . . . lesbianism puts women first while the society declares the male supreme. Lesbianism threatens male supremacy at its core." For a committed radical feminist, dedicated to fighting women's dependence on men at its root, lesbianism made a certain amount of ideological sense. In addition, the women's liberation movement really did attract the support of many lesbians, who without husbands to rely on for economic support, had more reason than most straight women to actively pursue gender equality.

Reform-minded feminists like Betty Friedan were, at first, very much opposed to incorporating lesbians and lesbianism into the women's movement. Friedan went so far as to call lesbians "the lavender menace." The reformers, quite simply, recognized that an overwhelming majority of Americans were unapologetically prejudiced against lesbians and homosexual men and they feared conflating the idea of feminism and lesbianism in the public mind—something that conservatives and many provincial Americans did anyway. Not until well into the 1970s did non-radical, straight feminists decide that it was simply wrong to allow political expediency to dictate morality; homophobia should have no place in their fight for an egalitarian society.

STONEWALL AND GAY RIGHTS

The rise of the lesbian question within the women's movement was part of a larger struggle that emerged at the very end of the 1960s: the gay liberation movement. Semi-secret, reform-minded homosexual rights and discussion groups had begun forming soon after World War II and a large and vital gay movement would not emerge until well into the 1970s. But in at least symbolic terms gay liberation burst onto the public stage very early in the morning on June 28, 1969, after police officers raided the Stonewall Inn, a gay bar in Greenwich Village.

A police raid on a gay bar was nothing new in New York City or elsewhere; gays were seen by most authorities as deviants who deserved to be harassed periodically. Traditionally, patrons of gay bars did their best to quietly walk away from the police raiders, knowing that they could lose their jobs and reputations if their homosexual activities were made public. But at the Stonewall that night something almost unprecedented occurred. As *The Village Voice* reported: "Limp wrists were forgotten. Beer cans and bottles were heaved at the windows and a rain of coins descended on the cops. . . . Almost by signal the crowd erupted into cobblestone and bottle heaving." In a fury, gay men, many of them working-class, several of whom were Hispanic, torched the Stonewall and a riot broke out. A defiant call to arms was spray-painted all over the Village: "Gay Power."

The new Gay Power activists were fueled by all the other civil rights, liberation, and protest movements that had preceded them. Many had gained organizational experience and a radical perspective working in such movements. Gay and lesbian activists were also building from the tiny "homophile" movement which had, in the 1960s, begun publicly lobbying government officials in Washington, D.C., New York, San Francisco, and elsewhere, asking for an end to discrimination and legal oppression. And by the late 1960s and early 1970s, in New York City and San Francisco, and to a lesser extent several other American cities, homosexuality was no longer "the love that dares not speak its name." Gay bars and other gay-oriented establishments, while under constant threat of police harassment, had begun to increase in number as gay men and women from around the country began to form semi-underground communities in the big cities. A series of books and articles, dating from the 1948 and 1953 Kinsey reports on American sexual behavior, while often far from sympathetic, had made it clear to many, gay and straight, that homosexuality was a far from rare phenomenon. This public knowledge, the increasing numbers of gays living in the big cities, combined with the less rigid sexual mores that prevailed by 1970 (at least on college campuses and among more cosmopolitan Americans), gave gay and lesbian activists a cultural and social platform from which to work.

THE STRUGGLE FOR GAY RIGHTS

Like the women's movement, the new gay activists fought on many fronts. At a fundamental level, they fought to turn around the society-wide certainty that homosexuality was, in the words of a brutal 1966 *Time* magazine article, "a pathetic little second-rate substitution for reality . . . a pernicious sickness." Many homosexuals, according to historian John D'Emilio, "absorbed [these] views of themselves as immoral, depraved, and pathological individuals." Part of the activists' fight, then, was to convince gay men and lesbians that they were not sick or bad people simply because of their sexual preference. They urged gay men and lesbians to "come out of the closet" and take pride in being gay. To this end they organized social events, fought to remove the stigma and danger attached to going to a gay bar or event, and on college campuses and elsewhere organized openly gay groups. To change heterosexual attitudes, activists targeted the American Psychiatric Association's official position that homosexuality was a mental disorder. In 1973, they succeeded in getting the APA to remove its stigmatizing label.

The new, militant activists continued the work of earlier reformers by fighting for simple civil rights. In New York City, for example, gay groups struggled to get the city government to pass a bill which would make discrimination by reason of sexual preference illegal—a bill which was finally passed in 1986. By 1973, nearly 800 openly gay organizations fought for the rights of homosexuals at both a local and national level. By the late 1970s, gay liberation had become a vital, multifaceted political movement increasingly accepted as a legitimate interest group by many big-city political establishments. Simultaneously, the relatively sudden visibility of openly gay men angered and frightened less tolerant Americans. Many people were appalled by those gay men who rejected what most Americans considered traditional sexual morality by practicing and publicly promoting sexual promiscuity, anonymous sex, and a more openly erotic way of life. The gay rights struggle was the most controversial civil rights or liberation movement to emerge out of the 1960s; by the late 1980s, conservative politicians would successfully use the question of homosexual rights to inflame and polarize Americans.

THE SIXTIES NEVER DIED

By the mid-1970s, most Americans' sense of economic security, which had influenced both liberals and radicals to believe that the times were right for fundamental political and social change, was gone. But it is incorrect to think that social activism came to an end with the 1970s. Throughout the 1970s, the women's movement, the gay movement, the environmental movement, as well as rapidly expanding movements of Chicanos, American Indians, disabled Americans, and others, gained adherents and power. In fact, much of what people remember as (or call pejoratively) "sixties" activism or "sixties" challenges to "traditional values" occurred in the first half of the 1970s. Just as most of the social activism and cultural rebellion Americans experienced in the 1960s had roots in previous decades, what activist Abbie Hoffman called "a sixties state of mind" continued to grow in new directions into the 1970s and after.

THE ENVIRONMENT AND THE CONSUMER

FREDERICK F. SIEGEL

The activist and student movements of the 1960s helped give rise to an important grassroots movement in the early 1970s: environmentalism. Frederick F. Siegel, a professor of history at Cooper Union in New York City and a columnist at the *New York Post*, discusses some of the strands of this broad-based movement.

Siegel notes that early concerns about the environment focused on overpopulation and the use of toxic pesticides. By 1970, the mass celebration of Earth Day and the creation of the Environmental Protection Agency (EPA) signaled widespread support for environmentalism. However, Siegel writes, popular support for environmental causes was diminished when some activists—including the consumer movement—sought to use environmental issues to lobby for increased regulation of business and industry.

America, Paul Ehrlich pointed out in his influential *The Population Bomb* (1969), accounted for only 6 percent of the world's population but 40 percent of its consumption and 50 percent of its pollution. The problem, as Ehrlich saw it, was that the newcomers to mass consumption, the unenlightened proles who "insisted on breeding excessively," mucked "up the environment with their plastic spray cans and electric baubles." The growth of this tasteless sort of throwaway consumption made life unpleasant for the more cultured members of the middle class, who found beaches and country lakes, which can't be mass-produced, becoming crowded and less pleasurable as more and more new people could afford access to them. If voluntary measures failed to halt this erosion in the quality of life, Ehrlich insisted, compulsory government population controls would be necessary. One of Ehrlich's colleagues, Martha Willing, suggested making it a crime to have more than two children, while another proposed inoculating both males and females against fertility at puberty. Ehrlich and the people associated with his upper-middle-class organization, ZPG [Zero Population Growth], conveyed a Malthusian sense of doom about the plagues that would follow unless we repented and repudiated the false gods of economic growth and mass consumption. By 1983, predicted Ehrlich, steak would be just a memory after a billion people had starved to death around the globe, while the use of dangerous chemical pesticides would lead the United States into a nuclear confrontation with Japan and the U.S.S.R. Fortunately, trend is not destiny and 1972 saw the beginning of a sharp and continuous drop in the American birth rate.

The population bomb fears were a case of a recurring middle-class panic, but the accompanying fears about pollution and the environment were not so easily discounted.

ENVIRONMENTAL TOXINS

Many of the hopes of the late 1940s and early 1950s were tied to the high-technology, high-energy methods of production developed during the war, which first promised to raise and then succeeded in raising the American standard of living. Until the early 1960s both scientists and lay public were generally unaware of the hidden costs imposed by vastly increased fluorocarbon consumption and the use of plastics and pesticides. But, beginning with the 1962 publication of Rachel Carson's pathbreaking *Silent Spring*, which exposed the malign effects of the wonder pesticide DDT, which had greatly increased crop yields, the nation became increasingly aware of the underside of high-tech productivity. High-tech mass production had raised living standards and vastly increased the number, type, and quality of goods available to Americans of limited means, but it also poisoned the nation's air, water, and soil. DDT killed off not only harmful insects but birds and wildlife as well, while petrochemical fertilizers "created vast nitrogenous wastes that drained into rivers and lakes," literally killing them. At the same time oil and strip-mined coal used increasingly to produce energy left the soil barren and the air filled with a smog which in Los Angeles and other cities became a direct threat to public health.

In "The Sources of Public Unhappiness," written for the upscale *New Yorker*, former [Lyndon] Johnson, [Joseph] McCarthy, and Robert Kennedy aide Richard Goodwin talked of how the awareness of environmental dangers had produced a sense of foreboding. For the "average citizen," said Goodwin, public life seemed to be running out of control. "The air around him is poisoned, parkland disappears under relentless bulldozers, traffic stalls and jams, airplanes cannot land. . . . Yet he cannot remember having decided that these things should happen, or ever having wished them. He has no sense that there is anything he can do to arrest the tide."

ENVIRONMENTAL MOVEMENT

By 1968 the growing awareness of the pollution and a muted version of the counterculture's anti-modernism created a response to the malaise Goodwin had identified. In the summer and fall of 1969, while the ghettos were quiet, the environmentalist movement became the new rage, receiving blanket coverage from the networks and top news magazines. "Suddenly, it seemed that every journalist in New York had turned with relief from worrying about 'the war and the cities' to worrying about the environment."

The environmental activists were drawn from the ranks of upper-middle-class whites who had filled the anti-war and civil rights movements, but environmentalism, as a plea for clean air and water, drew broader popular support. By April 1970, the date of the first Earth Day, environmentalism was so broadly popular that Congress adjourned for the day and 10 million schoolchildren took part in events to mark the occasion. "Ecology," cracked California Democrat Jesse Unruh, "has become the political substitute for the word 'mother.'" Responding to the popular outcry, Congress not only passed clean air, clean water, and safe waste disposal legislation; it also, with President Nixon's approval, created an Environmental Protection Agency in 1971, with the power to bring suit against the corporations or municipalities which violated the standards in the environmental legislation.

Like John Kennedy in 1960, Nixon, who focused on foreign policy, came to office with a set of attitudes but without a domestic program. Again like John Kennedy, "the marketing managers of Nixon Inc." had the "pragmatic" ideology of non-ideology. Nixon's position in the Republican Party had always been as a broker between the provincial wildmen, the Brickers, McCarthys, and Goldwaters, and the Eastern establishment. Elected by a narrow margin, Nixon began thinking about re-election almost as soon as he entered office. Governing became an extension of campaigning. Or as one aide put it, referring to Nixon's closest advisers, most of whom were public relations men, this administration gives "the impression of a four-year sales meeting." While searching for a salable domestic policy, he confided to Daniel Patrick Moynihan that the "real reason Hubert lost was not Vietnam"; he lost because the New Deal was over. Knowingly or not, he was echoing the words of the first Eisenhower administration. The New Deal, it seems, has been a long time dying. With his ball-and-socket flexibility, Nixon initially saw some of the left-liberal attacks made by Richard Goodwin and others on the efficacy and legitimacy of federal power as an opening for a moderate conservatism that lowered expectations while providing responsible government. To the surprise of many liberals, then, Richard Nixon took up a position at the head of the environmentalist parade. In signing environmental legislation, he caught the spirit of the moment when he proclaimed: "It is now or never for us to pay our debt to the past by reclaiming the purity of . . . our environment." Nixon went even further. In paying homage to the swelling feeling for the sanctity of nature, he struck a "radical" note, intoning that "we must learn not how to master nature but how to master ourselves, our institutions and our technology."

RALPH NADER

The broad consensus on conservation began to dissolve when environmentalism was used to challenge unchecked corporate power. The first challenge came from a young Harvard Law School graduate, Ralph Nader. In 1965 Nader published *Unsafe at Any Speed,* a devastating critique of the way the lack of competition in the auto industry allowed the three giants to engage in a mock rivalry over car styles while producing autos which, ignoring safety design, were unable to protect passengers in even a low-speed accident. Rewarded for his efforts by having General Motors turn its private spies on him, Nader went on to become a leading advocate of environmentalism. His basic message was simple. At a time, he argued, when giant economic concentrations are able to dominate markets, the free play of competition could no longer be relied on to protect the consumer. "Air pollution," wrote Nader, "is a new way of looking at an old American problem, concentrated and irresponsible corporate power." An age of monopoly required consumer organizations and government regulation designed to guarantee a minimum of social responsibility from organizations so large as to in effect be public but which were run solely for private profit. Nader's Raiders, task forces staffed by the veterans of social reform, studied topics ranging from air and water pollution to the depredations of agribusiness. The Nader task force on agriculture found that nearly half the land in America's most important agricultural state, California, was comprised of just forty-five farms, which received huge federal water subsidies of dubious legality. Agribusiness, the report noted, relied on machine harvesting and pest control methods which made food more expensive and threatened the land's ecological balance. "Corporate economic, product and environmental crimes," concluded Nader, "are part of a raging corporate radicalism which generates technological violence, undermines the integrity of government, breaks laws, blocks needed reforms, and repudiates a quality competitive system with substantial consumer sovereignty."

THE CONSUMER MOVEMENT

Nader's hopes that consumerism and environmentalism would spawn a mass reform movement were never fulfilled. In part Nader's trenchant criticism of corporate practices mobilized a political counter-response on the part of business, exemplified by Nixon's fierce assertion: "We are not going to allow the environmental issue to be used, sometimes falsely and sometimes in a demagogic way, basically to destroy the system." But Nader's hopes also received a blow from an unexpected source, the parallel and overlapping countercultural and ecological challenge to corporate business practices.

Though drawn like the Naderites from the sons and daughters of people who had already "made it," the ecologists, believers in the wilderness as a semi-sacred terrain threatened by the ravages of timber companies and snowmobiles, were an even wealthier group, sprinkled with "old money." Their vanguard organization, the Sierra Club, which had once preached a conventional brand of conservationism, turned increasingly during the turmoil of the 1960s to a religious view of nature that challenged traditional Western notions about the character of human existence. Where the Greek Protagoras had argued that "man is the measure of all things" and Christianity emphasized man's immortal soul, the ecologists' pantheistic view of nature was a mix of beat and Orientalist quietism and romantic aestheticism which preached a naturalist piety that seemingly rejected anthropocentric materialism.

The Sierra Club theology, one logical culmination of the revolt against mass society, was given its widest hearing in Charles Reich's best-selling *Greening of America*. Reich, a forty-two-year-old graduate of prep school and Yale, who described himself "as just like everyone else," was a former clerk to the backpacking civil libertarian Supreme Court Justice William O. Douglas and a member of a prestigious law firm before he joined the faculty at Yale. His book, which took pleasure in dividing the nation into warring cultures of grubby materialists on one side and bell-bottomed Beatles-humming lovers of peace and nature on the other, featured an endorsement from Senator George McGovern calling it one of the most profound books ever written about America. *The Times* of London, which serialized the book, caught its appeal in the subheads it gave to the sections. These read: "The Men with the Grey-Flannel Minds" . . ."A Generation Betrayed". . ."Plastic Lives in Plastic Homes" . . ."The Flowering of America." As the subheads indicate, the book was a virtual recapitulation of the countercultural litany. We live, said Reich, "in a society no one created and no one wants," but if "the most thoughtful and passionate of our youth" are given their heads, he foresaw an environmentalist-oriented revolution which promised "a higher reason, a more human community, and a new and liberated individual." The "new consciousness" promised "a new and enriching relationship of man to himself, to other men, to society, to nature, to land." But, warned Reich, if this new consciousness was denied, if the mechanized exploitation of nature which linked corporate profits to mass consumption was not halted, a terrible fate would befall the earth and all its inhabitants.

PREDICTIONS OF DOOM

In 1970 it was predicted that by 1980 "urban dwellers would have to wear gas masks to breathe," and that by 1985 new scientifically unleashed diseases that people lacked natural antibodies for would inflict the world with a plague of vast proportions. For some, like leftist environmentalist Barry Commoner, the coming catastrophe was an opportunity for "the radical reorganization of national economies and international commerce along lines that make ecological sense." But for the well-to-do bored with the homogeneity of modern life and the ugliness of industrial society, there was a "wish, barely disguised as a fear, that the era of economic growth may really be finished, and that a New Dark Age may be upon us." For the California mystic Theodore Roszak, living that New Dark Age promised an end to "the absurd affluence of middle-class America" and a return to a Paleolithic future of shamanistic spirituality and true community.

The stained-glass radicalism preached by Roszak and Reich, who complained about America's lack of "culture, tradition," and "social order," produced an angry response from middle America, which reacted to the attack on its position in society the way business responded to Nader. "Some people," wrote black leader Vernon Jordan, "have been too cavalier in proposing policies to preserve the physical environment for themselves while other poor people pay the costs." A popular labor union bumper sticker read: "If You're Hungry and Out of Work, Eat an Environmentalist." Like the first protest against consumption exemplified by John Kenneth Galbraith in the late 1950s, in which people driving Volvos told people driving Chevies to mind their social manners, environmentalism, despite its solid core of genuine concerns and often broad support, turned into a movement of "$20,000-a-year men telling all the $7,500-a-year men to simply stay where they are so we can all survive."

BORN ON THE FOURTH OF JULY

RON KOVIC

Ron Kovic was a young proud American who signed up for duty and was sent to Vietnam. While on duty, he was severely injured during an enemy attack and was unable to walk again. In the following excerpt from his book *Born on the Fourth of July*, Kovic describes his arrival back in the United States, where he finds himself in a veteran's hospital facing the pain of his lost youth and his destroyed body. Alternating between the first and third person, Kovic talks about his feelings of anger, confusion, and alienation.

Kovic published this book in 1976, at a time when the first major wave of literature about Vietnam began to emerge. Although the war finally ended on April 23, 1975, the memories and the horror of Vietnam dominated the lives of the many Americans who had fought there, and by the late 1970s, more and more Vietnam veterans began to write about their experiences. On the one hand, a flood of official recriminations sought to condemn the war: George Kennan, the architect of containment policy in the 1950s, called Vietnam "the most disastrous of all America's undertakings over the whole two hundred years of its history." On the other hand, the government wanted only to forget Vietnam as quickly as possible—but Kovic, and the tens of thousands of other Vietnam veterans whose minds and bodies had been shattered, could not forget so easily. Kovic turned his energies to political activism, joining the many Vietnam veterans in the 1970s who felt unappreciated and disillusioned and who felt their patriotic sacrifice to America had been simply a waste.

Excerpted from *Born on the Fourth of July*, by Ron Kovic (New York: Pocket Books, 1977). Copyright © 1976 by Ron Kovic. Reprinted with permission.

T he bus turned off a side street and onto the parkway, then into Queens where the hospital was. For the first time on the whole trip everyone was laughing and joking. He felt himself begin to wake up out of the nightmare. This whole area was home to him—the streets, the parkway, he knew them like the back of his hand. The air was fresh and cold and the bus rocked back and forth. "This bus sucks!" yelled a kid. "Can't you guys do any better than this? I want my mother, I want my mother."

The pain twisted into his back, but he laughed with the rest of them—the warriors, the wounded, entering the gates of St. Albans Naval Hospital. The guard waved them in and the bus stopped. He was the last of the men to be taken off the bus. They had to carry him off. He got the impression that he was quite an oddity in his steel frame, crammed inside it like a flattened pancake.

They put him on the neuro ward. It was sterile and quiet. I'm with the vegetables again, he thought. It took a long while to get hold of a nurse. He told her that if they didn't get the top of the frame off his back he would start screaming. They took it off him and moved him back downstairs to another ward. This was a ward for men with open wounds. They put him there because of his heel, which had been all smashed by the first bullet, the back of it blown completely out.

He was now in Ward 1-C with fifty other men who had all been recently wounded in the war—twenty-year-old blind men and amputees, men without intestines, men who limped, men who were in wheelchairs, men in pain. He noticed they all had strange smiles on their faces and he had one too, he thought. They were men who had played with death and cheated it at a very young age.

He lay back in his bed and watched everything happen all around him. He went to therapy every day and worked very hard lifting weights. He had to build up the top of his body if he was ever going to walk again. In Da Nang the doctors had told him to get used to the idea that he would have to sit in a wheelchair for the rest of his life. He had accepted it, but more and more he was dreaming and thinking about walking. He prayed every night after the visitors left. He closed his eyes and dreamed of being on his feet again.

Sometimes the American Legion group from his town came in to see him, the men and their wives and their pretty daughters. They would all surround him in his bed. It would seem to him that he was always having to cheer them up more than they were cheering him. They told him he was a hero and that all of Massapequa was proud of him. One time the commander stood up and said they were even thinking of naming a street after him. But the guy's wife was embarrassed and made her husband shut up. She told him the commander was kidding— he tended to get carried away after a couple of beers.

After he had been in the hospital a couple of weeks, a man appeared one morning and handed him a large envelope. He waited until the man had gone to open it up. Inside was a citation and a medal for Conspicuous Service to the State of New York. The citation was signed by Governor Rockefeller. He stuck the envelope and all the stuff in it under his pillow.

None of the men on the wards were civilian yet, so they had reveille at six o'clock in the morning. All the wounded who could get on their feet were made to stand in front of their beds while a roll call was taken. After roll call they all had to make their beds and do a general clean-up of the entire ward—everything from scrubbing the floors to cleaning the windows. Even the amputees had to do it. No one ever bothered him, though. He usually slept through the whole thing.

Later it would be time for medication, and afterward one of the corpsmen would put him in a wheelchair and push him to the shower room. The corpsman would leave him alone for about five minutes, then pick his body up, putting him on a wooden bench, his legs dangling, his toes barely touching the floor. He would sit in the shower like that every morning watching his legs become smaller and smaller, until after a month the muscle tone had all but disappeared. With despair and frustration he watched his once strong twenty-one-year-old body become crippled and disfigured. He was just beginning to understand the nature of his wound. He knew now it was the worst he could have received without dying or becoming a vegetable.

More and more he thought about what a priest had said to him in Da Nang: "Your fight is just beginning. Sometimes no one will want to hear what you're going through. You are going to have to learn to carry a great burden and most of your learning will be done alone. Don't feel frightened when they leave you. I'm sure you will come through it all okay.". . .

Oh God, what is happening to me? What is going on here? I want to get out of this place! All these broken men are very depressing, all these bodies so emaciated and twisted in these bed-sheets. This is a nightmare. This isn't like the poster down by the post office where the guy stood with the shiny shoes; this is a concentration camp. It is like the pictures of all the Jews that I have seen. This is as horrible as that. I want to scream. I want to yell and tell them that I want out of this. All of this, all these people, this place, these sounds, I want out of this forever. I am only twenty-one and there is still so much ahead of me, there is so much ahead of me.

I am wiped clean and pushed past the garbage cans. The stench is terrible. I try to breathe through my mouth but I can't. I'm trapped. I have to watch, I have to smell. I think the war has made me a little mad—the dead corporal from Georgia, the old man that was shot in the village with his brains hanging out. But it is the living deaths I am breathing and smelling now, the living deaths, the bodies broken in the same war that I have come from.

I am outside now in the narrow hallway. The young black woman is pushing my frame past all the other steel contraptions. I look at her face for a moment, at her eyes, as she pushes my frame up against another. I can hear the splashing of water next door in the shower room. The sun has come up in the Bronx and people are walking through the hallways. They can look into all the rooms and see the men through the curtains that never close. It is as if we are a bunch of cattle, as if we do not really count anymore.

They push me into the shower. The black woman takes a green plastic container and squirts it, making a long thin white line from my head to my legs. She is turning on the water, and after making sure it is not too hot she hoses me down.

It's like a car wash, I think, it's just like a big car wash, and I am being pushed and shoved through with the rest of them. I am being checked out by Tommy [a hospital aide] and hosed off by the woman. It is all such a neat, quick process. It is an incredible thing to run twenty men through a place like this, to clean out the bodies of twenty paralyzed men, twenty bloated twisted men. It is an incredible feat, a stupendous accomplishment, and Tommy is a master. Now the black woman is drying me off with a big white towel and shoving me back into the hallway.

Oh get me back into the room, get me back away from these people who are walking by me and making believe like all the rest that they don't know what's happening here, that they can't figure out that this whole thing is crazy. Oh God, oh God help me, help me understand this place. There goes the nurse and she's running down the hall, hitting the rubber mat that throws open the big green metal door with the little windows with the wire in them. Oh nurse please help me nurse, my stomach is beginning to hurt again like it does every time I come out of this place and my head is throbbing, pounding like a drum. I want to get out of this hall where all of you are walking past me. I want to get back into my bed where I can make believe this never happened. I want to go to sleep and forget I ever got up this morning.

Nixon and the Watergate Affair

William H. Chafe

The Watergate affair was perhaps the most important political event in 1970s America. The affair originated with a break-in at the Democratic Party headquarters at the Watergate Hotel in Washington, D.C., during the 1972 presidential election campaign. It initially appeared to be a minor incident, but when the crooks were identified as having government connections, Washington journalists, who had always strongly disliked Nixon, began to delve deeper into the event. Bob Woodward and Carl Bernstein were the two *Washington Post* reporters who spearheaded the investigation, suspecting that the Watergate break-in was only part of a complex network of illegal activity being managed by the Nixon White House. Aided by a friendly press, the Democratic Party refused to let the issue die. Although Nixon succeeded in winning the November 1972 election, events spiraled out of his control soon after, and he was forced to resign on August 9, 1974.

In the following excerpt from his book *The Unfinished Journey*, contemporary American historian William H. Chafe describes Nixon's downfall, from the Watergate break-in, through the increasing mound of evidence that piled up against him, to his exit from office in the face of impeachment. Some Nixon supporters argue that Nixon's crimes were no different from the buggings, tape recordings, and surveillance of opponents that had been going on in the White House for decades. Nixon's downfall, they suggest, was mainly due to a hostile press that systematically destroyed him. Others argue that although he committed the crime of perjury, by intentionally covering up his knowledge of the Watergate break-in, he in fact probably did not authorize or even know about the break-in beforehand: Perhaps if he had been honest about his connection rather than lying to the American people, he could have saved his presidency. And finally, there are those who suggest that Nixon's inability to come clean and extricate himself from the situation evidences a subconscious need to be punished for wrongs that he knew he committed. In this view, Nixon's seeming paralysis in acting (for example, he could have destroyed the incriminating tapes) reveals his latent guilt, which perhaps rendered him incapable of saving himself through decisive action.

O n the morning of June 17, 1972, Bob Woodward, a new reporter covering the metropolitan desk of the *Washington Post,* was awakened by his city editor and told to check on a break-in that had occurred the previous night at Democratic National Committee headquarters. He was joined by Carl Bernstein, a high school dropout and "counterculture type" who covered Virginia politics for the *Post.* The two reporters discovered that the five suspects had been arrested carrying expensive cameras and electronic equipment. Among them, the five had $2,300 in cash. All were well dressed, and all had given false names to the police. When they were arraigned, one of the suspects, James W. McCord, Jr., identified himself as a security consultant who had recently retired from government service. "Where in the government?" the judge asked. "The CIA," McCord answered. Subsequent investigation revealed that the other four suspects were all from Miami where they were reported to be heavily involved in CIA anti-Castro activities. The next day, an AP wire story revealed that James McCord was not only a retired CIA officer; he was also security coordinator for the Committee to Re-elect the President (CREEP).

Digging furiously, Bernstein and Woodward soon pieced together information that suggested a story potentially explosive in impact. One of the suspects had an address notebook containing the notation, "Howard E. Hunt, W. House." Another defendant's notebook carried sketches of McGovern headquarters at the Democratic Convention. A call to the White House confirmed that Hunt served as an associate to Charles Colson, Special Counsel to the President. Reached by telephone and asked why his name was in the address book of two men arrested at the Watergate, Hunt replied: "Good God!" Further investigation disclosed that a $25,000 check had been deposited in one of the defendant's Miami accounts with the name of Kenneth Dahlberg on it. Dahlberg, it turned out, was a fundraiser for the Nixon re-election committee. The check was part of a large sum that had been "laundered" through a Mexican bank, to obscure its sources as a political contribution. Later, a frightened secretary from CREEP told the enterprising reporters that three former White House aides now working with the reelection effort knew all about the bugging and break-in at the Watergate, including, she believed, [Attorney General] John Mitchell. The pieces were beginning to fall into place.

CONTAINING THE STORY

For the moment, the White House managed to contain the story. At an August press conference, Nixon declared that White House Counsel John Dean had "conducted a complete investigation" of the incident and found that "no one on the White House staff, no one in this administration presently employed, was involved in this very bizarre incident." A federal grand jury indicted only those conspirators already identified in the press. Nixon congratulated Dean for his good work. "You had quite a day today, didn't you?," the president said, praising Dean for "putting your fingers in the leaks that sprung here and sprung there." Although the *Washington Post* reported in early October that Watergate had been only a small part of a "massive campaign of political spying and sabotage conducted on behalf of President Nixon's re-election," the investigative efforts of Woodward and Bernstein were dismissed by many as an attempt by a vehemently anti-Nixon newspaper to cause trouble. In fact, however, Bernstein and Woodward were on target. The Watergate burglary was just the tip of the iceberg. Beneath the surface lay hidden stories of illegal fundraising, subversion of opposition political candidates, creation of a White House "plumbers" group authorized to conduct break-ins and wiretaps of political enemies, use of the Internal Revenue Service to discredit potential foes, and the mounting of counterintelligence operations against domestic dissidents. Nixon had reason to worry.

ILLEGAL FUNDRAISING

The first part of the hidden story involved massive illegal fundraising by CREEP. As early as 1970, the White House had furnished hundreds of thousands of dollars to an effort to defeat Governor George Wallace, the primary obstacle to Nixon's "Southern strategy." When the president's re-election campaign went into high gear, Nixon fundraisers, led by John Mitchell and Secretary of Commerce Maurice Stans, furiously solicited funds from the country's major corporations, asking for a minimum of $100,000 each. If campaign donations were given before April 7, 1972—the day a new campaign finance law went into effect—they did not have to be reported. More than $20 million was raised prior to the deadline, much of it "laundered" through Mexican banks and collected through implied threats that a failure to give would seriously impede a corporation's well-being. George Steinbrenner, a shipbuilding tycoon (and subsequently the owner of the New York Yankees), was told that the IRS, the Justice Department, and the Commerce Department would all be looking into his affairs if he failed to pay up. "You didn't have to draw a map for me to let me know what was going on," Steinbrenner told a friend. "It was a shakedown. A plain old-fashioned Goddamn shakedown." "Pay or die" was the short-hand message, and the scam seemed to be working to perfection.

Of the money collected, over $350,000 was squirreled away in a CREEP office safe for expenditure on "security" operations. Some of the money went to pay for a "dirty tricks" operation against Democratic opponents, orchestrated from the White House with the approval of H.R. Haldeman. Undercover operators purloined confidential documents from the files of Democratic candidates, wrote and distributed anonymous letters accusing Democrats of sexual indiscretions, and infiltrated the campaign staffs of every major candidate. In one bizarre episode, Donald Segretti authored a letter that appeared in New Hampshire's major newspaper two weeks before that state's primary, charging [Maine senator Edmund] Muskie with making offensive remarks about "Canucks"—French Canadians who lived in the state. So upset did Muskie become in response that he lost his composure, cried in front of TV cameras, and seriously damaged his reputation for self-possession and poise. Other campaign officials including G. Gordon Liddy, another former CIA agent, sought approval for spending as much as $1 million on projects such as "bugging" the Democratic opposition, seducing Democratic candidates at a yacht party where they would be offered sexual favors, and kidnapping dissident leaders. Told to come up with a less costly plan, Liddy responded with a blueprint for breaking into the Democratic National Committee headquarters, copying documents, and wiretapping phones. John Mitchell okayed the revised plan.

THE PLUMBERS

Liddy's ideas were ultimately traceable to the infamous White House Special Investigations Unit, nicknamed the "plumbers," that was created in the summer of 1971 to ferret out and destroy political enemies of the administration. A year earlier, after the Cambodia invasion had led to a series of harmful leaks to the press, Tom Houston, a White House aide, proposed a massive counterintelligence operation that would coordinate the work of the FBI, the CIA, and other intelligence agencies to combat the antiwar movement. Vetoed by FBI Director J. Edgar Hoover as excessive and illegal, the plan lay dormant for a year. But in June 1971, in the aftermath of the disastrous Laos invasion and Nixon's declining political popularity, the idea of a special investigation unit took on new life. The immediate occasion was the publication by the *New York Times* of the "Pentagon Papers," a detailed account of Johnson administration policy in Vietnam up to 1968. Profoundly offended by the role played by former Kissinger aide Daniel Ellsberg in leaking the classified documents, the White House determined to "get" Ellsberg, steal any other classified documents that he or his associates might publish, and stop the leaks coming from various government agencies. Under the ultimate supervision of John Ehrlichman, the "plumbers" included E. Howard Hunt from Charles Colson's office, Egil Krogh from Ehrlichman's staff, and others. Hunt and Colson had already embarked on a campaign to discredit the Kennedys, with Hunt both investigating Edward Kennedy's role in the Chappaquidick drowning of a young woman who had been a Robert Kennedy assistant, and composing fake cables from the State Department seeking to show that John Kennedy had ordered the assassination of South Vietnamese Premier Ngo Diem. Now the plumbers turned to Ellsberg, breaking into his psychiatrist's office to secure potentially damaging information regarding Ellsberg's sexual activities. They even planned to firebomb the Brookings Institution in Washington to obtain other classified documents. The entire operation was run out of the White House, and Nixon feared that any Watergate investigation would inevitably uncover the "plumbers" antics as well.

NIXON COVERS UP

As a result of his desire to prevent such disclosures, Nixon intervened directly after the Watergate burglary to divert attention from the crimes that he knew could bring down his administration. On June 20, and then again three days later, Nixon plotted with his chief aides to quash the Watergate inquiry, arranging for H.R. Haldeman to tell Deputy CIA Director Vernon Walters that the FBI investigation of Watergate would compromise sensitive CIA operations. Haldeman then had Walters steer Acting FBI Director L. Patrick Gray off the trail by implying that explosive national security secrets might be exposed if the FBI pursued its leads. The tactic worked, at least for the moment, although various FBI and Justice Department officials—smelling a setup—continued to leak information to Bernstein and Woodward. Politically sensitive Washingtonians sensed a cover-up, but no one fully understood how deep or pervasive the conspiracy of silence went. Still, when Majority Leader Tip O'Neill returned to Congress in January of 1973, he confided to House Speaker Carl Albert: "All my years tell me what's happening. They did so many bad things during that campaign that there is no way to keep it from coming out. . . . The time is going to come when impeachment is going to hit this Congress."

Then, suddenly, the lid blew off. On March 19, 1973, James McCord—former head of security for CREEP—presented a letter to Judge John Sirica prior to being sentenced for his participation in the burglary. The letter was a bombshell, alleging that high-ranking government officials had committed perjury during the investigation, that political pressure had been applied from "high" places to force the defendants to keep their silence, and that numerous participants in the Watergate crime had never been identified during the trial. Immediately, those with the most to lose from McCord's revelations saw the handwriting on the wall. John Dean, White House counsel, whose "investigation" Nixon had cited the previous August (there had never been one) went to the president and told him there was a "cancer" at the heart of the Nixon administration. Simultaneously, Dean started to talk to prosecutors, negotiating for immunity. Acting FBI Director L. Patrick Gray disclosed at a Senate confirmation hearing that he had "deep-sixed" documents critical to the case, allegedly on White House orders. That same day the judge in the Ellsberg case revealed the break-in at Ellsberg's psychiatrist's office. Each morning brought new headlines of scandal, and on April 30, Nixon fired Dean and accepted the resignations of Haldeman and Ehrlichman. While the president self-righteously denounced "any attempt to cover up in this case," the entire fabric of the White House conspiracy had begun to come apart.

THE TAPES ARE DISCOVERED

The ensuing months produced a bewildering array of startling new revelations, most of them witnessed firsthand by millions of Americans glued to their TV sets. In May, a Select Senate Committee chaired by North Carolina Senator Sam Ervin began televised hearings on Watergate. Although the White House attempted to invoke executive privilege to prevent senior officials from being grilled under oath, the tactic failed, and the nation watched—fascinated—as former Attorney General John Mitchell admitted meeting with the conspirators on three occasions prior to the break-in, and the "Disneyland mafia"—Haldeman, Ehrlichman, Chapin, and others—found themselves caught in embarrassing contradictions as they attempted to stonewall the Senate investigation. Ervin ("I'm just a country *law*yer") became a national hero with his feigned innocence and rapierlike wit, while Howard Baker, the ranking Republican on the committee, earned his place in history with the repeated inquiry: "What did the President know, and when did he know it." But all the revelations of other witnesses paled into insignificance when suddenly, in midsummer, White House Aide Alexander Butterfield announced that Nixon had installed a sophisticated tape system in the White House in early 1971 that recorded for posterity all the words spoken by the president or in his presence. Now, in addition to all the evidence accumulated on wiretapping, perjury, blackmail, and "dirty tricks," the country learned that there was indeed a source—a very reliable source—that could tell exactly "what the President knew, and when he knew it."

Inexorably, the drama unfolded. With every twist and turn Nixon took to evade accountability, he dug himself deeper into the quagmire. Responding to public clamor, Nixon had appointed a special prosecutor, Archibald Cox, to pursue the Watergate investigation. Both Cox and the Ervin committee subpoenaed critical tapes. Desperately seeking a way out, Nixon claimed executive privilege, arguing that conversations in the White House were as confidential as those between a patient and a doctor. Cleverly, Nixon attempted to work out a compromise with senators friendly to his cause, pledging to allow them to read transcripts of the tapes provided by the White House. But Special Prosecutor Cox refused to agree, petitioning the courts to coerce the surrender of evidence directly pertinent to a criminal investigation. In response, Nixon ordered Attorney General Elliot Richardson to fire the special prosecutor. When Richardson refused, he was dismissed. His deputy, William Ruckelshaus, also refused and he too was fired. Solicitor General Robert H. Bork finally carried out the president's order, but the public was outraged by the "Saturday night massacre" and demanded appointment of a new special prosecutor and release of the tapes.

NIXON SINKS DEEPER

Everything started to go wrong for Nixon during the fall of 1973. Just ten days before the "Saturday night massacre," Vice-President Spiro Agnew was forced to resign and to plead no contest in federal court on charges of income tax evasion and of accepting hundreds of thousands of dollars of bribes while governor of Maryland. The man who had fulminated against "permissiveness" and who had self-righteously proclaimed the administration's commitment to law and order had now been exposed as a common criminal. By December, Nixon's own personal finances had come under increasingly critical scrutiny. Congressional investigators reported that, although the president had received over $1.1 million in income during his first four years in office, he had paid less than $80,000 in taxes, largely because of a questionable deduction of almost $500,000 for donating his vice-presidential papers to the National Archives. Moreover, investigation of Nixon's personal assets showed that his houses at Key Biscayne and San Clemente had appreciated enormously in value, largely due to improvements made at public expense. As if all that were not bad enough, Judge John Sirica informed the public in late November that eighteen minutes had been erased from a critical June 20, 1972, tape subpoenaed by the Watergate prosecution. White House assistant Alexander Haig blamed the erasure on a defective recorder; and Nixon's secretary Rosemary Woods explained that she had erased the tape accidentally while transcribing it (the journalist Jimmy Breslin later described the posture she would have had to adopt to accomplish the erasure as like that of a runner "sliding into third base"). But subsequent expert testimony disclosed that the tapes had been deliberately tampered with by "manual" erasures. Yet the president proclaimed at a November 17 press conference, "I am not a crook." The country was no longer so sure.

By the spring of 1974, the entire house of cards began to topple. All during the early months of the year, reports had circulated that Special Prosecutor Leon Jaworski (Cox's replacement) had sufficient evidence to indict the president himself for criminal wrongdoing and was restrained from doing so only because he believed that a sitting president was not subject to indictment. When the grand jury completed its work on March 1, seven close Nixon aides were placed on trial, including Haldeman, Ehrlichman, Colson, and Mitchell. Central to the charges against these men was the allegation of perjury, yet as *New Republic* columnist John Osborne observed, "If Haldeman had lied, the President had lied." At issue was the payment of $75,000 in "hush" money to Watergate defendants immediately after a conversation with the president. Having heard the tape, the Watergate grand jury concluded that Haldeman had perjured himself when he swore under oath that Nixon had opposed paying the money. Significantly, Judge John Sirica announced that he would give *all* the evidence pertaining to the president's conversation to the House Judiciary Committee.

With meticulous thoroughness and consummate skill, the legislative branch of government enacted the next to last scene of the Nixon drama. Guided by politically astute Majority Leader Tip O'Neill, the House placed authority for the impeachment investigation with the Judiciary Committee headed by Peter Rodino. Careful, moderate, and above all respectable, Rodino promised to conduct the proceedings in a manner designed to avoid sensationalism and ensure that an indictment of the president would have the maximum opportunity of winning conviction in a trial before the U.S. Senate.*

Wisely, Rodino chose Republican John Doar, a former Justice Department attorney, widely respected for his prudence and restraint, as counsel for the impeachment hearing. From the very beginning, Doar concentrated on the events immediately surrounding the Watergate burglary. "From what we've got al-

---

* Under the rules governing impeachment, the House of Representatives determines whether an indictment is justified, and the Senate constitutes the jury for the trial.

ready," Doar told his associates, "I think the one tape I want to hear, if I had to hear any tape, is June 23." The House leadership understood that to be successful in its investigation of the president, it would need to forge a coalition of moderate Republicans, liberal Democrats, and Southern conservatives so that no one could charge that the proceedings were stacked ideologically against the president. To the consternation of many liberals, Doar took weeks to amass his evidence and prepare his case. In the meantime, Nixon continued to fight back, appealing to the conservative majority that had elected him and charging that the Watergate investigation represented a conspiracy of the Eastern establishment. Traveling abroad, he sought to use his role as world statesman to counter the political infighting back home and, astonishingly, succeeded in retaining the loyalty of countless millions of Americans who believed the president and were unwilling to acknowledge his complicity in the crimes alleged against him. As yet, no "smoking gun" had directly revealed the president's criminal involvement.

THE SUPREME COURT RULES

But when the Supreme Court ruled unanimously on July 24 that Nixon had to turn over the tapes of fifty-four conversations, including that of June 23, to the Judiciary Committee, the "smoking gun" finally appeared. The country was already familiar with many Nixon tapes, including the "expletives deleted" that riddled the president's conversations and his ethnic slurs against Italians, blacks, and Jews. But there had never been any hard evidence that Nixon himself had committed a crime. Now, Nixon ordered his counsel, Fred Buzhardt, to listen to the June 23 tapes and determine whether they were as devastating as Nixon remembered them to be. When the answer came back "yes," Nixon still weaseled, asking his colleagues whether there was any "air" in the Supreme Court decision—any way to avoid compliance. Finally, concluding that there was not, Nixon released the June 23 tapes—documenting beyond any doubt that just six days after the Watergate burglary, the president himself had ordered the cover-up and engaged in a criminal conspiracy to obstruct justice. Stunned and disillusioned, White House staff members who had retained their faith in Nixon suddenly understood the enormity of the crime that had been committed. No longer was escape possible. Led by Senator Barry Goldwater, a delegation of the most senior members of Congress waited on the president to insist that he resign. And on August 8, in a rambling, wavering voice that acknowledged nothing more than a "few mistakes of judgment," Nixon announced his resignation as president. At noon the next day, Vice-President Gerald Ford was sworn in as the country's new chief executive. "Our long national nightmare," he declared, "is over."

THE ENERGY CRISIS AND WORLD ORDER

HENRY KISSINGER

The energy crisis had its roots in the Yom Kippur war of October 6, 1973, when Egypt and Syria attacked Israel on the holiest day of the Jewish year. Caught by surprise, as most Israelis were observing the Day of Atonement, the Israelis suffered heavy losses both in lives and in military equipment. The Soviets had supplied their allies, the Arab states, with arms, tanks, and airplanes, so Israel, America's historical ally, turned to the White House for assistance. America responded with an enormous emergency airlift to Israel, and within two weeks the Israeli army had chased its invaders almost back to their respective capitals of Damascus in the north and Cairo to the south.

The Arab states initially responded to U.S. support of Israel by hiking up the price of oil. Then, on October 20, 1973, eleven members of the Organization of Petroleum Exporting Countries (OPEC) placed an embargo on all sales to the United States. Four days later, Secretary of State Henry Kissinger managed to negotiate a peace treaty directly with Soviet leader Leonid Brezhnev. However, even after the OPEC countries lifted the ban on sales, prices skyrocketed, causing major shortages in the United States. By December 1973, oil prices had nearly quadrupled.

Since 1971 the American economy had been caught in a cycle of runaway inflation and recession nicknamed "stagflation." The oil embargo only worsened this economic slump in the United States. By the mid-1970s Americans had accepted the fact that the days of cheap energy that had been the norm since World War II were over. In 1973, over the complaints of environmentalists, Nixon gave the go-ahead for the Alaska pipeline

Excerpted from Henry Kissinger's remarks to the annual meeting of the National Conference of State Legislators in Detroit, Michigan, August 3, 1977.

in order to decrease America's reliance on foreign sources of oil. Even so the prices of OPEC oil jumped from $1.80 per barrel in early 1971 to $20 per barrel by the late 1970s.

Henry Kissinger, born in Germany, served first as Richard M. Nixon's security advisor (1969–1975) and then as secretary of state (1973–1977) in the Nixon and Ford administrations. In the following speech made to the National Conference of State Legislators in Detroit, Michigan, on August 3, 1977, he discusses the energy crisis then affecting the United States and explores its economic and political ramifications. He traces America's increasing dependence on oil (and oil-producing countries) during the 1950s through the 1970s and outlines a national strategy aimed at overcoming this dependence, which includes developing America's own oil supplies and cutting down on oil consumption. In addition, Kissinger suggests, diplomacy must be aimed at building more reliable relations with OPEC countries and strengthening alliances among other Western oil-consuming nations.

T he energy crisis is not just a technical problem; it is not an abstract playground for specialists. It has wide-ranging implications for our daily lives and some of our deepest values. Energy is central to our own economy. It affects our jobs, prices, and prosperity. And internationally the energy crisis has global dimensions; it is one of the most fundamental challenges to international stability in a generation. It threatens the vitality of the world economy. And for the first time in our history, a small group of nations controlling a scarce resource could over time be tempted to pressure us into foreign policy decisions not dictated by our national interest.

The question is quite simply whether energy will bring about the destruction of the system of world order we have been building slowly and painfully over the last two decades, or whether it will serve as the instrument and vital proof of our common progress. The energy crisis therefore goes beyond the technical problem of establishing a better balance between supply and demand. It is the supreme test of nations' ability to live together on this shrinking planet, to prevent this increasingly scarce resource from leading to major conflict, and, above all, to understand and act upon the mutual dependence of different nations—of producer and consumer, developed and developing nations, the wealthy and debt-ridden.

I believe that in the final analysis the interests of the nations of the world are, though different, complementary. But that complementarity is not self-evident; a new commitment to international cooperation will not emerge from the crisis of the last four years automatically. It is the supreme task of statesmanship for our age to create out of the elements of our mutual dependence a new dedication to positive collaboration, and in this way to turn the energy challenge into a powerful positive force for world cooperation, order, and progress.

THE ENERGY CHALLENGE AND ITS CONSEQUENCES

What is the energy crisis?

The last three decades have been a history of our increasing dependence on imported energy. In 1950, the United States was virtually self-sufficient in oil. In 1960, our reliance on foreign oil had grown to 16 percent of our requirements. In 1973, the year of the embargo and the massive price increase, America's dependence had doubled to 35 percent. Since then our dependence has *grown*, not diminished; in the winter months of this year, oil imports for the first time in our history reached 50 percent of our oil consumption—a development which only two years ago was not expected until the 1980s.

When the United States was self-sufficient, or a net exporter of oil, not only were we invulnerable to embargoes but we also had some influence over the world price. We could go far toward ensuring that the world economy had available to it adequate supplies of oil at reasonable prices.

In the last two decades conditions have changed dramatically. We have become net importers of oil and on a growing scale. Western Europe's and Japan's energy needs increased rapidly. Developing countries around the world began their own efforts toward industrialization, and in consequence became for the first time major consumers of energy. Prices remained low. And so for two decades the world economic system was based on the expectation of cheap and plentiful petroleum, while supply, except in the Middle East, fell far behind the explosive energy demand.

The effect on the United States of this structural change in the world energy market was dramatic. As we grew increasingly dependent on outside oil, we became vulnerable to external manipulation of price and interruption of our supply.

It was against this background that OPEC began to make its influence felt. Forged into an effective mechanism for agreement on prices and production among the few nations in the world that were oil exporters, OPEC embarked on what in 1973 became a successful effort to quadruple the world price of oil. In the same year, in an added demonstration of the central role of petroleum in the world's economy, the major producers cut off their exports to certain countries during the Arab-Israeli war.

These events made explicit the energy crisis which had been building for decades. They caused an immediate economic crisis both in this country and around the world. A drop of only 10 percent of our imported oil, lasting less than half a year, cost Americans half a million jobs and over ten billion dollars of national output. The massive price increases of 1973 added at least five percentage points to the price index, contributing to our worst inflation since World War II. It set the stage for a serious recession, in this country and worldwide, from which we are only now recovering.

OIL AND THE ECONOMY

Internationally, the energy crisis reduced the annual growth rate of the industrial countries by 1.2 percent and accelerated the average rate of inflation in the industrialized world by 3 percent. It has also had a massive adverse effect on the balance of payments of all the industrial nations. Since 1973, the oil-consuming countries have paid $367 billion in oil import bills to the thirteen OPEC countries; this is the equivalent of a huge excise tax and constitutes one of the greatest and most sudden transfers of wealth in human history. Today, each 10 percent price increase adds an additional $14 billion to the OPEC balances. For the United States, the quadrupled oil price worsened our balance of payments by $36.4 billion in 1976 alone. To put it another way: President Carter has stated that this year our balance of payments deficit is running at a rate of $25 billion a year; without oil imports, we would be running a surplus of $20 billion a year. Oil imports mark a $45 billion difference, which over time could spell an economic disaster.

The enormous surplus earnings of the oil producers overhang the world economy. They are a factor of instability even if not manipulated for political motives. In another Middle East crisis the vast accumulated petrodollars could become a weapon against the world monetary and financial system.

Since the dramatic events of 1973, America's dependence on imported oil has increased by nearly 50 percent despite the efforts of three Presidents to mobilize an effective national response to the energy challenge. This growing dependence is intolerable. Even when the oil producers behave responsibly and seek to be moderate—as they have in recent years—their decisions are determined by *their* conception of their interests, priorities, and political choices, and not by ours. Our ability to conduct a fair and responsible foreign policy according to *our* values and *our* choices is constrained. Our country's freedom of action in foreign policy is to that degree circumscribed.

POLITICAL REPERCUSSIONS

If the economic and political consequences of the energy crisis are severe for the United States, the impact on other countries more dependent on imported oil is correspondingly greater. Simultaneous recession and inflation—stagflation—has created severe problems in many countries, including many of our allies in Europe. Political and social difficulties that were already at the margin of governments' ability to manage threaten in some cases to get out of control. Economic crisis was a rude shock to large numbers of ordinary people in Western Europe whose aspirations had been raised so dramatically in the years since the war.

Thus, too much of Western Europe of the Seventies has become fertile ground for social friction and political turmoil within nations, and for economic conflict between them. The energy crisis has hampered the progress of European unity. It has strengthened the hand of opponents of democracy as democratic governments and moderate leaders have come under severe attack for failing to solve their economic problems, to a degree not experienced since the Twenties and Thirties. If Communist parties come to power in Western Europe, it will mark a tragic watershed in America's relationship to its alliances, transforming the North Atlantic Alliance as well as the purposes and practices of European integration. The irony is that some of the most conservative and anti-Communist governments in the world will have contributed to this state of affairs.

Even short of this prospect, the consequences for the cohesion of the Western Alliance are grave. Nations in economic travail are inevitably tempted to resort to protectionism in a desperate effort to keep jobs and markets at home. The result can be a vicious spiral of shrinking trade and further economic deterioration for all nations. Today, even while the industrial democracies are embarked on the difficult process of recovery, protectionist pressures are high and still mounting. This is because the recovery is uneven, and unemployment remains a problem almost everywhere. . . .

In short, the energy crisis has placed at risk the entire range of our foreign policy. It mortgages the prospects of our own economy; it weakens the industrial democracies economically and potentially militarily; it undermines the world economy; and it frustrates the hope for progress of most of the new nations.

RESPONDING TO THE ENERGY CHALLENGE

. . . The United States needs, most of all, an energy strategy. First, there must be recognition of the severity of our present circumstances—by leaders, legislatures, and public. The steps that are taken must not be random responses but elements of a coherent strategy that links both domestic and foreign concerns. Such a strategy requires above all a determined national energy program for the United States. It must mobilize the solidarity of the industrial democracies. It must address the international financial implications of the crisis. It must accommodate the needs of the developing nations. And it must engage the oil-producing nations as constructive participants and partners in a thriving global economic system. . . .

An effective national energy strategy to bring about this result must include the following elements:
- conservation;
- development of new supply;
- collaboration among the consumer nations, including safeguarding the world financial system; and
- shaping of a reliable long-term relationship between the consumers and producers. . . .

President Carter's conservation aim is to reduce the annual growth of national energy demand to less than 2 percent by 1985, from the present 4.6 percent; to limit gasoline consumption to 10 percent below its present level by 1985; to reduce oil imports from a potential level of 16 million barrels per day to 6 million; to establish a Strategic Petroleum Reserve of 1 billion barrels as insurance against emergencies; to increase coal production by two thirds to more than 1 billion tons annually; to insulate 90 percent of existing homes and all new buildings; and to install solar energy in more than 2.5 million homes.

The United States is theoretically capable of reducing its energy consumption by as much as 30 percent *without* affecting the rate of growth of our GNP or our standard of living. In 1975, Americans *wasted* more fossil fuel than was *used* by two thirds of the world's population. Energy is wasted whenever energy expenditure can be reduced without higher economic or social costs. To give but one example: In the past two decades architects have more and more tended toward sealed constructions, that is to say, buildings whose windows cannot be opened—especially office constructions. But in most cities of America, temperatures for many months each year are comfortable. Thus, in sealed buildings a great deal of energy is wasted in achieving a temperature that already exists outside and that would be available for free if windows could be opened. This simple conservation measure would obviously impose no hardship and could be rapidly achieved by changing building codes. . . .

DEVELOPING NEW ENERGY SUPPLIES

The second essential element of an energy strategy is *development of new and alternative energy supplies.* Conservation alone, crucial as it is, cannot permanently reduce our dependence on OPEC oil. Even the most ambitious conservation plan could not expect to do more than reduce our dependence on imported oil to the level of 1973—when an embargo caused the most serious recession since the 1930s. . . .

Much more can and must be done to develop new sources of oil. We should provide every incentive to maximize domestic production. We should also pursue a conscious policy of diversification of foreign sources. Any new source of oil is additional insurance against an embargo and a contribution to equilibrium in the international energy dialogue.

It is clearly in the interest of the United States and all the industrial democracies to diversify technologically as well as geographically. It has been said that the United States is the Saudi Arabia of coal, so vast are our deposits. Moreover, the industrial democracies have the technical skill and resources to create fuels from shale oil, tar sands, and coal gasification and liquefaction. And much progress has been made—and more can be made—on advanced methods such as nuclear power, fusion, and solar power.

Iran and the Hostage Crisis

George Lenczowski

In November 1979, a group of militant Islamic students took over the U.S. embassy in Tehran, Iran, and captured sixty-six American hostages. Thirteen of the hostages were soon released, but the other fifty-three were held captive for 444 days. In the following selection, George Lenczowski recounts the events leading up to the crisis and the manner in which it was resolved. As Lenczowski explains, the students took the hostages in protest of U.S. support of Iran's former leader, Shah Muhammad Reza Pahlavi. At one point, President Jimmy Carter authorized a military mission to rescue the hostages by force, but the mission failed tragically, resulting in the death of eight U.S. servicemen. Eventually an agreement was reached with the Iranian government, and the hostages were released on January 20, 1981. Lenczowski teaches political science at the University of California at Berkeley and is the author of *American Presidents and the Middle East*, from which this selection was excerpted.

E ver since Nixon's presidency, Iran had enjoyed a special, almost unique, status in U.S. foreign policy. In conformity with the Nixon Doctrine, Iran had become a virtual American surrogate in the Persian Gulf area. Iran's willingness and, as was believed in Washington, ability to replace Britain as the guardian of the Gulf's security were welcome from the American point of view. Nixon's decision to give Iran a blank check for arms supplies was translated into a consistent U.S. policy, of which Iran took full advantage by becoming one of the principal recipients of American weapons and by modernizing and enlarging its military establishment. The shah of Iran, Mohammed Reza Pahlavi, was, in American eyes, virtually identified with his country. His periodic consultations with a succession of American presidents since Truman had established him as a friend and ally whose foreign policy priorities, especially his resistance to Communism and Soviet imperialism, had found admiration and approval in Washington. . . .

CARTER AND THE SHAH

Jimmy Carter's advent to the presidency in 1977, as one observer noted, was a blow to the shah. This was because of Carter's frequently emphasized two goals of foreign policy: human rights and arms reductions. Insistence on human rights meant that authoritarian or repressive practices, even those engaged in by U.S. friends, would be viewed with a jaundiced eye by the new administration; and a policy of more careful scrutiny on the quality and quantity of arms supplied to foreign recipients would mean possibly severe limitations on the shah's ambitious military modernization program. In fact, soon after Carter's advent to power Iran's ambassador in Washington, Ardeshir Zahedi, voiced in private conversations his concern that the presidential human rights slogans were likely to cause confusion and disarray in Iran. This was so, as the ambassador knew well, because of the characteristic trait of Iranian political mentality—namely, to seek or suspect foreign clandestine inspiration of any significant event in Iran. A call for respect of human rights could easily be interpreted as American disapproval of the shah's domestic policies and as encouragement to the opposition.

For a number of years opposition in Iran was muted and almost clandestine. It had taken the shah a decade, since his countercoup in 1953, to consolidate his power and silence the dissidents. After launching his White Revolution the shah became the only and supreme wielder of power. Opposition to his rule did exist, but it was virtually equated with treason and subversion and, as a political force, was disorganized and ineffective. The shah did not conceal his role as the sole source of authority but preferred to have it known as royal authoritarianism rather than a dictatorship. There was, in his mind, a difference between these two notions: a king had a legal and historical legitimacy, a dictator ruled by naked force. Moreover, objectively, a dictatorship had a proclivity toward totalitarianism, that is, penetration of the all-powerful state into every area of individual and collective life, aiming at complete control of all human activities. By contrast, his royal authoritarianism tolerated a good deal of individual or collective freedom. Such matters as religion and its practice, education of one's children, pursuit of economic gains, ability to travel abroad and have foreign contacts, freedom to emigrate, and freedom to form clubs and associations were left to individual choice with no intrusion by the state, provided they were not a manifestation of political opposition.

Politically, however, the shah was not only supreme but was an "activist" aiming at a rapid transformation of Iran, a country lagging behind the West in many areas, into a modern industrial state, high in production and consumption, militarily strong, and culturally advanced. In the earlier days of his reign the shah had benefited from the advice of some experienced counselors who had the courage to tell him which policies or decisions were useful and safe and which were not. But as the shah advanced in age, experience, and power, while his erstwhile advisers died out or faded away, he became less tolerant of open or implied criticism; instead of independent advice, he began receiving words of praise and adulation. Surrounded by "yes" men, he was the constant object of obsequiousness, genuine or faked. Those praising his moves were often engaging in the time-tested Iranian exercise of "takieh" (or "ketman"), that is, a behavior calculated to conceal one's true feelings and to pretend that there was loyalty, conformity, and devotion where none of these existed.

GROWING TENSIONS IN IRAN

So long as the economic boom, generated by huge oil revenues since 1973–74, lasted the shah could proceed successfully with his policies of modernization, development, and building a powerful military apparatus. But when a recession began in 1975–76, cracks appeared in the ostensibly stable structure. A number of negative aspects of the regime became increasingly visible. Urban construction demand had brought about disquieting demographic dislocations: the village poor flocked to the cities and crowded the peripheral shantytowns in unsanitary conditions, aggravating the conspicuous contrasts between the wealth of the upper classes and the poverty of the migrants. Corruption, always a bane in the Third World, became rampant and involved members of the royal family. Western-educated entrepreneurs, with easier access to the government and the imperial court, were amassing quick fortunes and becoming objects of envy by traditional bazaar-based merchant classes. Prosperity and development brought to Iran dangerously large numbers of foreign technicians and managers, including some 35,000 Americans whose relatively high standard of living provoked the resentment of the Iranian populace. Inflation hurt the masses. Popular alienation from the regime grew apace; individual or small group acts of violence (including some assassinations) began to multiply, to be met with severe (but apparently not very effective) acts of repression by the shah's secret police, the SAVAK. Opposition to the regime began to crystallize by 1976–77 into a coalition composed of four discernible elements: (1) the National Front liberal-democratic intelligentsia, mostly consisting of professional classes, bureaucrats, and students, all still full of nostalgia for the past idealism of the Premier Mohammad Mossadegh era of the 1950s; (2) the bazaar merchants and their numerous artisan retainers and acolytes; (3) the Leftists of various brands (Tudeh Party, Mujahedin-e-Khalq, etc.); and (4) the Shiite clerical strata, consisting of the mullas and led by the *mojtaheds* (jurisprudents), of whom the highest ranking carried the title of ayatollahs. These groups had little in common with each other; their ideologies and political objectives were often mutually incompatible. But together they formed a formidable negative coalition with one common denominator: hatred of the shah and his regime.

While President Carter was aware of some violations of human rights in Iran, he was also impressed by the progress and development achieved under the shah's rule. Broadly, his attitude toward the shah in 1977, the first year of his presidency, could be described as ambivalent. It is fairly certain that he was not well informed of the depth and scope of opposition to the shah and was not cognizant of the influence that the words or policies of an American president were bound to have on the attitudes of the Iranians and of the shah himself. . . .

THE REBELLION BEGINS

The circumstances in Iran very soon took a turn for the worse. In early January 1978 an article in the popular Teheran daily *Etelaat* (apparently planted by the Ministry of Information) attacked Iran's religious leadership, singling out Ayatollah Ruhollah Khomeini with allegations of immoral conduct and treasonous lack of patriotism. The reaction to the article was immediate. Under the aegis of religious leaders violent riots erupted in the holy city of Qum and other urban centers. Iranian security forces responded harshly. Their fire caused the death of a number of demonstrators. It is the Iranian Shiite custom to mourn their dead in forty-day intervals. These mourning processions invited further clashes between the aroused populace and the security forces, resulting in new victims and thus perpetuating the cycles of violence which in due time spread to such major cities as Tabriz and Isfahan.

In the meantime the principal target of the government's hostility, Ayatollah Khomeini, in exile in Najaf (Iraq) since the 1960s, took full advantage of his sheltered asylum to wage an unrelenting propaganda war against the shah, by preaching to the numerous Iranian pilgrims visiting Najaf and Kerbela the need for resistance to the regime, and by sending hundreds of cassettes with tapes of his inflammatory speeches to Iran. These speeches and sermons were subsequently broadcast in Iran's mosques, inciting the people to rise in revolt against the godless and corrupt monarchy and calling upon the soldiers to disobey orders and desert.

THE SHAH IS INCONSISTENT

The Iranian government's response was inconsistent. On the one hand it used its security forces in harsh reprisals. These forces confronted the rioting mobs with lethal weapons because they lacked the nonlethal riot control equipment generally available to police in the Western world. On the other the shah began making conciliatory moves toward the opposition. . . .

The shah oscillated between an urge to introduce a strict military regime and his frequently expressed (to foreign envoys) reluctance to use massive force against his own subjects. He was clearly looking for guidance from Washington while suspecting it of working for his downfall. Moreover, he suffered from an incurable disease—lymphatic cancer—which he kept to himself as a deep secret. This perhaps could, at least partly, explain his changing moods, switching from bouts of depression to unwarranted optimism. In the fall of 1978 the shah appointed a new prime minister, hitherto chief of the Imperial General Staff, General Gholam Reza Azhari, to head what was popularly referred to as "the military government." Actually, most of the ministerial portfolios were, after a brief period, entrusted to civilians and, to avoid bloodshed, the shah opposed repressive measures against the dissenters on a massive scale. Moreover, General Azhari was a rather mild-mannered man, suffering from a heart ailment, who could hardly fit the definition of a rigid military leader. Furthermore the shah, as is often the case of more timid individuals, distrusted his own military chiefs and, to protect himself against a possible conspiracy, insisted that the commanders of the army, navy, and air force report to him separately rather than act jointly. . . .

As for the president himself, he seemed never to make up his mind whether insistence on human rights in Iran or Iran's strategic value to the United States should be given priority. This question certainly transcended conceptual theorizing because the United States had a vast array of means to influence the course of events in Iran, perhaps decisively. These means included public presidential pronouncements, private advice to the shah, arms supplies policies, sales of riot-control equipment, training and upgrading Iran's military forces, or even using clandestine methods (as had been done in 1953 during the Mossadegh crisis) to effect changes in Iran. As the crisis worsened, Carter became more inclined to support the shah against his adversaries and on a few occasions sent him direct messages and once called him on the telephone. Thus in the fall of 1978 the president informed the shah "that whatever action he took, including setting up a military government, I would support him."

Later, as the year was drawing to a close, Carter still persevered in his policy of amity to the shah, but as he himself stated, this friendly attitude was almost always conditioned by advice that the shah should liberalize and reach accommodation with the dissidents. "Personally and through the State Department," he wrote, "I continued to express my support for the Shah, but at the same time we were pressing him to act forcefully on his own to resolve with his political opponents as many disputes as possible." As [the president's national security adviser Zbigniew] Brzezinski described it in his memoirs, "The Shah was never explicitly urged to be tough; U.S. assurances of support were watered down by simultaneous reminders of the need to do more about progress toward genuine democracy; coalition with the opposition was mentioned always as a desirable objective.". . .

November and December 1978 as well as January 1979 witnessed numerous—almost frantic—activities of the U.S. government to salvage what remained of the Iranian royal authority and American interests. A special task force on Iran was formed, directed by David Newsom, undersecretary of state. To supplement these efforts Brzezinski, with Carter's approval, established telephone communications with Iran's Washington ambassador, Zahedi, who spent some time in Iran in the fall of 1978. (This direct contact was highly resented by [Secretary of State Cyrus] Vance and [the U.S. ambassador to Iran, William] Sullivan.) Various emissaries were sent to Teheran to evaluate and report on the situation, which, especially during the holy month of Moharram (December), worsened appreciably. American visitors included Secretary of the Treasury Michael Blumenthal, Robert Bowie of the CIA, and Senator Robert Byrd. In late November former Under Secretary of State George Ball was invited by the president to study and report on the Iranian situation. His recommendations were more in line with Sullivan's and Vance's thinking: he favored gradual transfer of power from the shah to the opposition and urged opening of U.S. contacts with Khomeini. Although Ball's report was rejected by the White House, Vance chose Theodore L. Eliot, former ambassador to Afghanistan, to contact Khomeini in Paris. However, before Eliot could set out on his trip, his mission was canceled by the White House, and Sullivan was instructed to inform the shah that the U.S. government no longer intended to have any talks with Khomeini.

This ostensible stiffening of the American attitude was, within a few days, countermanded by a new message to be relayed to the shah that "the United States government felt it was in his best interests and in Iran's for him to leave the country.". . .

THE SHAH ESCAPES

The shah, accompanied by his family, left Iran for an extended "leave" on January 16, 1979. Formally, a regency council took over his duties. For the military there remained only three alternatives: (1) to support Shahpour Bakhtiar [premier of Iran], (2) to seize power by a coup (for itself or for the shah), or (3) to surrender to the opposition. The first alternative, as we have seen, was most unlikely; the third assumed that the opposition would emerge victorious; hence Brzezinski (and some Iranian generals) favored, until the very last minute, a military coup. [U.S. Air Force general Robert] Huyser, though not successful in ensuring the army's support for Bakhtiar, nevertheless succeeded in persuading its leading generals not to stage a coup.

Thus a sort of psychological vacuum occurred. On February 1, 1979, Khomeini returned triumphantly from Paris and on February 10–11 a mutiny of *homofars* (air force technicians) resulted in a popular uprising that put an end to the monarchy in Iran. The military leaders capitulated, and some offered their services to the revolution. Appearing as supreme leader of Iran's Islamic Republic, Khomeini promptly appointed Mehdi Bazargan, a respected and pious figure of the liberal opposition, as prime minister. In spite of an attack on and temporary occupation of the American embassy by a frenzied revolutionary mob (during which Ambassador Sullivan comported himself with cool professionalism, thus avoiding bloodshed), the U.S. government recognized Bazargan's government and continued regular diplomatic relations with Iran. In contrast to the early predictions of American experts, religious leaders in Iran not only assumed full authority but actually emerged as executives and active participants in the new government. Moreover, there was no question of introducing democracy. Khomeini as the supreme leader (*fakigh*) established a medieval-type religious totalitarian state that soon attracted the world's attention by its acts of intolerance, vengefulness, and repression, expressed in numerous imprisonments, torture, and executions. In fact the excesses of the shah's secret police paled in comparison with the cruelties of the new regime. A major exodus, by legal or illegal routes, of the Iranian secular intelligentsia and managerial class took place, while the religious leaders engaged in confiscations of private property, occupation of private homes, coercive measures toward women wearing Western dress, and haphazard distribution of available funds among the "deprived" classes. Revolutionary *komiteh*s terrorized the population, seconded by the Revolutionary Guards (*pasdaran*) and youth volunteers (*basij*). Universities and schools were "Islamicized" as well as the military academies. Production in many sectors of the economy decreased, and some rationing was introduced.

In spite of the basically anti-American and anti-Western stance of the Khomeini regime, a semblance of normalcy returned to Iranian-American relations. A special Pentagon emissary, Eric von Marbod, concluded with Bazargan's government a "memorandum of understanding" calling for termination and restructuring of major arms contracts—an important step that prevented untold complications likely to ensue if the matter had been left unattended.

The highest point in this process of normalization was reached when, at an anniversary celebration in Algiers on November 1, 1979, Brzezinski met and conversed with Premier Bazargan and two other Iranian ministers (all three laymen).

THE HOSTAGE CRISIS

The gradual resumption of normalcy in U.S.-Iranian relations, however, suffered a complication when the exiled shah was admitted to the United States in November 1979 to undergo treatment in a New York hospital. The shah had been invited to live in the United States at the time of his departure from Iran and had he accepted the offer at that time probably no crisis would have occurred. But he delayed his arrival, choosing to stay in Egypt, Morocco, and the Bahamas for periods of time, until he found himself in Mexico, where his physical condition worsened. The White House and the State Department were aware of a danger to the American embassy in Iran should the shah be admitted to the United States. But his swiftly deteriorating health and the lack of appropriate medical facilities in Mexico led two prominent Americans, David Rockefeller and Henry Kissinger, to urge the president to permit his entry for humanitarian reasons and out of respect for the American tradition of political asylum, especially to a former ally now in need. Whatever misgivings he had had, Carter concurred with their judgment and agreed to the shah's admission.

By the time the shah came to the United States the mood in Iran had changed. Iranian revolutionary leaders had developed a suspicion that the American government might be plotting to restore the shah to power. As soon as the shah arrived in New York, Iran's militants (a street rabble and some fanatical students) on November 4 assaulted the American embassy in Teheran and captured a total of sixty-six individuals. The only staff members who avoided capture were Bruce Laingen, the U.S. chargé d'affaires, and two aides, who just happened to be in the Ministry of Foreign Affairs at that time, where they remained as virtual prisoners. There is no definite evidence whether the attackers were working entirely on their own initiative or had been abetted and instructed beforehand by Khomeini and his religious aides. Their action took the Bazargan government by surprise; Acting Foreign Minister Ibrahim Yazdi assured chargé Laingen that the captives would be released within forty-eight hours. Contrary to the expectations and promises of Yazdi and Bazargan, Khomeini's son Ahmad arrived at the U.S. embassy and in the name of his father praised the captors for their deed. As soon as Khomeini's attitude became known to Bazargan, he tendered his resignation and along with him Yazdi was also relieved of his duties. Thus the slender influence that secular democratic liberals had had on Iran's political process came to an end, and the religious figures, noted for their Shia fundamentalism and hatred of the "American Satan" and Western values, emerged dominant and monopolized most of the commanding posts in the Islamic republic.

What followed was a saga of Iranian cruelty, duplicity, violation of diplomatic rules, and utter disregard of elementary human rights on the one hand and, on the other, of American indecision, confusion, vacillation between the use of diplomacy and force to rescue the hostages, and of serious humiliation suffered by the U.S. government and military establishment.

By the norms of the civilized world Iranian behavior was noted for its barbarity and cynicism. Khomeini's regime soon released the captured women and, in a move calculated to exploit American racial dilemmas, the black male employees as well. But the white male captives underwent all sorts of indignities and ordeals, with Iranian captors repeatedly pointing loaded guns at their heads, blindfolding and chaining them, keeping them bound and stretched on bare floors for hours, etc. The hostages were also threatened with a possible trial on spy charges. At the same time the Iranian regime formulated far-reaching demands: that the shah should be extradited to Iran and that his wealth abroad should be seized and returned to the revolutionary authorities. It is interesting to note in this connection that, according to available information, in anticipation of a similar move against itself the Soviet government sternly warned the Khomeini regime that any act of violence committed against the Soviet embassy or personnel in Iran would be met with a swift and strong retribution. There is no record of any Iranian attack on Soviet institutions or employees during the Khomeini era.

The American government tried to resolve the dilemma by diplomatic means, through the use of various intermediaries (because diplomatic relations were in due time broken and the Iranian embassy expelled from Washington). "We . . . asked the

Algerians, Syrians, Turks, Pakistanis, Libyans, P.L.O., and others," wrote Carter, "to intercede on behalf of the release of our hostages." In mid-November Carter issued orders to stop U.S. imports of Iranian oil and to freeze some $12 billion of Iranian funds on deposit in the United States. Further sanctions followed. The administration also made efforts to remove the shah from U.S. territory and find a place for him abroad. The matter was complicated by the refusal of President Lopez Portillo to readmit the shah to Mexico despite his earlier offer to do so when the shah was leaving for New York. Eventually, after presidential aide Hamilton Jordan made a trip to Panama, its "strongman," General Omar Torrijos, offered the shah asylum on the island of Contadora, which the deposed ruler of Iran finally reached after a transitional stay at Lackland Air Force Base in Texas.

As negotiations with the Khomeini regime about the hostages dragged on through a variety of emissaries, certain Iranian leaders appeared anxious to reach a settlement, both to relieve the economic pressure caused by American sanctions and to restore some of Iran's reputation which had become grossly tarnished in the international community. But whenever it seemed that an agreement for the release of the hostages was in sight, Khomeini would throw his support to the militants' extreme demands and the contemplated deal would be called off.

USING FORCE

Exasperated, Carter and his advisers finally decided to resort to force. A seemingly ingenious plan of rescue was prepared, involving precise synchronization of moves among various branches of U.S. military and intelligence services. A special team, code-named "Delta," under the command of Colonel Charlie Beckwith, was to fly to a desert destination not far from Teheran from a gathering point on Masira Island in Oman and, through intricate maneuvers, rescue the hostages between April 24 and 26, 1980. Unfortunately, the planning was not flawless: it did not foresee a possible loss of any of the few helicopters to be employed in the action. So, when one of them was accidentally destroyed in the course of the operation (with several men killed), the rescue mission was aborted. To Carter it was a major blow to his and American prestige and possibly contributed to his failure to be reelected to the second term. Moreover, the whole episode further accentuated the simmering feuds within the administration and led to the resignation of Secretary Vance, already frustrated by his disagreements with the president and Brzezinski.

A month before this tragic failure, the shah, fearful for his safety in Panama, had left for Egypt, his plane refueling in the Azores. He claimed that Torrijos had been planning, in response to Iranian demands (and possibly for gain), to extradite him to Iran. Although Carter in his memoirs asserted that the shah's claim was false, there is reason to believe that it was true because Torrijos had informed a French intermediary in negotiations with Iran that he would detain the shah in Panama under certain conditions. Moreover, acting on his own authority, Carter's chief of staff, Hamilton Jordan, gave instructions to stop the shah's plane in the Azores until further orders. These came somewhat later, rescinding the original instruction, and the shah left without further impediment. His hasty departure from Panama in a chartered plane had been arranged by certain private American friends. In late July the shah died in Cairo.

PROFITABLE NEGOTIATIONS

In early September an emissary from Khomeini expressed—via West Germany—interest in resolving the hostage crisis. Later that month a war broke out between Iraq and Iran, thus causing Khomeini's regime to be more amenable to serious talks about the fate of American captives. Such talks were conducted in the fall of 1980 by Deputy Secretary of State Warren Christopher and Khomeini's delegate, Taba-Tabai, with the aid of Algeria. They resulted in a tentative agreement which covered four principal areas: (1) hostages to be released, (2) Iranian assets in the U.S. to be unfrozen, (3) Iranian claims on the shah's personal assets to be resolved in U.S. courts, and (4) Iranian claims and U.S. counterclaims regarding corporate and financial problems to be subjected to decisions of the International Court of Justice at The Hague. Even though Iran's revolutionary parliament approved these points in early November, the Iranians procrastinated with formal signing and, shortly before Christmas 1980, demanded that the United States transfer to Algeria $25 billion as a guarantee against the settlement of future claims and counterclaims. Although through the summer and the fall the president had vacillated between use of force and compromise (for example by ordering the aircraft carrier *Constellation* to sail from the Philippines to the Persian Gulf and then canceling his orders), this time he rejected Iran's demand as ridiculous and unacceptable and, in anticipation of a breakdown in further talks, prepared to declare a state of emergency or to ask Congress to declare war on Iran.

Ultimately, on January 19, 1981, the agreement was signed but, with a typically mean streak, Khomeini delayed the release of the hostages until 12:30 P.M. January 20, that is, thirty minutes after Carter relinquished his office as president. Thus came to an end one of the most heartrending and humiliating chapters in America's history.

Even at the time of the crisis it seemed clear that Khomeini, while satisfying his irrational craving to hurt and humiliate America, used the hostage crisis to consolidate his Islamic revolution. Although the captors inflicted much physical and psychological suffering on the hostages, they did not kill any. In fact, depriving the American captives of their lives would not have served Khomeini's purpose; it could have aroused so much indignation among the American people as to lead to war against Iran and elimination of the Khomeini regime. Hence Carter's hesitant policy, geared above all to the safeguarding of the hostages' lives, and his reluctance to use force or the threat of it, though understandable perhaps lacked political realism.

Carter became a victim of indecision as to which principle should receive priority: a principle of restraint, which was consistently advocated by Vance and which, it could be claimed, helped extricate the hostages from captivity, or a principle of placing broadly conceived national interest and honor above all other considerations, as promoted by Brzezinski. There is no doubt that, to Khomeini and other radical militants around the world, the hostage crisis revealed an element of vulnerability in the United States and other democracies, demonstrating that terrorist methods could be used successfully to achieve their objectives.

Reagan, Gorbachev, and the End of the Cold War: 1980–1992

CHAPTER 6

REAGAN'S FOREIGN POLICY STYLE

MICHAEL SCHALLER

Ronald Reagan, fortieth president of the United States, held office from 1981 to 1989 and is considered an icon of 1980s America. He entered politics after a successful career as a movie star and as governor of California from 1966 until 1974. His relaxed and unpretentious manner, his skill at talking in layman's terms, and his assertive rhetoric made him an appealing change for the American electorate after the unfocused political vision of the former president, Democrat Jimmy Carter.

In the following excerpt, Reagan biographer Michael Schaller discusses Reagan's foreign policy. Schaller is sometimes critical of Reagan, suggesting that he lacked a strong foreign policy vision and relied excessively on his quarreling advisers. According to Schaller, the main feature of Reagan's foreign policy was a costly arms buildup, which included the controversial Strategic Defense Initiative (SDI), known as Star Wars in the popular media. SDI, which Reagan announced in a televised address on March 23, 1983, was a proposed system of satellite-based missiles and lasers designed to shield the United States from incoming nuclear missiles.

Schaller argues that the disproportionate expenditure on arms negatively impacted the United States, as funds were cut from education and welfare measures. Many Americans opposed Reagan's costly arms program, and especially the SDI initiative, as evidenced by the enormous June 1982 demonstration in New York City protesting nuclear arms.

Although the Star Wars shield incurred much criticism, Schaller suggests that the arms buildup did prove to be a highly

Excerpted from *Reckoning with Reagan: America and Its President in the 1980s*, by Michael Schaller (New York: Oxford University Press, 1992). Copyright © 1992 by Oxford University Press, Inc. Reprinted with permission.

effective way of financially exhausting the USSR, which lacked the resources to compete with the United States. In this way, Reagan was perhaps responsible for hastening the demise of the Soviet Union. Reagan's term ended in 1989 on an extremely positive note as he negotiated dramatic arms reductions programs with Russian premier Mikhail Gorbachev. Although Reagan began the 1980s as a staunch cold warrior, he ended the decade as a willing negotiator for peace with the Soviet Union.

A s with the president's domestic program, a yawning gap existed between the rhetoric and reality of foreign policy. Ronald Reagan lived in a world of myths and symbols, rather than facts and programs. In spite of his reputation as an ideological activist, the president gave little specific direction to his foreign policy advisers. Until 1983, it is uncertain whether Reagan even thought in terms of a coherent strategy. He and his advisers were determined to stress domestic issues during the first two years of office. Foreign policy consisted largely of assertive rhetoric, the arms buildup, and covert paramilitary operations. Reagan hoped these actions would wring concessions from Moscow and reduce Soviet influence.

The president often began National Security Council meetings by reading letters or press clippings sent to him by citizens. Each week the White House Communications Office (called by some irreverent staff members the "Schlock Capital of the World" because of the many needlepoint inspirational sayings and similar items sent by the president's admirers) selected about thirty letters for Reagan to read. On Friday afternoons he answered many of these in longhand notes. He devoted more time to this than to scheduled meetings with many of his senior Cabinet members.

When the president was under the influence of these letters, Chief of Staff Donald Regan later remarked, the "goddamnest things would come out of him. We had to watch what he read." But after he read a few letters or told an anecdote, the president usually fell silent and seldom asked questions. After a few minutes, he soon exhibited what aides called a "glassy look."

ALEXANDER HAIG

In 1981 Reagan named former Henry Kissinger aide and Nixon chief of staff Gen. Alexander Haig as Secretary of State. The president promised him full authority to act as "Vicar of For-eign Policy," in Haig's phrase and the new Secretary of State lost no time in trying to assert his leadership. On inauguration day he handed Edwin Meese a memorandum on his priorities and awaited the president's reply. When none came, he asked Meese what had happened. Meese told him it "was lost," which should have, but did not, shatter Haig's illusions.

During the first months of the new administration, Haig urged Reagan to confront the guerrillas in El Salvador and Fi-del Castro's Cuba. "Give me the word and I'll make that island a fucking parking lot," Michael Deaver recorded him as shout-ing. According to Deaver, Haig's fury "scared the shit" out of Reagan and prompted the White House staff to undermine the Secretary of State at every turn.

Haig lasted 18 unhappy months in the State Department be-fore Reagan replaced him in June 1982. Afterward, Haig de-scribed the administration's policy-making apparatus as a "ghost ship." You heard "the creak of the rigging and the groan of the timbers and sometimes even glimpsed the crew on deck . . . but which of the crew had the helm . . . was impossible to know for sure."

Throughout the first term, the White House triumvirate of James Baker, Michael Deaver, and Edwin Meese influenced for-eign policy by controlling access to Reagan. For example, Haig seldom got into the Oval Office, never alone. The White House guard knew that failure to monitor Reagan's visitors sometimes led to radical changes in policy. For example, in 1983 Joseph Coors, a friend of the president's, escorted nuclear physicist Ed-ward Teller past the presidential doorkeeper. Teller beguiled the president with exaggerated stories of an anti-missile defense. Shortly afterward, "Star Wars" emerged as a national priority.

A FOLLOWER, NOT A LEADER

Except on a few points, Reagan preferred to follow the lead of his advisers on foreign policy matters. This presented a prob-lem since many disagreed among themselves. In the absence of any direction besides anti-communism, Secretary of State Haig (replaced by George Shultz in 1982), Secretary of Defense Cas-par Weinberger, CIA director William Casey, and six successive directors of the National Security Council (Richard Allen, William Clark, Robert McFarlane, John Poindexter, Frank Car-lucci, and Colin Powell) often followed their own instincts. For example, Secretary of State Shultz supported negotiations with the Soviets over arms control and a punitive military approach toward minor enemies, such as the Sandinistas in Nicaragua. Secretary of Defense Caspar Weinberger distrusted the Soviets completely and favored an arms buildup over any agreement to limit armaments.

Yet Weinberger proved quite reluctant to use military force in the Third World, test it undermine public support for rearmament. At one cabinet meeting an exasperated Shultz snapped, "If you are not willing to use force, maybe we should cut your budget." Reagan tried to settle disputes among his contentious advisers by asking them to compromise, a solution NSC head Robert McFarlane described as "intrinsically unworkable.". . .

MORE BANG FOR MORE BUCKS: THE NEW ARMS RACE

More than anything, the staggering arms buildup begun in 1981 emerged as the centerpiece of Reagan's foreign policy. Defense spending rose steadily through 1985, peaking at just over $300 billion per year. At full throttle, the Pentagon spent over $30 per hour, every day on procuring weapons, maintaining forces, and exploring new technologies. The administration, many suspected, believed a stepped-up arms race would beggar the Soviet Union. To a degree, this may have proved true, though at a great cost to the United States as well.

During this period, the United States, in effect, substituted an arms budget and covert operations for foreign policy. The administration invested heavily in weapons designed during the Ford-Carter years, many of which were envisioned for fighting a nuclear war with the Soviet Union. These included enhanced radiation neutron bombs and artillery shells designed to irradiate Soviet tanks and troops in central Europe; 100 MX intercontinental missiles capable of carrying ten nuclear warheads with pinpoint accuracy into Soviet territory; the B-1 intercontinental bomber (cancelled by Carter but revived by Reagan) to replace the fleet of aging B-52s; the B-2 or "stealth" bomber and "stealth" fighter, secret radar-avoiding planes able to penetrate deep inside the Soviet Union; powerful and highly accurate D-5 missiles for mounting on Trident submarines; cruise missiles and Pershing II missiles which, when launched from Europe could hit targets inside Russia in a few minutes; and a 600-ship navy.

MOUNTING ANXIETY OVER ARMS

These immensely powerful and expensive weapons sparked a great deal of controversy. Critics of the MX missile complained that its power and accuracy meant that in a crisis the Soviets would be tempted to strike first in order to destroy the missiles in their vulnerable silos before they could be launched. (After Utah's two Republican senators, Jake Garn and Orin Hatch, objected to basing the MX in multiple shelters in their state as Carter had proposed, Reagan opted to put the new missile into existing but "hardened" Minuteman silos. Experts doubted these could withstand a nuclear attack.) American commanders, knowing this, might feel impelled to fire the missiles first, lest the Soviets score an early knockout. Thus, instead of enhancing deterrence, the MX might create a hairtrigger situation in which both sides struck first out of fear.

Until 1986, the Democratic-controlled House and Republican Senate approved most of Reagan's arms requests. Like the public, many Democratic representatives favored a more assertive foreign policy and appreciated the president's tough rhetoric. Also, the results of two decades of effort to negotiate arms limitations with the Soviets seemed to have borne little fruit. The Democratic Party suffered an intense identity crisis, persisting since the Iran stalemate, which diffused organized opposition to the administration's foreign and military policies. . . .

The administration adopted a contradictory policy toward arms limitations treaties. Reagan denigrated as "fatally flawed" Carter's still unratified SALT [Strategic Arms Limitation Treaty] II treaty, charging that it locked in a Soviet advantage and left the United States vulnerable. The president deplored the treaty's limits and promised to develop more nuclear weapons to close the "window of vulnerability." But the joint Chiefs of Staff disagreed with Reagan. They believed that SALT II, despite imperfections, restrained the Soviets from deploying even more missiles. Although Reagan refused to concede this point, in practice he adhered to most of the provisions of the SALT II treaty. In 1982 Reagan agreed to resume arms control talks with Moscow. But negotiations to reduce long-range missiles (Strategic Arms Reduction Talks, or START) and medium-range weapons (Intermediate Nuclear Forces, or INF) quickly foundered over political, technical, and military objections raised by both sides. In December 1983, when the United States began deployment of cruise and Pershing II missiles in Western Europe, Soviet negotiators walked out.

The Soviet Union claimed that its own intermediate range SS-20 missiles targeted on Europe merely matched British and French missiles as well as weapons aboard American planes and submarines around Europe. Washington disputed this assertion. Influenced by Defense Secretary Weinberger and his hardline deputy, Richard Perle, Reagan proposed a "Zero Option," involving the removal of all Soviet SS-20 missiles in return for no future U.S. deployment of cruise and Pershing missiles in Europe. As Weinberger and Perle hoped, this scuttled negotiations when the Soviets protested that the American stance locked in a U.S. advantage.

The domestic debate grew quite bizarre when another Weinberger aide, T.K. Jones, tried to calm popular alarm with assurances that most Americans would survive, or even prosper, after a nuclear war. Jones explained that in case of attack citizens need only "dig a hole, cover it with a couple of doors, and then throw three feet of dirt on top. If there are enough shovels around," Jones predicted, "everybody's going to make it." He forecast rapid economic recovery. To some, this glib assertion made it seem that the administration was preparing to fight a nuclear war in the belief it would be survivable.

STAR WARS

Reagan held seemingly contradictory views about nuclear war. Perhaps because of his early religious upbringing, he often referred to nuclear conflict as the manifestation of Armageddon, a biblical prophesy of the destruction of the world. Since he maintained that the Bible foretold all events, this presumably meant he expected an unavoidable war. Still, the prospect of such a holocaust horrified him.

During a tour in 1979 of the Strategic Air Command center at Cheyenne Mountain in Colorado, he was shocked when told that if the Soviets fired even one missile, the United States could do nothing but track it and fire back. His friend Martin Anderson quoted Reagan as saying "we have spent all that money and have all that equipment, and there is nothing we can do to prevent a nuclear missile from hitting us." Reagan especially disliked the chilling acronym—MAD, or Mutual Assured Destruction—that described American strategy.

The president's idea of a solution to the nuclear threat

stemmed partly, like many of his notions, from the movies. In the otherwise forgettable 1940 adventure film *Murder in the Air,* secret agent Brass Bancroft (Ronald Reagan) foiled the effort of foreign agents to steal a secret "inertia projector," a device that could stop enemy aircraft from flying. As one of the characters remarks, it would "make America invincible in war and therefore the greatest force for peace ever invented." Reagan often recalled the early 1950s film *The Day the Earth Stood Still* in which an alien from another planet stops all machines on Earth as a warning to mankind to seek peace.

During the late-1970s physicist Dr. Edward Teller and retired Air Force Lt. General Daniel Graham, who headed a group called High Frontier, impressed Reagan with talk of an anti-missile shield. During a 1983 meeting in the Oval Office, Teller told Reagan about progress in building an X-ray laser powered by a nuclear bomb. In theory, the device could produce energy beams capable of shooting down Soviet missiles after their launch and before they deployed their multiple warheads. Mounted on orbiting platforms, they could provide a space shield, or "astrodome," over America. As Teller expected, the president liked the idea of a high technology "fix" and neglected to probe for details.

In March 1983, when Reagan unveiled his updated secret weapon, his words paraphrased those spoken in his 1940 film. The president revealed a startling vision of a peaceful future in which a "Strategic Defense Initiative" (SDI) would render nuclear weapons "impotent and obsolete." Reagan proposed a vast research and development program to develop an anti-missile system. Most critics, and many supporters, dubbed the concept "Star Wars."

Only a handful of White House insiders knew in advance of Reagan's initiative. The Joint Chiefs of Staff and the secretaries of state and defense were skeptics, while National Security Adviser Robert McFarlane favored SDI as a bargaining chip with the Soviets rather than as an actual system. However, the White House public relations staff had been consulted more closely. Michael Deaver arranged for testing the idea on focus groups and found solid support for a "space shield." Deaver admitted he and those queried had no idea how such a shield would work but that they liked "the concept."

Many people inside and outside the administration worried that SDI violated the ABM treaty, which barred the United States and Soviet Union from testing or deploying any new anti-missile systems. A majority of scientists doubted that Star Wars, which depended on many types of untested technology, would ever work. Even a shield 90% effective would allow through enough enemy warheads to obliterate this country. Some critics judged SDI little more than a fig leaf to mask substantial assistance for American companies engaged in high technology competition against Japan. For example, the Rockwell Corporation issued a promotional brochure for investors describing SDI as a vast new "Frontier for Growth, Leadership and Freedom." Other critics of the program speculated that SDI proponents did not really expect to shoot down missiles, but wanted to provoke Moscow into a bankrupting high technology contest.

The space shield described by the president and advertised on television by groups such as High Frontier never stood a chance of being built. The huge costs and daunting technical problems compelled weapons researchers to concentrate on developing systems to protect American *nuclear missile silos*, not cities or civilians, against a Soviet nuclear strike. They reasoned that SDI might knock out enough incoming warheads to permit sufficient American missiles to survive and launch a punishing retaliatory blow. This likelihood, presumably, would deter the Soviets from attacking. In effect, SDI would do little more than enhance, at great cost, the MAD strategy.

From Moscow's perspective, SDI appeared as one more threat. For example, the United States might launch a nuclear first strike that would destroy most Soviet missiles in their silos. An SDI antimissile system might be good enough to shoot down a small Soviet retaliatory barrage. American leaders, confident of escaping destruction, might be tempted to initiate nuclear war under these conditions.

Between 1983 and 1989, the United States spent almost $17 billion on SDI research, but achieved few results. The much-touted X-ray laser failed to work and the estimated cost of even a limited space shield literally skyrocketed. The disappointing record of the space shuttle left the United States with little ability to even carry components of SDI into space. A decade after the president unveiled the scheme, it remained a distant prospect.

THE IRAN-CONTRA AFFAIR

REPORT OF THE CONGRESSIONAL COMMITTEES

In 1986, several high-ranking Reagan administration officials were implicated in a scandal that would become known as the Iran-Contra affair. The administration had engaged in two illegal covert operations: supporting the rightist Contra rebels in their war against the left-wing regime in Nicaragua, and selling arms to Iran in an attempt to win the release of American hostages in Lebanon. These illegal operations were linked by the fact that funds from the sale of arms to Iran were funneled to the Contra rebels.

The following selection is excerpted from the official *Report of the Congressional Committees Investigating the Iran-Contra Affair*. The report concludes that although President Reagan and his staff insisted that the president did not know of the diversion of funds to the Contras, the chief executive bears the ultimate responsibility for the crimes and the attempts to cover them up.

T he full story of the Iran-Contra Affair is complicated, and, for this Nation, profoundly sad. In the narrative portion of this Report, the Committees present a comprehensive account of the facts, based on 10 months of investigation, including 11 weeks of hearings. . . .

SUMMARY OF THE FACTS

The Iran-Contra Affair had its origin in two unrelated revolutions in Iran and Nicaragua.

In Nicaragua, the long-time President, General Anastasio So-

Excerpted from *The Report of the Congressional Committees Investigating the Iran-Contra Affair: With Supplementary, Minority, and Additional Views*, by the U.S. Congress House and Senate Select Committee to Investigate Covert Arms Transactions with Iran, 1987.

moza Debayle, was overthrown in 1979 and replaced by a Government controlled by Sandinista leftists.

In Iran, the pro-Western Government of the Shah Mohammed Reza Pahlavi was overthrown in 1979 by Islamic fundamentalists led by the Ayatollah Khomeini. The Khomeini Government, stridently anti-American, became a supporter of terrorism against American citizens.

NICARAGUA

United States policy following the revolution in Nicaragua was to encourage the Sandinista Government to keep its pledges of pluralism and democracy. However, the Sandinista regime became increasingly anti-American and autocratic; began to aid a leftist insurgency in El Salvador; and turned toward Cuba and the Soviet Union for political, military, and economic assistance. By December 1981, the United States had begun supporting the Nicaraguan Contras, armed opponents of the Sandinista regime.

The Central Intelligence Agency (CIA) was the U.S. Government agency that assisted the Contras. In accordance with Presidential decisions, known as Findings, and with funds appropriated by Congress, the CIA armed, clothed, fed, and supervised the Contras. Despite this assistance, the Contras failed to win widespread popular support or military victories within Nicaragua.

Although the President continued to favor support of the Contras, opinion polls indicated that a majority of the public was not supportive. Opponents of the Administration's policy feared that U.S. involvement with the Contras would embroil the United States in another Vietnam. Supporters of the policy feared that, without U.S. support for the Contras, the Soviets would gain a dangerous toehold in Central America.

Congress prohibited Contra aid for the purpose of overthrowing the Sandinista Government in fiscal year 1983, and limited all aid to the Contras in fiscal year 1984 to $24 million. Following disclosure in March and April 1984 that the CIA had a role in connection with the mining of the Nicaraguan harbors without adequate notification to Congress, public criticism mounted and the Administration's Contra policy lost much of its support within Congress. After further vigorous debate, Congress exercised its Constitutional power over appropriations and cut off all funds for the Contras' military and paramilitary operations. The statutory provision cutting off funds, known as the Boland Amendment, was part of a fiscal year 1985 omnibus appropriations bill, and was signed into law by the President on October 12, 1984.

Still, the President felt strongly about the Contras, and he ordered his staff, in the words of his National Security Adviser, to find a way to keep the Contras "body and soul together." Thus began the story of how the staff of a White House advisory body, the NSC, became an operational entity that secretly ran the Contra assistance effort, and later the Iran initiative. The action officer placed in charge of both operations was Lt. Col. Oliver L. North.

A COVERT OPERATION

Denied funding by Congress, the President turned to third countries and private sources. Between June 1984 and the beginning of 1986, the President, his National Security Adviser, and the NSC staff secretly raised $34 million for the Contras from other countries. An additional $2.7 million was provided for the Contras during 1985 and 1986 from private contributors, who were addressed by North and occasionally granted photo opportunities with the President. In the middle of this period, Assistant Secretary of State A. Langhorne Motley—from whom these contributions were concealed—gave his assurance to Congress that the Administration was not "soliciting and/or encouraging third countries" to give funds to the Contras because, as he conceded, the Boland Amendment prohibited such solicitation.

The first contributions were sent by the donors to bank accounts controlled and used by the Contras. However, in July 1985, North took control of the funds and—with the support of two National Security Advisers (Robert McFarlane and John Poindexter) and, according to North, Director Casey—used those funds to run the covert operation to support the Contras.

At the suggestion of Director Casey, North recruited Richard V. Secord, a retired Air Force Major General with experience in special operations. Secord set up Swiss bank accounts, and North steered future donations into these accounts. Using these funds, and funds later generated by the Iran arms sales, Secord and his associate, Albert Hakim, created what they called "the Enterprise," a private organization designed to engage in covert activities on behalf of the United States.

The Enterprise, functioning largely at North's direction, had its own airplanes, pilots, airfield, operatives, ship, secure communications devices, and secret Swiss bank accounts. For 16 months, it served as the secret arm of the NSC staff, carrying out with private and non-appropriated money, and without the accountability or restrictions imposed by law on the CIA, a covert Contra aid program that Congress thought it had prohibited.

Although the CIA and other agencies involved in intelligence activities knew that the Boland Amendment barred their involvement in covert support for the Contras, North's Contra support operation received logistical and tactical support from various personnel in the CIA and other agencies. Certain CIA personnel in Central America gave their assistance. The U.S. Ambassador in Costa Rica, Lewis Tambs, provided his active assistance. North also enlisted the aid of Defense Department personnel in Central America, and obtained secure communications equipment from the National Security Agency. The Assistant Secretary of State with responsibility for the region, Elliott Abrams, professed ignorance of this support. He later stated that he had been "careful not to ask North lots of questions."

By Executive Order and National Security Decision Directive issued by President Reagan, all covert operations must be approved by the President personally and in writing. By statute, Congress must be notified about each covert action. The funds used for such actions, like all government funds, must be strictly accounted for.

The covert action directed by North, however, was not approved by the President in writing. Congress was not notified about it. And the funds to support it were never accounted for. In short, the operation functioned without any of the accountability required of Government activities. It was an evasion of the Constitution's most basic check on Executive action—the power of the Congress to grant or deny funding for Government programs.

DENIAL OF OPERATIONS

Moreover, the covert action to support the Contras was concealed from Congress and the public. When the press reported in the summer of 1985 that the NSC staff was engaged in raising money and furnishing military support to the Contras, the President assured the public that the law was being followed. His National Security Adviser, Robert C. McFarlane, assured Committees of Congress, both in person and in writing, that the NSC staff was obeying both the spirit and the letter of the law, and was neither soliciting money nor coordinating military support for the Contras.

A year later, McFarlane's successor, Vice Admiral John M. Poindexter, repeated these assurances to Congressional Committees. Then, with Poindexter's blessing, North told the House Intelligence Committee he was involved neither in fundraising for, nor in providing military advice to, the Contras.

When one of Secord's planes was shot down over Nicaragua on October 5, 1986, the President and several administration spokesmen assured the public that the U.S. Government had no connection with the flight or the captured American crew member, Eugene Hasenfus. Several senior Government officials, including Elliott Abrams, gave similar assurances to Congress.

Two months later, McFarlane told Congressional Committees that he had no knowledge of contributions made by a foreign country, Country 2, to the Contras, when in fact McFarlane and the President had discussed and welcomed $32 million in contributions from that country. In addition, Abrams initially concealed from Congress—in testimony given to several Committees—that he had successfully solicited a contribution of $10 million from Brunei.

North conceded at the Committees' public hearings that he had participated in making statements to Congress that were "false," "misleading," "evasive and wrong."

During the period when the Administration was denying to Congress that it was involved in supporting the Contras' war effort, it was engaged in a campaign to alter public opinion and change the vote in Congress on Contra aid. Public funds were used to conduct public relations activities; and certain NSC staff members, using the prestige of the White House and the promise of meetings with the President, helped raise private donations both for media campaigns and for weapons to be used by the Contras.

S/LPD

Pursuant to a Presidential directive in 1983 the Administration adopted a "public diplomacy" program to promote the President's Central American policy. The program was conducted by an office in the State Department known as the Office for Public Diplomacy for Latin America and the Caribbean, (S/LPD). . . .

S/LPD produced and widely disseminated a variety of pro-Contra publications and arranged speeches and press confer-

ences. It also disseminated what one official termed "white propaganda": pro-Contra newspaper articles by paid consultants
who did not disclose their connection to the Administration.
Moreover, under a series of sole source contracts in 1985 and
1986, S/LPD paid more than $400,000 for pro-Contra public re-
lations work to International Business Communications (IBC),
a company owned by Richard Miller, whose organization was
described by one White House representative as a "White
House outside the White House.". . .

Private funds were also used. North and Miller helped Carl
R. "Spitz" Channell raise $10 million, most of which went to
Channell's tax-exempt organization, the National Endowment
for the Preservation of Liberty ("NEPL"). They arranged numerous "briefings" at the White House complex on Central
America by Administration officials for groups of potential contributors. Following these briefings, Channell reconvened the
groups at the Hay-Adams Hotel, and made a pitch for tax-
deductible contributions to NEPL's Central America "public education" program or, in some individual cases, for weapons.
Channell's major contributors were given private briefings by
North, and were afforded private visits and photo sessions with
the President. On one occasion, President Reagan participated
in a briefing. . . .

IRAN

The NSC staff was already engaged in covert operations
through Secord when, in the summer of 1985, the Government
of Israel proposed that missiles be sold to Iran in return for the
release of seven American hostages held in Lebanon and the
prospect of improved relations with Iran. The Secretaries of
State and Defense repeatedly opposed such sales to a government designated by the United States as a supporter of international terrorism. They called it a straight arms-for-hostages
deal that was contrary to U.S. public policy. They also argued
that these sales would violate the Arms Export Control Act, as
well as the U.S. arms embargo against Iran. The embargo had
been imposed after the taking of hostages at the U.S. Embassy
in Tehran on November 4, 1979, and was continued because of
the Iran-Iraq war.

Nevertheless, in the summer of 1985 the President authorized
Israel to proceed with the sales. The NSC staff conducting the
Contra covert action also took operational control of imple-

menting the President's decision on arms sales to Iran. The President did not sign a Finding for this covert operation, nor did he notify the Congress.

THE HAWK TRANSACTIONS

Israel shipped 504 TOW anti-tank missiles to Iran in August and September 1985. Although the Iranians had promised to release most of the American hostages in return, only one, Reverend Benjamin Weir, was freed. The President persisted. In November, he authorized Israel to ship 80 HAWK antiaircraft missiles in return for all the hostages, with a promise of prompt replenishment by the United States, and 40 more HAWKs to be sent directly by the United States to Iran. Eighteen HAWK missiles were actually shipped from Israel in November 1985, but no hostages were released.

In early December 1985, the President signed a retroactive Finding purporting to authorize the November HAWK transaction. That Finding contained no reference to improved relations with Iran. It was a straight arms-for-hostages Finding. National Security Adviser Poindexter destroyed this Finding a year later because, he testified, its disclosure would have been politically embarrassing to the President.

The November HAWK transaction had additional significance. The Enterprise received a $1 million advance from the Israelis. North and Secord testified this was for transportation expenses in connection with the 120 HAWK missiles. Since only 18 missiles were shipped, the Enterprise was left with more than $800,000 in spare cash. North directed the Enterprise to retain the money and spend it for the Contras. The "diversion" had begun.

North realized that the sale of missiles to Iran could be used to support the Contras. He told Israeli Defense Ministry officials on December 6, 1985, one day after the President signed the Finding, that he planned to generate profits on future arms sales for activities in Nicaragua.

On December 7, 1985, the President and his top advisers met again to discuss the arms sales. Secretaries Shultz and Weinberger objected vigorously once more, and Weinberger argued that the sales would be illegal. After a meeting in London with an Iranian interlocutor and the Israelis, McFarlane recommended that the sales be halted. Admiral John Poindexter (the new National Security Adviser), and Director Casey were of the opposite opinion.

AN ARMS/HOSTAGE EXCHANGE

The President decided to go forward with the arms sales to get the hostages back. He signed a Finding on January 6, 1986, authorizing more shipments of missiles for the hostages. When the CIA's General Counsel pointed out that authorizing Israel to sell its U.S.-manufactured weapons to Iran might violate the Arms Export Control Act, the President, on the legal advice of the Attorney General, decided to authorize direct shipments of the missiles to Iran by the United States and signed a new Finding on January 17, 1986. To carry out the sales, the NSC staff turned once again to the Enterprise.

Although North had become skeptical that the sales would lead to the release of all the hostages or a new relationship with Iran, he believed that the prospect of generating funds for the Contras was "an attractive incentive" for continuing the arms sales. No matter how many promises the Iranians failed to keep throughout this secret initiative, the arms sales continued to generate funds for the Enterprise, and North and his superior, Poindexter, were consistent advocates for their continuation. What North and Poindexter asserted in their testimony that they did not know, however, was that most of these arms sales profits would remain with the Enterprise and never reach the Contras.

In February 1986, the United States, acting through the Enterprise, sold 1,000 TOWs to the Iranians. The U.S. also provided the Iranians with military intelligence about Iraq. All of the remaining American hostages were supposed to be released upon Iran's receipt of the first 500 TOWs. None was. But the transaction was productive in one respect. The difference between what the Enterprise paid the United States for the missiles and what it received from Iran was more than $6 million. North directed part of this profit for the Contras and for other covert operations. Poindexter testified that he authorized this "diversion."

The diversion, for the Contras and other covert activities, was not an isolated act by the NSC staff. Poindexter saw it as "implementing" the President's secret policy that had been in effect since 1984 of using non-appropriated funds following passage of the Boland Amendment. . . .

In May 1986, the President again tried to sell weapons to get the hostages back. This time, the President agreed to ship parts for HAWK missiles but only on condition that all the American hostages in Lebanon be released first. A mission headed by

Robert McFarlane, the former National Security Adviser, traveled to Tehran with the first installment of the HAWK parts. When the mission arrived, McFarlane learned that the Iranians claimed they had never promised to do anything more than try to obtain the hostages' release. The trip ended amid misunderstanding and failure, although the first installment of HAWK parts was delivered.

The Enterprise was paid, however, for all of the HAWK parts, and realized more than an $8 million profit, part of which was applied, at North's direction, to the Contras. Another portion of the profit was used by North for other covert operations, including the operation of a ship for a secret mission. The idea of an off-the-shelf, stand-alone covert capacity had become operational.

On July 26, 1986, another American hostage, Father Lawrence Jenco, was released. Despite all the arms sales, he was only the second hostage freed, and the first since September 1985. Even though McFarlane had vowed at the Tehran meeting not to deliver the remainder of the HAWK parts until all the hostages were released, the Administration capitulated again. The balance of the HAWK parts was shipped when Father Jenco was released.

ALBERT HAKIM

In September and October 1986, the NSC staff began negotiating with a new group of Iranians, the "Second Channel," that Albert Hakim had opened, in part, through promises of bribes. Although these Iranians allegedly had better contacts with Iranian officials, they, in fact, represented the same principals as did the First Channel and had the same arrangement in mind: missiles for hostages. Once again, the Administration insisted on release of all the hostages but settled for less.

In October, after a meeting in London, North left Hakim to negotiate with the Iranians. Hakim made no secret of his desire to make large profits for himself and General Secord in the $15 billion-a-year Iranian market if relations with the United States could be restored. Thus, he had every incentive to make an agreement, whatever concessions might be required.

As an unofficial "ambassador" selected by North and Secord, Hakim produced a remarkable nine-point plan, subsequently approved by North and Poindexter, under which the United States would receive "one and one half" hostages (later reduced to one). Under the plan, the United States agreed not only to sell the Iranians 500 more TOWs, but Secord and Hakim promised to develop a plan to induce the Kuwaiti Government to release the Da'wa prisoners. . . . The plan to obtain the release of the Da'wa prisoners did not succeed, but the TOW missiles were sold for use by the Iranian Revolutionary Guard. Following the transfer of these TOWs, a third hostage, David Jacobsen, was released on November 2, 1986, and more profit was generated for the Enterprise.

Poindexter testified that the President approved the nine-point plan. But other testimony raises questions about this assertion. Regardless of what Poindexter may have told the President, Secretary Shultz testified that when he informed the President on December 14, 1986, that the nine-point plan included a promise about the release of the Da'wa prisoners in Kuwait, the President reacted with shock, "like he had been kicked in the belly."

During the negotiations with the Second Channel, North and Secord told the Iranians that the President agreed with their position that Iraq's President, Saddam Hussein, had to be removed and further agreed that the United States would defend Iran against Soviet aggression. They did not clear this with the President and their representations were flatly contrary to U.S. policy.

The decision to designate private parties—Secord and Hakim—to carry out the arms transactions had other ramifications. First, there was virtually no accounting for the profits from the arms deals. Even North claimed that he did not know how Secord and Hakim actually spent the money committed to their custody. . . .

Second, by permitting private parties to conduct the arms sales, the Administration risked losing control of an important foreign policy initiative. Private citizens—whose motivations of personal gain could conflict with the interests of this country—handled sensitive diplomatic negotiations, and purported to commit the United States to positions that were anathema to the President's public policy and wholly unknown to the Secretary of State.

THE COVERUP

The sale of arms to Iran was a "significant anticipated intelligence activity." By law, such an activity must be reported to Congress "in a timely fashion" pursuant to Section 501 of the National Security Act. If the proposal to sell arms to Iran had been reported, the Senate and House Intelligence Committees would likely have joined Secretaries Shultz and Weinberger in object-ing to this initiative. But Poindexter recommended—and the President decided—not to report the Iran initiative to Congress.

Indeed, the Administration went to considerable lengths to avoid notifying Congress. The CIA General Counsel wrote on January 15, 1986, "the key issue in this entire matter revolves around whether or not there will be reports made to Congress." Shortly thereafter, the transaction was restructured to avoid the pre-shipment reporting requirements of the Arms Export Con-trol Act, and place it within the more limited reporting require-ments of the National Security Act. But even these reporting re-quirements were ignored. The President failed to notify the group of eight (the leaders of each party in the House and Sen-ate, and the Chairmen and Ranking Minority Members of the Intelligence Committees) specified by law for unusually sensi-tive operations. . . .

WHO WAS RESPONSIBLE

Who was responsible for the Iran-Contra Affair? Part of our mandate was to answer that question, not in a legal sense (which is the responsibility of the Independent Counsel), but in order to reaffirm that those who serve the Government are ac-countable for their actions. Based on our investigation, we reach the following conclusions.

At the operational level, the central figure in the Iran-Contra Affair was Lt. Col. North, who coordinated all of the activities and was involved in all aspects of the secret operations. North, however, did not act alone.

North's conduct had the express approval of Admiral John Poindexter, first as Deputy National Security Adviser, and then as National Security Adviser. North also had at least the tacit support of Robert McFarlane, who served as National Security Adviser until December 1985.

In addition, for reasons cited earlier, we believe that the late Director of Central Intelligence, William Casey, encouraged North, gave him direction, and promoted the concept of an extra-legal covert organization. Casey, for the most part, insu-lated CIA career employees from knowledge of what he and the NSC staff were doing. Casey's passion for covert operations—dating back to his World War II intelligence days—was well known. His close relationship with North was attested to by sev-eral witnesses. Further, it was Casey who brought Richard Secord into the secret operation, and it was Secord who, with Albert Hakim, organized the Enterprise. These facts provide strong reasons to believe that Casey was involved both with the diversion and with the plans for an "off-the-shelf" covert capacity.

The Committees are mindful, however, of the fact that the evidence concerning Casey's role comes almost solely from North; that this evidence, albeit under oath, was used by North to exculpate himself; and that Casey could not respond. Although North told the Committees that Casey knew of the diversion from the start, he told a different story to the Attorney General in November 1986, as did Casey himself. Only one other witness, Lt. Col. Robert Earl, testified that he had been told by North during Casey's lifetime that Casey knew of the diversion.

The Attorney General recognized on November 21, 1986, the need for an inquiry. His staff was responsible for finding the diversion memorandum, which the Attorney General promptly made public. But as described earlier, his fact-finding inquiry departed from standard investigative techniques. The Attorney General saw Director Casey hours after the Attorney General learned of the diversion memorandum, yet he testified that he never asked Casey about the diversion. He waited two days to speak to Poindexter, North's superior, and then did not ask him what the President knew. He waited too long to seal North's offices. These lapses placed a cloud over the Attorney General's investigation.

There is no evidence that the Vice President was aware of the diversion. The Vice President attended several meetings on the Iran initiative, but none of the participants could recall his views.

The Vice President said he did not know of the Contra resupply operation. His National Security Adviser, Donald Gregg, was told in early August 1986 by a former colleague that North was running the Contra resupply operation, and that ex-associates of Edwin Wilson—a well known ex-CIA official convicted of selling arms to Libya and plotting the murder of his prosecutors—were involved in the operation. Gregg testified that he did not consider these facts worthy of the Vice President's attention and did not report them to him, even after the Hasenfus airplane was shot down and the Administration had denied any connection with it.

The central remaining question is the role of the President in the Iran-Contra Affair. On this critical point, the shredding of documents by Poindexter, North, and others, and the death of Casey, leave the record incomplete.

PRESIDENT REAGAN'S ROLE

As it stands, the President has publicly stated that he did not know of the diversion. Poindexter testified that he shielded the President from knowledge of the diversion. North said that he never told the President, but assumed that the President knew. Poindexter told North on November 21, 1986, that he had not informed the President of the diversion. Secord testified that North told him he had talked with the President about the diversion, but North testified that he had fabricated this story to bolster Secord's morale.

Nevertheless, the ultimate responsibility for the events in the Iran-Contra Affair must rest with the President. If the President did not know what his National Security Advisers were doing, he should have. It is his responsibility to communicate unambiguously to his subordinates that they must keep him advised of important actions they take for the Administration. The Constitution requires the President to "take care that the laws be faithfully executed." This charge encompasses a responsibility to leave the members of his Administration in no doubt that the rule of law governs.

Members of the NSC staff appeared to believe that their actions were consistent with the President's desires. It was the President's policy—not an isolated decision by North or Poindexter—to sell arms secretly to Iran and to maintain the Contras "body and soul," the Boland Amendment notwithstanding. To the NSC staff, implementation of these policies became the overriding concern.

Several of the President's advisers pursued a covert action to support the Contras in disregard of the Boland Amendment and of several statutes and Executive orders requiring Congressional notification. Several of these same advisers lied, shredded documents, and covered up their actions. These facts have been on the public record for months. The actions of those individuals do not comport with the notion of a country guided by the rule of law. But the President has yet to condemn their conduct.

The President himself told the public that the U.S. Government had no connection to the Hasenfus airplane. He told the public that early reports of arms sales for hostages had "no foundation." He told the public that the United States had not traded arms for hostages. He told the public that the United States had not condoned the arms sales by Israel to Iran, when in fact he had approved them and signed a Finding, later destroyed by Poindexter, recording his approval. All of these statements by the President were wrong.

Thus, the question whether the President knew of the diversion is not conclusive on the issue of his responsibility. The President created or at least tolerated an environment where those who did know of the diversion believed with certainty that they were carrying out the President's policies.

This same environment enabled a secretary who shredded, smuggled, and altered documents to tell the Committees that "sometimes you have to go above the written law;" and it enabled Admiral Poindexter to testify that "frankly, we were willing to take some risks with the law." It was in such an environment that former officials of the NSC staff and their private agents could lecture the Committees that a "rightful cause" justifies any means, that lying to Congress and other officials in the executive branch itself is acceptable when the ends are just, and that Congress is to blame for passing laws that run counter to Administration policy. What may aptly be called the "cabal of the zealots" was in charge.

In a Constitutional democracy, it is not true, as one official maintained, that "when you take the King's shilling, you do the King's bidding." The idea of monarchy was rejected here 200 years ago and since then, the law—not any official or ideology—has been paramount. For not instilling this precept in his staff, for failing to take care that the law reigned supreme, the President bears the responsibility.

Fifty years ago Supreme Court Justice Louis Brandeis observed: "Our Government is the potent, the omnipresent teacher. For good or for ill, it teaches the whole people by its example. Crime is contagious. If the Government becomes a lawbreaker, it breeds contempt for law, it invites every man to become a law unto himself, it invites anarchy."

The Iran-Contra Affair resulted from a failure to heed this message.

THE RISE OF THE YUPPIES

BRUCE J. SCHULMAN

In the 1980s, the sagging economy that had been suffering cycles of recession and inflation since the early 1970s finally began to regain its health. The newly implemented theories of supply-side economics led to slashed taxes and reduced government controls to encourage investment. The formula worked, and in mid-1983, the economy boomed and entered its longest period of growth in American history. Soon after, the new wealth was being flashed around in highly visible ways.

A big part of this economic growth was in financial services, where mergers and acquisitions between companies occurred rapidly, the stock indexes boomed, and the large corporations were filled with young, urban professionals labeled "yuppies." In the following excerpt, Bruce J. Schulman, a Boston University professor of American history who received his Ph.D from Stanford, discusses the phenomenon of the yuppie. In addition to his recent book on the 1970s and his earlier work, *Lyndon B. Johnson and American Liberalism*, Schulman has written about the transformation of the sunbelt states during World War II and in the following decades.

According to Schulman, the central tenet of yuppie culture was the accumulation of wealth, both as a good in itself and for the freedom and power that it was believed to buy. The yuppie label also tended to imply a certain conformity: an identity based on good education, corporate employment, an urban lifestyle, and the embrace of money and luxury goods. Schulman notes that by the late 1980s, this suit-wearing, credit-card wielding crew began to dislike their appellation, but the label stuck nonetheless.

Schulman traces the origins of the yuppie identity, pointing out that many of the yuppies were actually former hippies from the late 1960s and 1970s. For example, Jerry Rubin, one of the leaders of Yippie!, a group founded in 1967 to critique society through street theater and absurd pantomime, became a successful investment banker in the 1980s. The transformation from Yippie! to yuppie implied a rejection of the 1960s idealism and an embrace of corporate culture and a consumerist ethic.

On December 31, 1984, *Newsweek* magazine devoted its year-end issue to "The Year of the Yuppie." "The young urban professionals have arrived," the newsweekly declared, "they're making lots of money, spending it conspicuously and switching political candidates like they test cuisines." In that same year, a satirical how-to guide, *The Yuppie Handbook*, climbed the best-seller lists, and all the major news outlets focused on the yuppie phenomenon—charting its effects on American consumption patterns, popular culture, religion, politics, and economic life.

THE ORIGINS OF THE YUPPIE

The very term *yuppie* remains shrouded in mystery and controversy. Most chablis-swilling sociologists believe the word first saw print in March 1983, when syndicated columnist Bob Greene dropped it offhandedly into a piece on ex-Sixties radical (and ex-Seventies New Ager) Jerry Rubin and his reemergence as an investment banker. Still, San Francisco Bay–area humorist Alice Kahn probably deserves the credit (or the blame) for defining and delineating this new social class—developing *yuppie* as a modified acronym for young urban professional.

Kahn's June 1983 article in the *East Bay Express* created the familiar profile of the typical yuppie that the national press would soon adopt. Kahn wrote about how well-off young professionals—who worked long hours at basically unfulfilling jobs, but earned loads of money—formed their identities through luxurious leisure activities and consumption of big-name purchased goods. She noticed yuppies driving out community shops with their preferences for upscale boutiques.

A few months later, Americans began discovering yuppies everywhere. Carmakers, demographers, academics, film and television producers, record company executives, journalists, and politicians began to see yuppiedom as the new, influential wave in American life. Corporate America developed new marketing strategies for the yuppie market: "Detroit's New Goal—Putting Yuppies in the Driver's Seat," reported *Business Week* in 1984. "Saab Hitches Its Star to the Yuppie Market." Advertisers, a *U.S. News and World Report* survey concluded, "say yuppies are disproportionately important in the marketplace."

Young urban professionals also flexed their muscles in the political and cultural arenas. Colorado senator Gary Hart's upstart 1984 campaign for the Democratic presidential nomination credited his hip appeal to yuppie voters. "Now that the Gary Hart campaign is more or less over," *New Republic* columnist Michael Kinsley joked in the summer of 1984, the "specter of a federal quiche stamps program has passed. There will be no transatlantic Perrier pipeline, no National Tennis Elbow Institute, no Department of Life Style." *U.S. News* ran a story on "How Churches Try to Woo the Yuppies." A strange new illness—chronic fatigue syndrome—was renamed "yuppie flu."

YUPPIE, YIPPIE, HIPPIE, PREPPIE

The term *yuppie* proved so contagious because it evoked the yippies—the most outrageous, anarchic cultural radicals of the 1960s. Many observers fastened onto Jerry Rubin's odyssey from yippie to yuppie. Rubin had helped to mastermind the disturbances at the 1968 Democratic National Convention in Chicago. In 1968, he and Abbie Hoffman had thrown dollar bills onto the floor of the New York Stock Exchange, laughing as the brokers scurried madly for the cash and the television cameras rolled. Now, fifteen years later, Rubin himself scurried for cash. It struck many as a fitting emblem of failed idealism.

Yuppie also implied an alternative to, even a rejection of, *hippie*. Young professionals rejected the values of the counterculture, or at least they had thoroughly tamed and domesticated them. The yuppie lifestyle drained from the hippie ideal the spirit of rebellion, the need to create alternative institutions, families, and selves. As journalist and former Carter speechwriter Hendrik Hertzberg put it, "Yuppiedom carried over from hippiedom an appreciation for things deemed 'natural,' an emphasis on personal freedom, and the self-absorption of that part of the counterculture known as the human-potential movement." But, Hertzberg jibed, "Hippies thought property was theft; yuppies think it's an investment. Hippies were interested in karma; yuppies prefer cars."

At the same time, *yuppie* echoed the term *preppie*. It evoked a sense of entitlement—a privileged way of life and its exclusive accoutrements. Still, yuppiedom diverged from preppiedom in one crucial respect: birth, family, and upbringing made a preppie, but anyone with money could enter the terrain of the yuppies. Just don't forget your American Express Gold Card.

Fleeting as it was, the yuppie phenomenon represented the ascendance of a new cultural style. In many ways, the boisterous, consumerist spirit of the mid-1980s signaled the triumph of Reaganism. After all, the president had long wished to restore the imagined nation of his youth, his image of America as a place where anyone could get rich. The *Wall Street Journal* aptly referred to the elderly president as the nation's most aged yuppie.

Still, yuppie values never implied respect for tradition or nostalgia for the small-town values Reagan liked to evoke in his signature anecdotes. Yuppies challenged the ossified structures of corporate America, the sacred rituals of academia, the bloated bureaucracies of government. According to *Newsweek,* they were three times as likely as other Americans to carry American Express cards, travel overseas, and work out in health clubs. Their primary loyalties lay not with family, corporation, or country but with their networks—"informal associations of mutual friendship that cut across corporate lines to unite people of similar ages, professional levels and interests, principally money and sex."

What formed the key tenets of yuppie ideology, if they even deserved such a grandiose designation? What ideas percolated along with the gourmet coffee? First, raw accumulation of wealth for its own sake was not tawdry or immoral but worthy. Personal empowerment depended on having money; finding yourself costs!

WALL STREET

In the 1987 film *Wall Street,* Oliver Stone's attempt to critique yuppie values, the evil character played by Michael Douglas, a ruthless capitalist named Gordon Gecko, stole the show and the audience with a now-legendary disquisition. Criticized for being greedy, Gecko does not deny but instead celebrates his avarice. "Greed is good," Gecko lectures a shareholders' meeting of an underperforming corporation. "Greed, in all its forms, greed for life, greed for love, greed for knowledge—has marked the upsurgence of man since the beginning of time. . . . Greed, gentlemen, can not only save this company, but it can save that other malfunctioning institution known as the United States of America." Real young professionals agreed that economic accumulation represented a good in and of itself.

But that zest for wealth did not foreclose the possibility of social reform. On the contrary, the second key tenet of yuppie ideology held that moneymaking was not antithetical to meaningful social change, but absolutely essential for it. For yuppies, the entrepreneur had replaced the reformer or radical. One could change the world by providing it with natural, caring, environmentally safe, politically sensitive goods and services.

Geoffrey Lewis, a self-identified yuppie, explained this in a *Newsweek* feature. By 1984, the former antiwar radical had become an immensely successful New York City attorney, living in a $200,000 co-op on Manhattan's tony Upper East Side. Once tear-gassed at 1971 May Day demonstrations in Washington, Lewis remained engaged in politics, although his causes and his tactics had matured. "I will always be a community-minded person," he soberly reflected. "It's just that the shape of my concerns may change as I grow older." While Lewis and his fellow yuppies did not "want money to rule your life. You have to realize what money can bring you. In our case, I would like to think it can bring us more than just a VCR."

THE ANTI-HIPPIE

Lewis's new sobriety reflected a third crucial tenet of yuppie ideology: a rejection of hippies, a repudiation of the cultural and political critique of the Sixties counterculture. Yuppies dismissed the antimaterialism of the counterculture as naive; they replaced the hippie quest for freedom from the aerosol and vinyl institutions of American capitalism with an equally passionate search for the best that consumer culture could offer. "The name of the game," *The Yuppie Handbook* affirmed, "is the *best*—buying it, owning it, using it, eating it, wearing it, growing it, cooking it, driving it, doing whatever with it."

Yuppie-era popular culture mocked the idea of altered consciousness and decried the Sixties counterculture for its supposed naiveté. Compare, as many 1980s film critics did, the 1967 classic *The Graduate* to the 1983 blockbuster *Risky Business*. Both films focused on graduating seniors with dim prospects—Benjamin Braddock, the eponymous college graduate with no hopes or plans played by Dustin Hoffman, and Joel Goodsen, a high school senior struggling to gain admission to an elite college despite his low SAT scores. Both protagonists journeyed toward personal fulfillment—literally traveling in sports cars and on public transportation. Both also receive sexual initiation by an experienced older woman. But in one reviewer's words, "Benjamin Braddock moves out of his house; Joel stays and turns it into an enterprise. Benjamin rejects further education; Joel pimps his way into Princeton. When barging into a frat house, Benjamin looks like an illegal alien; Joel probably cannot wait for rush."

Benjamin Braddock's 1967 graduate ultimately rejected the materialism around him. Terminating his affair with Mrs. Robinson and her corrupt society, Benjamin escapes on a bus with the woman he loves and becomes something of a countercultural hero. But Joel finds love and success with the seductive, fallen older woman. "It was great the way her mind worked," Joel enthused. "No doubts, no fears, just the shameless pursuit of immediate material gratification. What a capitalist!" Benjamin's discomfort with wealth and luxury reflected the values of the counterculture; however dumbed down, Risky Business reflected a growing sentiment that capitalism offered liberation and empowerment.

In the mid-1980s, during the high tide of Reaganism, Americans celebrated yuppiedom in films, television, recordings, magazine articles, marketing surveys, and sociological analyses. The nation trumpeted unabashedly the influence of yuppies; even if the media exaggerated their actual numbers, they remained the trendsetters, the opinion makers. And yuppie values seemed the perfect complement to the age of Reagan. Yuppies ruled!

The yuppie phenomenon would be short-lived. By the time Reagan left the White House, *yuppie* would become a curse word—a derogatory term that corporations, journalists, and young professionals themselves strived to avoid. Even yuppies hated yuppies. No one willingly answered to the name. BMW, the automobile that had become synonymous with yuppies on the make, launched a $30 million advertising campaign to shed itself of just that image. But by then, while brand names might become clichéd, the core beliefs of yuppiedom had become so well entrenched that no one even noticed them any more. A broad consensus had emerged: Americans affirmed the superiority of the private sphere to the public sector; entrepreneurship, not political activism, marked the path to personal liberation and social transformation.

THE END OF THE COLD WAR

MIKHAIL GORBACHEV

For many historians, the following speech given by Soviet premier Mikhail Gorbachev at the United Nations in December 1988, marked the end of the cold war. It ushered in a new era of U.S. history in which the specter of communism was over, the arms race was nullified, and the terms "communist" and "capitalist" were no longer used to signal enemy camps. Some argue that the United States "won" the cold war, for the demise of communism in the USSR validated democratic capitalism as an ideology; others insist that there were no real winners.

This historic address came three years after Gorbachev had assumed power in 1985 and had initiated unprecedented economic, political, and social reforms known as perestroika (restructuring) and glasnost (freedom) in an attempt to save the flailing Soviet economy and the corrupt and inefficient Communist Party. Perestroika encouraged market forces, decentralized management, and democratized the Communist Party organization. Glasnost allowed discussion of elements of Soviet society previously banned from discussion, such as rampant crime, corruption, alcoholism, and prostitution.

Opposed to the nuclear race for its enormous cost, which was draining the already weak Soviet economy, Gorbachev had proposed substantial arms reductions to Reagan within a few months of the former's presidency. Reagan's arms buildup and aggressive "evil empire" rhetoric notwithstanding, the U.S. president had proved to be quite open to negotiations. As part of his plan to focus on developing the USSR's internal infrastructure rather than squandering funds on international ven-

Excerpted from Mikhail Gorbachev's speech to the General Assembly of the United Nations, December 8, 1988.

tures, Gorbachev pushed forward with arms reductions proposals as well as honoring his promise to pull Soviet troops out of Afghanistan.

In the following speech, Gorbachev expands on these peaceful initiatives by rejecting the imposition of foreign (Communist) doctrine on any country and jettisoning the use of force in foreign policy. He describes a vision of a world in which cooperation and peace triumph over aggression and nuclear threats. In effect, Gorbachev announces the freedom of the Eastern bloc satellites in this dramatic speech. Shortly after this address, and throughout the course of 1989, Soviet troops left several Eastern European states such as Czechoslovakia and Romania and these countries overthrew their Communist rulers. The Baltic states of Lithuania, Latvia, and Estonia, part of the Soviet empire for centuries, yet with a memory of their brief independence between the world wars, similarly declared their freedom. The Berlin Wall, which divided the communist east from the democratic west also came down in 1989—attacked by Berliners with pickaxes until only a pile of rubble remained. In 1991, the Soviet Union itself fractured into fifteen independent republics. Russia, headed by Boris Yeltsin, emerged as the largest and most powerful state, and throughout the 1990s the smaller republics of the former USSR remained in the Russian sphere of influence.

W e have come here to show our respect for the United Nations, which increasingly has been manifesting its ability to act as a unique international center in the service of peace and security.

The world in which we live today is radically different from what it was at the beginning or even in the middle of this century. And it continues to change as do all its components.

The advent of nuclear weapons was just another tragic reminder of the fundamental nature of that change. A material symbol and expression of absolute military power, nuclear weapons at the same time revealed the absolute limits of that power. The problem of mankind's survival and self-preservation came to the fore.

It is obvious, for instance, that the use or threat of force no longer can or must be an instrument of foreign policy. This applies above all to nuclear arms, but that is not the only thing that matters. All of us, and primarily the stronger of us, must exercise self-restraint and totally rule out any outward-oriented use of force.

That is the first and the most important component of a non-violent world as an ideal which we proclaimed together with India in the Delhi Declaration and which we invite you to follow.

The new phase also requires de-ideologizing relations among states. We are not abandoning our convictions, our philosophy or traditions, nor do we urge anyone to abandon theirs.

But neither do we have any intention to be hemmed in by our values. That would result in intellectual impoverishment, for it would mean rejecting a powerful source of development—the exchange of everything original that each nation has independently created.

In the course of such exchange, let everyone show the advantages of their social system, way of life or values—and not just by words or propaganda, but by real deeds.

That would be a fair rivalry of ideologies. But it should not be extended to relations among states.

ROMANTIC? NO, REALISTIC

We are, of course, far from claiming to be in possession of the ultimate truth. But, on the basis of a thorough analysis of the past and newly emerging realities, we have concluded that it is on those lines that we should jointly seek the way leading to the supremacy of the universal human idea over the endless multitude of centrifugal forces, the way to preserve the vitality of this civilization, possibly the only one in the entire universe.

Could this view be a little too romantic? Are we not overestimating the potential and the maturity of the world's social consciousness? We have heard such doubts and such questions both in our country and from some of our Western partners.

I am convinced that we are not floating above reality.

We regard prospects for the near and more distant future quite optimistically.

Just look at the changes in our relations with the United States. Little by little, mutual understanding has started to develop and elements of trust have emerged, without which it is very hard to make headway in politics.

In Europe, these elements are even more numerous. The Helsinki process is a great process.

I am convinced that our time and the realities of today's world call for internationalizing dialogue and the negotiating process.

This is the main, the most general conclusion that we have come to in studying global trends that have been gaining momentum in recent years, and in participating in world politics.

In this specific historical situation we face the question of a new role for the United Nations.

We feel that states must to some extent review their attitude to the United Nations, this unique instrument without which world politics would be inconceivable today.

The recent reinvigoration of its peacemaking role has again demonstrated the United Nations' ability to assist its members in coping with the daunting challenges of our time and working to humanize their relations.

External debt is one of the gravest problems. Let us not forget that in the age of colonialism the developing world, at the cost of countless losses and sacrifices, financed the prosperity of a large portion of the world community. The time has come to make up for the losses that accompanied its historic and tragic contribution to global material progress.

We are convinced that here, too, internationalizing our approach shows a way out.

Looking at things realistically, one has to admit that the accumulated debt cannot be repaid or recovered on the original terms.

THE BURDEN OF WORLD DEBT

The Soviet Union is prepared to institute a lengthy moratorium of up to 100 years on debt servicing by the least developed countries, and in quite a few cases to write off the debt altogether.

As regards other developing countries, we invite you to consider the following:

- Limiting their official debt servicing payments depending on the economic performance of each of them or granting them a long period of deferral in the repayment of a major portion of their debt;
- Supporting the appeal of the United Nations Conference on Trade and Development for reducing debts owed to commercial banks;
- Guaranteeing government support for market arrangements to assist in Third World debt settlement, including the formation of a specialized international agency that would repurchase debts at a discount.

The Soviet Union favours a substantive discussion of ways

to settle the debt crisis at multilateral forums, including consultations under the auspices of the United Nations among heads of government of debtor and creditor countries.

International economic security is inconceivable unless related not only to disarmament but also to the elimination of the threat to the world's environment. In a number of regions, the state of the environment is simply frightening.

Let us also think about setting up within the framework of the United Nations a center for emergency environmental assistance. Its function would be promptly to send international groups of experts to areas with badly deteriorating environment.

The Soviet Union is also ready to cooperate in establishing an international space laboratory or manned orbital station designed exclusively for monitoring the state of the environment.

In the general area of space exploration, the outlines of a future space industry are becoming increasingly clear.

The position of the Soviet Union is well known: activities in outer space must rule out the appearance of weapons there. Here again, there has to be a legal base. The groundwork for it—the provisions of the 1967 treaty and other agreements—is already in place.

We have put forward our proposal to establish it on more than one occasion. We are prepared to incorporate within its system our Krasnoyarsk radar station. A decision has already been taken to place that radar under the authority of the U.S.S.R. Academy of Sciences.

Soviet scientists are prepared to receive their foreign colleagues and discuss with them ways of converting it into an international center for peaceful cooperation by dismantling and refitting certain units and structures, and to provide additional equipment.

The entire system could function under the auspices of the United Nations.

The whole world welcomes the efforts of this organization and its Secretary General, Mr. Perez de Cuellar, and his representatives in untying knots of regional problems. Allow me to elaborate on this. Paraphrasing the words of the English poet that Hemingway took as an epigraph to his famous novel, I will say this: The bell of every regional conflict tolls for all of us.

This is particularly true, since those conflicts are taking place in the Third World, which already faces many ills and problems of such magnitude that is has to be a matter of concern to us all.

The year 1988 has brought a glimmer of hope in this area of our common concerns as well. This has been felt in almost all regional crises. On some of them, there has been movement. We welcome it and we did what we could to contribute to it.

I will single out only Afghanistan.

Ending the Afghan War

The Geneva accords, whose fundamental and practical significance has been praised throughout the world, provided a possibility for completing the process of settlement even before the end of this year. That did not happen.

This unfortunate fact reminds us again of the political, legal and moral significance of the Roman maxim "pacta sunt servanda"—treaties must be observed.

I don't want to use this rostrum for recriminations against anyone.

But it is our view that, within the competence of the United Nations, the General Assembly Resolution adopted last November could be supplemented by some specific measures.

In the words of that resolution, for the urgent achievement of a comprehensive solution by the Afghans themselves of the question of a broad-based government the following should be undertaken:

- A complete cease-fire effective everywhere as of Jan. 1, 1989, and the cessation of all offensive operations or shellings, with the opposing Afghan groups retaining, for the duration of negotiations, all territories under their control;
- Linked to that, stopping as of the same date any supplies of arms to all belligerents;
- For the period of establishing a broad-based government, as provided in the General Assembly resolution, sending to Kabul and other strategic centres of the country a contingent of United Nations peacekeeping forces;
- We also request the secretary general to facilitate early implementation of the idea of holding an international conference on the neutrality and demilitarization of Afghanistan.

We shall continue most actively to assist in healing the wounds of the war and are prepared to cooperate in this endeavor both with the United Nations and on a bilateral basis.

We support the proposal to create under the auspices of the

United Nations a voluntary international Peace Corps to assist in the revival of Afghanistan.

Letting Arafat Speak

In the context of the problem of settling regional conflicts, I have to express my opinion on the serious incident that has recently affected the work of this session. The chairman of an organization which has observer status at the United Nations was not allowed by U.S. authorities to come to New York to address the General Assembly. I am referring to Yasir Arafat.

What is more, this happened at a time when the Palestine Liberation Organization has made a constructive step which facilitates the search for a solution to the Middle East problem with the involvement of the United Nations Security Council.

This happened at a time when a positive trend has become apparent toward a political settlement of other regional conflicts, in many cases with the assistance of the Soviet Union and the United States. We voice our deep regret over the incident and our solidarity with the Palestine Liberation Organization.

I would like to join the voice of my country in the expressions of high appreciation of the significance of the Universal Declaration of Human Rights adopted 40 years ago, on Dec. 10, 1948.

Today, this document retains its significance. It, too, reflects the universal nature of the goals and objectives of the United Nations.

The most fitting way for a state to observe this anniversary of the declaration is to improve its domestic conditions for respecting and protecting the rights of its own citizens.

Before I inform you on what specifically we have undertaken recently in this respect I would like to say the following.

Our country is going through a period of truly revolutionary uplifting.

The process of perestroika is gaining momentum. We began with the formulation of the theoretical concept of perestroika. We had to evaluate the nature and the magnitude of problems, to understand the lessons of the past and express that in the form of political conclusions and programmes. This was done.

Theoretical work, a reassessment of what is happening, the finalization, enrichment and readjustment of political positions have not been completed. They are continuing.

But it was essential to begin with an overall concept, which, as now confirmed by the experience of these past years, has generally proved to be correct and which has no alternative.

For our society to participate in efforts to implement the plans of perestroika, it had to be democratized in practice. Under the sign of democratization, perestroika has now spread to politics, the economy, intellectual life and ideology.

ECONOMIC CHANGES AT HOME

We have initiated a radical economic reform. We have gained experience. At the start of next year the entire national economy will be redirected to new forms and methods of operation. This also means profoundly reorganizing relations of production and releasing the tremendous potential inherent in socialist property.

Undertaking such bold revolutionary transformations, we realized that there would be mistakes, and also opposition, that new approaches would generate new problems. We also foresaw the possibility of slowdowns in some areas.

But the guarantee that the overall process of perestroika will steadily move forward and gain strength lies in a profound democratic reform of the entire system of power and administration.

With the recent decisions by the Supreme Soviet on amendments to the Constitution and the adoption of the Law on Elections, we have completed the first stage of the process of political reform.

Without pausing, we have begun the second stage of this process with the main task of improving the relationship between the center and the republics, harmonizing interethnic relations on the principles of Leninist internationalism that we inherited from the Great Revolution, and at the same time reorganizing the local system of Soviet power.

A great deal of work lies ahead. Major tasks will have to be dealt with concurrently.

We are full of confidence. We have a theory and a policy, and also the vanguard force of perestroika—the party, which also is restructuring itself in accordance with new tasks and fundamental changes in society as a whole.

What is most important is that all our peoples and all generations of citizens of our great country support perestroika.

We have become deeply involved in building a socialist state based on the rule of law. Work on a series of new laws has been completed or is nearing completion.

Many of them will enter into force as early as in 1989, and we expect them to meet the highest standards from the standpoint of ensuring the rights of the individual.

Soviet democracy will be placed on a solid normative base. I am referring, in particular, to laws on the freedom of conscience, glasnost, public associations and organizations, and many others.

In places of confinement there are no persons convicted for their political or religious beliefs.

Additional guarantees are to be included in the new draft laws that rule out any form of persecution on those grounds.

Naturally this does not apply to those who committed actual criminal offenses or state crimes such as espionage, sabotage, terrorism, etc., whatever their political or ideological beliefs.

Draft amendments to the penal code have been prepared and are awaiting their turn. Among the articles being revised are those related to capital punishment.

The problem of exit from and entry to our country, including the question of leaving it for family reunification, is being dealt with in a humane spirit.

As you know, one of the reasons for refusal to leave is a person's knowledge of secrets. Strictly warranted time limitations on the secrecy rule will now be applied. Every person seeking employment at certain agencies or enterprises will be informed of this rule. In case of disputes, there is a right of appeal under the law.

This removes from the agenda the problem of the so-called "refuseniks."

We intend to expand the Soviet Union's participation in the United Nations and Conference of Security and Cooperation in Europe human rights monitoring arrangements. We believe that the jurisdiction of the International Court of Justice at the Hague as regards the interpretation and implementation of agreements on human rights should be binding on all states.

We regard as part of the Helsinki process the cessation of jamming of all foreign radio broadcasts beamed at the Soviet Union.

Overall, this is our credo. Political problems must be solved only by political means; human problems, only in a humane way.

REDUCTIONS IN ARMED FORCES

Now let me turn to the main issue—disarmament, without which none of the problems of the coming century can be solved.

Today, I can report to you that the Soviet Union has taken a decision to reduce its armed forces.

Within the next two years their numerical strength will be reduced by 500,000 men. The numbers of conventional armaments will also be substantially reduced. This will be done unilaterally, without relation to the talks on the mandate of the Vienna meeting.

By agreement with our Warsaw Treaty allies, we have decided to withdraw by 1991 six tank divisions from East Germany, Czechoslovakia and Hungary, and to disband them.

Assault landing troops and several other formations and units, including assault crossing units with their weapons and combat equipment, will also be withdrawn from the groups of Soviet forces stationed in those countries.

Soviet forces stationed in those countries will be reduced by 50,000 men and their armaments, by 5,000 tanks.

All Soviet divisions remaining, for the time being, in the territory of our allies are being reorganized. Their structure will be different from what it is now; after a major cutback of their tanks it will become clearly defensive.

At the same time, we shall reduce the numerical strength of the armed forces and the numbers of armaments stationed in the European part of the Soviet Union.

In total, Soviet armed forces in this part of our country and in the territories of our European allies will be reduced by 10,000 tanks, 8,500 artillery systems and 800 combat aircraft.

Over these two years we intend to reduce significantly our armed forces in the Asian part of our country, too. By agreement with the government of the Mongolian People's Republic a major portion of Soviet troops temporarily stationed there will return home.

In taking this fundamental decision the Soviet leadership expresses the will of the people, who have undertaken a profound renewal of their entire socialist society.

THE ECONOMY OF DISARMAMENT

We shall maintain our country's defense capability at a level of reasonable and reliable sufficiency so that no one might be tempted to encroach on the security of the Soviet Union and our allies.

By this action, and by all our activities in favor of demilitarizing international relations, we wish to draw the attention of the international community to yet another pressing problem—the problem of transition from the economy of armaments to an economy of disarmament.

Is conversion of military production a realistic idea? I have already had occasion to speak about this. We think that, indeed, it is realistic.

For its part, the Soviet Union is prepared to do these things:

- In the framework of our economic reform we are ready to draw up and make public our internal plan of conversion;
- In the course of 1989 to draw up, as an experiment, conversion plans for two or three defense plants;
- To make public our experience in providing employment for specialists from military industry and in using its equipment, buildings and structures in civilian production.

It is desirable that all states, in the first place major military powers, should submit to the United Nations their national conversion plans.

It would also be useful to set up a group of scientists to undertake a thorough analysis of the problem of conversion as a whole and as applied to individual countries and regions and report to the secretary-general of the United Nations, and, subsequently, to have this matter considered at a session of the General Assembly.

FUTURE RELATIONS WITH THE UNITED STATES

And finally, since I am here on American soil, and also for other obvious reasons, I have to turn to the subject of our relations with this great country. I had a chance to appreciate the full measure of its hospitality during my memorable visit to Washington exactly a year ago.

The relations between the Soviet Union and the United States of America have a history of five and a half decades. As the world changed, so did the nature, role and place of those relations in world politics.

For too long a time they developed along the lines of confrontation and sometimes animosity—either overt or covert.

But in the last few years the entire world could breathe a sigh of relief thanks to the changes for the better in the substance and the atmosphere of the relationship between Moscow and Washington.

No one intends to underestimate the seriousness of our differences and the toughness of outstanding problems. We have, however, already graduated from the primary school of learning to understand each other and seek solutions in both our own and common interests.

ELIMINATING NUCLEAR ARMS

The Soviet Union and the United States have built the largest nuclear and missile arsenals. But it is those two countries that, having become specifically aware of their responsibility, were the first to conclude a treaty on the reduction and physical elimination of a portion of their armaments which posed a threat to both of them and to all others.

Both countries possess the greatest and the most sophisticated military secrets. But it is those two countries that have laid a basis for and are further developing a system of mutual verification both of the elimination of armaments and of the reduction and prohibition of their production.

It is those two countries that are accumulating the experience for future bilateral and multilateral agreements.

We value this. We acknowledge and appreciate the contribution made by President Ronald Reagan and by the members of his administration, particularly Mr. George Shultz.

All this is our joint investment in a venture of historic importance. We must not lose this investment, or leave it idle.

The next U.S. administration, headed by President-elect George Bush, will find in us a partner who is ready—without long pauses or backtracking—to continue the dialogue in a spirit of realism, openness and good will, with a willingness to achieve concrete results working on the agenda which covers the main issues of Soviet-U.S. relations and world politics.

I have in mind, above all, these things:

- Consistent movement toward a treaty on 50 percent reductions in strategic offensive arms while preserving the ABM treaty;
- Working out a convention on the elimination of chemical weapons—here, as we see it, prerequisites exist to make 1989 a decisive year;
- And negotiations on the reduction of conventional arms and armed forces in Europe.

I also have in mind economic, environmental and humanistic problems in their broadest sense.

I would like to believe that our hopes will be matched by our joint effort to put an end to an era of wars, confrontation and regional conflicts, to aggressions against nature, to the terror of hunger and poverty as well as to political terrorism.

This is our common goal and we can only reach it together. Thank you.

Operation Desert Storm and America's Post–Cold War Middle East Policy

Robert E. Hunter

Iraqi president Saddam Hussein invaded neighboring Kuwait on August 2, 1990. The United States responded by sending troops to the region and spearheading the passage of a U.N. resolution demanding Iraq's withdrawal from the region. When these efforts failed, a U.S.-led coalition began Operation Desert Storm, a military campaign aimed at forcing Iraq out of Kuwait. This effort succeeded within five weeks.

Framing his discussion of American responses to Iraq's invasion of Kuwait in the context of the post–cold war era, Robert E. Hunter suggests that Middle-Eastern geopolitics was irrevocably altered following the demise of the Soviet Union. The author ascribes American policy miscalculations to the U.S. government's failure to gauge Saddam Hussein's desire to stand up to America as the last remaining superpower. During the cold war, the Iraqi leader Saddam Hussein had been, in Hunter's words, "to some degree a Soviet client," whose actions would have been regulated according to U.S.-Soviet relations. The collapse of the Soviet Union facilitated a U.S.-led coalition of in-

Excerpted from "U.S. Policy Toward the Middle East After Iraq's Invasion of Kuwait," by Robert E. Hunter, in *The Middle East After Iraq's Invasion of Kuwait*, edited by Robert O. Freedman (Gainesville: University Press of Florida, 1993). Copyright © 1993 by Robert E. Hunter. Reprinted with permission.

ternational partners that eventually led to the defeat of the invading Iraqi army in Kuwait.

According to Hunter, the Gulf War highlighted the need for a clearer articulation of American policies toward the Persian Gulf region, and specifically toward the Arab-Israeli conflict. Lacking opposition from the now-dissolved Soviet Union, the United States had an opportunity to revive the peace process and fulfill long-range strategic policies. Long-term American geopolitical aims included the protection of the world oil supply, stanching the flow of weapons to the region, and the containment of radical Islamic fundamentalism.

Hunter is vice president for regional programs and director of European studies at the Center for Strategic and International Studies in Washington, D.C.

W hen the United States awoke on the morning of August 2, 1990, to learn that Iraq had invaded Kuwait, it found itself in a new era in world history. For some time, U.S. citizens had understood intellectually that the cold war was over and that the United States was achieving a preeminence in global politics that it had never known before— save, perhaps, for a few fleeting moments at the end of World War II. But the shock of Saddam Hussein's aggression against his small neighbor was needed to begin turning the idea of a new era into reality.

TAKEN BY SURPRISE

The United States was taken by surprise on two levels. Most obvious was a patent miscalculation of Iraqi intentions. In retrospect, Saddam Hussein had made clear his ambitions toward Kuwait and had almost defied the world to do something to thwart them. And he had defined a larger strategic perspective that centered on the collapse of Soviet power, the emergence of the United States "in a superior position," and the risk that the "Arab Gulf region will be governed by U.S. will." When the evidence of Saddam's intentions and the warnings of a few prescient individuals were analyzed, they formed a dismal commentary on the failure of the U.S. government to recognize the obvious. Saddam Hussein, after all, was not supposed to invade Kuwait or take any other action hostile to Western interests. For nearly a decade, he had been a U.S.-chosen instrument in the region, first to prevent an Iranian victory in the war that Iraq had started, then to help obscure the domestic political blunder of the Reagan administration in secretly selling weapons to Iran, putatively in exchange for U.S. hostages held in Lebanon.

Such was the power of myth making, wishful thinking, and a U.S.-Middle East policy gone wild over the years that Saddam Hussein could even lay down the gauntlet to the U.S. ambassador in Baghdad as late as a week before the invasion, without setting off alarm bells in Washington. The ambassador promptly went on vacation and thus was not on post when the war began.

At a broader level, the United States was taken by surprise by the changed circumstances of East-West relations. During the cold war, an action such as that taken by Saddam Hussein, who was to some degree a Soviet client, was not supposed to happen. By traditional practice, a crisis aborning would have been relatively quickly sorted out by the superpowers, its limits tacitly or explicitly agreed upon, and the offending rascal soon brought to heel. Even though both Washington and Moscow had taken risks in the region on more than one occasion, they had a healthy appreciation of what they could and could not get away with, while preserving their mutual interest, to prevent Middle East events from jeopardizing their broader relationship. Yet by mid-1990, the old rules no longer applied, and perhaps the first person to articulate the new reality was the Iraqi president, in a speech before the Arab Cooperation Council at Amman in February 1990. On that occasion, he said that there was now only one superpower in the region—namely, the United States—and that someone had to counter its hegemonic ambitions in the Middle East.

On the morrow of Iraq's invasion, the United States had rapidly to come to terms both with its miscalculation about Iraq—indeed, with the weaknesses of its overall Persian Gulf strategy—and with the new dimensions of the post–cold war era. To his credit, President George Bush responded vigorously, if a bit uncertainly, during the first few days of the growing crisis. Saddam Hussein could be forgiven, in fact, if he were bewildered by both the alacrity and the strength of the U.S. response. Such a response was not to be expected—had he not recently been assured on this point by the U.S. ambassador to Iraq?—and thus it was doubly unwelcome, having deprived the Iraqi dictator of room to calculate his moves. . . .

DESERT SHIELD

On August 6, President Bush ordered a U.S. military buildup in the Persian Gulf that was to reach the level of 500,000 U.S. men and women in the brief period of five and a half months, or about the level of U.S. deployments in Vietnam, which had been achieved over more than five and a half years. Desert Shield, as this buildup was called, was an unprecedented achievement in logistics, with a stunning flow of weaponry, personnel, equipment, and supplies sent a long way in a short period of time. The buildup was aided by the fact that there was no air or sea challenge from Iraq and that there was a ready availability of first-class bases in Saudi Arabia and in some of the smaller Persian Gulf states, but even with these advantages Desert Shield was an impressive feat.

The original declared U.S. strategy, however, was not to use military force to achieve the goal of forcing Iraq's retreat from Kuwait. The military buildup was aptly named: it was to be the shield, the protection for Saudi Arabia in particular, while the sword was to be economic sanctions, endorsed and put in place by the UN Security Council, beginning with Resolution 661 of August 6, the second of fourteen resolutions aimed at Iraq.

FORGING A COALITION

Early on in the crisis, it also became clear in Washington that there was virtue in not going it alone in the Persian Gulf. Obviously, such a course was mandated by the decision to impose economic sanctions: their success required widespread cooperation that was secured and that led to modern history's most effective trade embargo against any country. But there were other reasons for the United States to seek cooperation that were not so obvious. The Soviet Union was clearly not going to pose the kind of challenge to U.S. unilateral actions that, prior to the radical internal and external changes set in train by President Mikhail S. Gorbachev, would have been second nature.

Desert Shield may have been represented as defensive, while the offense was composed of economic sanctions, but it did represent incipient conflict and was so understood by the U.S. public. The prospect of open conflict came under intense public scrutiny because of the size of the buildup and the sudden reversal of U.S. policy toward Iraq and because it came in the immediate aftermath of the cold war's end—which had been, in effect, a stunning victory for U.S. and Western policy sustained over more than four decades. Ironically, this scrutiny was applied to an operation whose risks, measured in terms of East-West relations, were far less than many other military activities undertaken by the United States during the cold war.

It rapidly became clear that U.S. popular support for administration policy was more likely to be forthcoming if the United States were joined by other states, especially close allies. What, in fact, was the United States trying to achieve? Or, put another way, if confrontation came to war, for what would the United States be fighting? The Bush administration cited several concerns, including oil, jobs at home, and even the American way of life, but all fell largely on deaf ears. In the post–cold war era, there was suddenly a reversion to an earlier style of popular expectation about U.S. war fighting: now it must be justified in terms of principle, not of realpolitik. But if a fight were truly needed to protect the flow of oil, military action could certainly be justified in terms of critical interests of the United States and its allies; in fact, following the arrival of the first U.S. forces in Saudi Arabia, the basic Western concern was that Iraq's unredressed aggression would give it a whip hand in the politics of oil, if not physical control over that vital Persian Gulf resource. . . .

In the event, the United States gained direct military support in the Persian Gulf from Britain, France (which had not placed its forces under U.S. military command since World War II), and several other European allies. Their willingness to cooperate was facilitated by a critical development: the decision of the Soviet Union not to obstruct U.S. policy and, in the main, to support it—witness Moscow's affirmative votes on all UN Security Council resolutions as well as its general support, at critical times, for overall U.S. policy, despite occasional diplomatic maneuvering. Thus this was the first crisis played out beyond the traditional area covered by the North Atlantic Treaty Organization (NATO) during which the European allies of the U.S. did not have to calculate the potentially negative consequences for East-West détente in Europe if they were to follow the U.S. lead. To underscore this point Secretary of State James A. Baker stopped in Moscow on August 3 and joined Foreign Minister Eduard Shevardnadze in condemning the invasion, and President Bush elicited a declaration of support from President Gorbachev at Helsinki on September 9. No doubt, the Soviets calculated that gaining access to the global economy was more important than pursuing classical regional ambitions, now paling in importance compared with the death throes of an empire. Germany and Japan, however, were constrained by historical memory and legal requirements and did not send combat forces to the Persian Gulf. Rather they acceded to U.S. requests for financial support. (Germany sent some forces to Turkey, within the formal NATO area, and Japan sent some non-combatants to the Gulf.) The aftershocks of this diplomacy are still being felt.

The U.S. forging of a coalition of states to address the crisis in the Persian Gulf also developed a further purpose. Saddam Hussein was not idle while the forces of Desert Shield were being assembled and the sanctions drawn more tightly. Among other things, he countered by attempting to portray himself as the victim of the "imperialists and Zionists," a line he pursued throughout the crisis. Saddam's charges that the crisis was linked to Jerusalem and the Palestinian problem, to the maldistribution of oil resources within the Arab world, and to the presence of Western military forces in Saudi Arabia—the land of the Prophet— found receptive ears in much of the Arab and Islamic worlds. The U.S. countered by broadening the coalition to include several Arab states, four non-Arab Islamic states (Bangladesh, Pakistan, Senegal, and Niger), and other Third World states, for a total of more than thirty countries. The battle of ideas was thus joined, and through its deft diplomacy both bilaterally and at the United Nations the United States made a good showing for itself. . . .

DESERT STORM

A full, public, and widely watched debate in the U.S. Congress led to its endorsement of war, along with that of the UN Security Council. Failing to withdraw from Kuwait—indeed, even to pursue the option of disgorging part of the fruits of his aggression—Saddam Hussein thus brought war upon himself. It began in the early hours of January 16, 1991, soon after the expiration of the period set by the United Nations for the use of only nonmilitary means to force Iraqi compliance with its demands.

The U.S. strategy in the Persian Gulf War, code name Desert Storm, was relatively simple: to exploit vastly superior air power and high technology until Iraq's capacity to resist militarily was severely damaged and only then to expel Iraqi forces from Kuwait physically. In fact, the United States pursued three objectives in the following rough order of priority: to cripple Iraq's future capacity to make war with either conventional arms or weapons of mass destruction; to limit coalition casualties; and to liberate Kuwait. It also had a fourth, undeclared objective of removing Saddam Hussein from power, but it did not elevate this objective to the point of wishing to occupy Iraq. By some calculations—erroneous, as events turned out—the Iraqi dictator's military defeat would inevitably provoke his overthrow by domestic opponents.

THE AFTERMATH

The ground war ended on February 28 with the U.S.-led coalition forces occupying about one-quarter of Iraq and having liberated Kuwait. Afterwards, there was debate about whether the war was halted too soon, especially before the Iraqi Republican Guards had been destroyed. These arguments, however, ignored the potential penalties of U.S. occupation of the entire country, the risks of higher casualties, and the splintering of the coalition if the initial declared and agreed-upon war aims were exceeded. Events that occurred soon after the war's end were more controversial. President Bush had called upon the people of Iraq to revolt against their leader, but when Shi'ites in the south and Kurds in the north did so—representing most of Iraq's population—the United States stood by while Saddam Hussein's forces decimated them. This U.S. policy was adopted in large part at the suggestion of Saudi Arabia, which feared that gains for the Shi'ites would either stir up its own Shi'ite population in the oil-rich Eastern Province or play into the hands of Iran (which in fact provided little or no help to its fellow Shi'ites in Iraq) and in part at the suggestion of Turkey, which feared the impact on its own Kurdish population. Ankara reversed its stance, however, when it became clear that the problem could not be contained, and the United States then sponsored an unprecedented UN-sanctioned mission, Operation Provide Comfort, to protect the Iraqi Kurds for a time against Baghdad.

Saddam Hussein remained in power, however. This became a problem for the Bush administration because of the president's characterization of Saddam Hussein as a Hitler and his pledge that sanctions against Iraq would remain in place so long as the dictator remained in power. In major part, this characterization of Saddam reflected a U.S. tactic to build popular support for Desert Shield and Desert Storm, and, having focused on the role of the Iraqi president, the administration was stuck with its symbol. The dilemma of what to do about Iraq remained unresolved

by the end of 1992 and will no doubt complicate U.S. calculations of a viable strategy for the region in the future.

On March 6, 1991, President Bush spoke to a joint session of
Congress and presented his postwar strategy for the Middle
East. It included U.S. support for regional security efforts—
which has come to mean a particular focus on the Gulf Cooperation Council (GCC); some joint military exercises; a continuing U.S. naval presence in the region; a concerted effort "to
control the proliferation of weapons of mass destruction and the
missiles used to deliver them"; progress in Arab-Israeli peacemaking, and regional economic development. On the last, Secretary Baker proposed a Middle East Development Bank but
did not pursue the subject.

Notably, the president was silent on the issue of constraining
the flow of conventional weapons to the region; indeed, a new
arms buildup began immediately after the war, fueled by recognition of vulnerability plus admiration for the performance of
U.S. weaponry. In May 1991, the five permanent powers of the
UN Security Council met in Paris to consider the problem, and
in December the permanent members of the UN Security Council approved the creation of a register of worldwide arms trans-
fers. But a U.S.-led policy of permissiveness had already guaranteed that, following the collapse of confrontation in Central
Europe, the Middle East would remain the most heavily armed
region on earth. Indeed, the United States has been unstinting in
its arms sales to the region. With the possibility of major regime
changes during the next few years, at least in part as a delayed
reaction to the Persian Gulf War, this lack of U.S. attention to a
central aspect of the long-term security structure of the region
could be laying the groundwork for future conflicts. . . .

In general, a year after Desert Storm, the United States had
still not sorted out its long-term security policies toward the
Persian Gulf region. The United States voiced support for the
GCC, indicated that it would retain some force presence in the
region, that it was selling arms to regional countries, and that it
was still seeking to contain Iraq. But it had not come to terms
with reality: both Iraq and Iran are regional states whose interests must be dealt with. The goal of deposing Saddam Hussein
begs the question of what could follow. Some form of pluralism—democracy adapted to regional circumstances—is desirable, but in the short term it could lead to the breakup of Iraq,
with unforeseen consequences. The original U.S. hope—that

Iraq could be ruled by a military regime without Saddam Hussein—is likely beyond the U.S. ability to engineer, and it is not clear that, from the perspective of regional states, this outcome would be much better than Saddam's rule. . . .

THE ARAB-ISRAELI CONFLICT

U.S. preoccupation with the Persian Gulf during the latter half of 1990 and the first part of 1991 did not mean that it had lost interest in the Arab-Israeli conflict. Indeed, this part of the Middle East was the central focus of the Bush administration's regional policy during 1989–90. The new administration had to address two new basic elements: the continuing Intifada, or uprising, of Palestinians in the West Bank and Gaza, and the declaration by the Palestine Liberation Organization in December 1988 that it was meeting the three U.S. conditions for opening a dialogue (acceptance of U.N. Security Council Resolutions 242 and 338, recognition of Israel's right to exist, and renunciation of terrorism). The Reagan administration took the PLO at its word and promptly opened diplomatic contacts.

In the early months of the Bush administration, Secretary Baker embarked on a revival of Arab-Israeli peacemaking that turned on the creation of a legitimate authority in the occupied territories for negotiations with Israel. This effort centered on ideas advanced by the United States and the Israeli government, led by Prime Minister Yitzhak Shamir, for elections in the territories. By the time of Iraq's invasion of Kuwait, however, these efforts had achieved little tangible progress.

Following the Persian Gulf War, however, the United States began a diplomatic initiative of a skill and intensity that had not been seen since President Jimmy Carter left office more than a decade before. Most remarkable, perhaps, was the motivation. On the surface, there was no particular strategic rationale for doing so, although the U.S. commitment to gain peace for Israel was still important. With the collapse of the Soviet Union, the so-called Arab confrontation states had lost their superpower patron. Iraq had been defeated in battle. The PLO had supported Saddam Hussein and thus alienated many of its Arab supporters. In sum, there was little risk of an Arab-Israeli war and no risk that the United States and the Soviet Union would find themselves confronting each other.

U.S. motives were thus more complex than they had been in the past. They derived in part from promises made by President

Bush during the effort to forge the Desert Shield coalition. In his address to the United Nations on October 1, 1990, the president said that if Iraq withdrew from Kuwait, he believed that "there may be opportunities . . . for all the states and the peoples of the region to settle the conflicts that divide the Arabs from Israel." He reiterated this commitment in his address to Congress on March 6, 1991. But why? The administration was likely responding to U.S. emergence from the Persian Gulf conflict as the unchallenged, preeminent external power in the Middle East, to a degree not rivaled by any other outsider at least in this century. This fact, plus the other developments cited, opened possibilities for Arab-Israeli peacemaking that could take place without opposition from the Soviet Union or unhelpful advice from European friends. Indeed, as part of its overall policy of putting primacy on economic relations with the West, the Soviet Union supported U.S. objectives by permitting the migration of hundreds of thousands of Jews to Israel and by reestablishing diplomatic relations with Israel that Moscow had broken during the 1967 Six-Day War.

In addition, there is the long-term question of the flow of oil, set against the background of incipient political and social changes within the region that were likely given further impetus by the war. U.S. efforts to resolve the Arab-Israeli conflict, certainly one of the principal irritants in U.S. relations with many regional countries, could encounter potentially hostile currents of opinion—including Islamic fundamentalism of various stripes. The revival of the peace process represented one of the few examples of long-range strategic planning in modern U.S. foreign policy. . . .

THE EMERGING AGENDA

The aftermath of both the cold war and the Persian Gulf War has left the United States with a greater range of worldwide geostrategic flexibility than it has enjoyed for at least half a century. A partial exception is the Middle East. While the possibility of open conflict is currently remote, old and new problems still require U.S. engagement and enlightened action. Most novel is the requirement to develop sensible and productive relations both with newly independent former Soviet republics in Central Asia and with neighbors contending for influence in them. Risks lie in inadequate knowledge, combined with a temptation to try affecting events beyond U.S. capacity or understanding of alternatives and consequences—practicing geo-mechanics rather than geopolitics. . . .

Ironically, the United States also faces a greater need for knowledge and understanding about the Middle East now, especially as its practical confines are extended northward, than during the more dangerous times of the cold war. Greater flexibility in political and other relationships poses more complex, if potentially less consequential or risky, demands. This risk will be particularly true in dealing with deep-seated cultural factors, the most puzzling of which for the United States is religion, especially the role that Islam will play in different societies. There is still a risk that the United States will blunder into confrontation with various Islamic states, because of misunderstanding or lack of adequate leadership to give expression to common interests. It is remarkable how simple distinctions like that between Sunnis and Shi'ites are blurred in American commentary, and fear produced by such ignorance can have unfortunate consequences.

Following the Persian Gulf War, it was possible to argue that U.S. responsibilities in the region, from taking part in security to prompting peace between Israel and its neighbors, would decline—possible but wrong. In fact, by becoming the region's preeminent outside power, the United States also increased expectations on the part of regional leaders and peoples about its role, for good or ill. Some view it as the legatee of Western imperialism and fully expect it to follow suit; others view it as the ultimate arbiter of all the region's ills. Neither view is just, but both must be countered by what the United States does, from taking the lead in controlling the spread of lethal weaponry, to helping resolve the Arab-Israeli conflict and championing the cause of political and economic modernization, regionwide. The United States cannot alone be held responsible for advancing this agenda, but neither can it escape its own essential part in the next act of the continuing Middle East drama.

CHRONOLOGY

1945

During the week of February 4–12, the Yalta Conference is held between Franklin Roosevelt, Joseph Stalin, and Winston Churchill to discuss World War II. On April 12, President Roosevelt suddenly dies, and Harry S. Truman replaces him. On April 25 the United Nations is founded. The war ends in Europe on May 8. The United States drops an atomic bomb on Hiroshima on August 6 and on Nagasaki three days later. On August 14 Japan surrenders, ending the war.

1946

In February, in a famous speech, Stalin declares communism and capitalism to be incompatible. In late February, George Kennan wires Washington from Moscow, opining that Soviet-style communism must not be allowed to spread; this view forms the basis of "containment policy." Churchill gives his "Iron Curtain" speech on March 5. In September civil war breaks out in Greece between Communist guerrillas and the British-backed government. In November the "Loyalty Program" begins: Civil servants are compelled to take loyalty oaths, and thousands leave or are fired from their jobs on the suspicion that, based on former liberal or radical left beliefs, they could potentially support Communist activities in the future.

1947

On March 12, in a proposal later known as the Truman Doctrine, the U.S. president officially commits his country to helping the nations of Europe fight communism and, specifically, to assisting Greece and Turkey resist the Communists. On June 5, at the Harvard College Commencement, Secretary of State George Marshall announces the Marshall Plan of economic aid to Europe. The National Security Act of July 26, 1947, creates the National Security Council and the CIA, which are

. not responsible to Congress and are thus free of congressional control. In October the House Un-American Activities Committee (HUAC) begins its Hollywood hearings.

1948

In February the Soviets stage a coup in Czechoslovakia and impose a Communist regime there. On March 31 Congress approves the Marshall Plan of billions of dollars in loans, goods, and services to resuscitate the flailing European economies. On June 24 the Berlin Blockade begins as Soviets block road and water access to the German capital of Berlin in an attempt to prevent the reunification of Germany. French, British, and American pilots fly food and supplies into West Berlin for fifteen months. Truman desegregates the armed forces and presents Congress with a list of other civil rights proposals—antilynching laws, job-discrimination protection, and a permanent Commission on Civil Rights— but Congress rejects these measures. In August, Whittaker Chambers, a former Soviet spy, accuses Alger Hiss, a former U.S. diplomat and head of the Carnegie Endowment, of spying for Russia. The U.S. Communist Party is accused of attempting to overthrow the government. In May the State of Israel is declared, and President Truman formally recognizes it within eleven minutes, initiating a strong diplomatic friendship between the two countries.

1949

On April 4 the North Atlantic Treaty Organization (NATO) agreement is signed between the United States, Canada, and the countries of Western Europe, agreeing that an attack on one of them constitutes an attack on all. On May 12 the USSR concedes defeat and reopens land routes to Berlin, ending the blockade. The USSR detonates its first atom bomb on September 23. In October the Communist forces led by Mao Zedong gain control of the government and establish the People's Republic of China.

1950

In January, Alger Hiss is convicted of perjury. Ethel and Julius Rosenberg are arrested and tried for channeling atomic secrets to the Soviets. In February, Senator Joseph McCarthy makes a famous speech in which he declares his fight on communism, contrasting Christians with Communist atheists. Following the invasion of South Korea by pro-Soviet Northern troops on June 25, the United States sends troops to South Korea to repel the North Koreans and prevent the unification of Korea under Communist rule. In mid-September U.S. troops led by General Douglas MacArthur repel the North Koreans from the South. In early October the UN/U.S. force crosses into North Korea. On November 25 China intervenes in the war in Korea.

1951

In March, Ethel and Julius Rosenberg are convicted of nuclear espionage. In April, Truman demands General MacArthur's resignation as head of the NATO forces deployed in Korea.

1952

In November the United States explodes its first hydrogen bomb. Dwight D. Eisenhower wins the November presidential election.

1953

Stalin dies on March 5 and a power struggle ensues. Nikita Khrushchev emerges victorious as the secretary of the Communist Party, and Georgy Malenkov becomes premier. Ethel and Julius Rosenberg are executed on June 19. The Korean War ends on July 27. By August the USSR has detonated its own version of the hydrogen bomb.

1954

In April, McCarthy is found guilty of falsely accusing prominent army personnel of having Communist leanings. He is formally condemned by the U.S. Senate in December for abuses of justice. In August, Mohammed Mossadegh's pro-Soviet regime in Iran is overthrown. In the *Brown v. Board of Education* ruling, the U.S. Supreme Court declares that segregated public schools are unconstitutional.

1955

West Germany joins the United Nations on May 5. On May 14 the Warsaw Pact is signed between the USSR and the Eastern European satellites. Montgomery, Alabama, resident Rosa Parks is arrested for refusing to relinquish her seat on a bus to a white person. The citizens of Montgomery boycott the city's segregated bus system for over a year until the buses are desegregated.

1956

After the United States retracts offers to fund Aswan Dam, Egypt's President Gamal Nasser nationalizes the British-owned Suez Canal on July 26, provoking a combined British, French, and Israeli attack. In October the Hungarian revolution begins, led by Imre Nagy. Soviet troops roll into Budapest and kill the dissidents. In late October the French, British, and Israelis attack Egypt in retaliation for its terrorism.

1957

President Eisenhower announces the Eisenhower Doctrine, relating to policy in the Middle East. In June, Khrushchev becomes the Soviet premier. In September, in Little Rock, Arkansas, officials refuse to comply with the federal mandate to integrate schools; violence results. Eisenhower sends in troops to enforce the law. On October 4 the Soviets launch *Sputnik*, the first earth-orbiting satellite, thus prompting a frantic space race as the United States attempts to close the feared technological gap with the Soviet Union.

1958

In January the United States launches *Explorer I*, which orbits Earth. In July the National Aeronautics and Space Administration (NASA) is founded.

1959

Revolution in Cuba brings Fidel Castro to power on New Year's Day. In mid-September, Khrushchev visits the United States (a first for a Soviet president).

1960

In February four African American college students in Greensboro, North Carolina, begin a series of sit-ins all over the racially segregated South. In May the Soviets shoot down an American U-2 spy plane and capture the pilot. In April the Student Nonviolent Coordinating Committee (SNCC) is formed. In November, John F. Kennedy is elected president and Lyndon B. Johnson becomes vice president.

1961

On January 3 the United States breaks off official relations with Cuba. President Kennedy establishes the Peace Corps in March. Soviet astronaut Yuri Gagarin orbits Earth on April

12. On April 17 U.S.-trained and armed Cubans land at the Bay of Pigs in Cuba as part of a CIA plot to overthrow the pro-Soviet leader. The invasion is poorly planned and executed and proves to be an embarrassing failure for the Americans. In May, James Farmer of the Congress of Racial Equality (CORE) organizes the Freedom Rides to protest segregated transport. The United States sends "advisers" to South Vietnam. On August 13 the Berlin Wall is erected to stop easterners from fleeing to the west.

1962

In February American John Glenn orbits Earth. In October American officials discover that Soviet missiles are being shipped to Cuba. After a tense thirteen days of negotiations, the Soviets agree to remove the missiles if the United States agrees not to attack Cuba. Students for Democratic Change write the Port Huron statement. James Meredith, an African American, is prevented from registering at the University of Mississippi by a local mob headed by Mississippi governor Ross Barnet; Kennedy sends in the National Guard to enforce desegregation.

1963

In May, President Kennedy makes a famous speech announcing that the government will not tolerate southern racism. Later that night Medgar Evers, head of the Mississippi NAACP is gunned down outside his home by white racists. In August, 250,000 people gather on the mall in Washington, D.C., for the historic civil rights march at which Martin Luther King Jr. gives his "I Have a Dream" speech. A partial Nuclear Test Ban Treaty is signed in Moscow on August 25 by the United States, Britain, and the USSR. On November 22, John F. Kennedy is assassinated in a Dallas motorcade by Lee Harvey Oswald. As the nation mourns, Jack Ruby shoots and kills Oswald as he is being transferred from city jail to state prison.

1964

On August 7 the Tonkin Gulf Resolution is passed by Congress, authorizing military action in Vietnam and committing the United States to eleven more years of war. In the spring, the University of California at Berkeley shuts down for two months amid antiwar rallies, sit-ins, and violence between students and police. During the Mississippi Freedom Summer, a thousand white college students go to Mississippi to help local residents register voters for a new wing of the Democratic Party, the Mississippi Freedom Democratic Party. Six volunteers and locals are murdered by the Ku Klux Klan. Congress passes the Civil Rights Act, which is shepherded through Congress by Kennedy's successsor, Lyndon B. Johnson. Soviet leader Khrushchev is replaced by Leonid Brezhnev. In October, China detonates its first nuclear bomb. Johnson wins the November presidential election.

1965

Civil rights leader Malcolm X is assassinated on February 21. In March intense bombing of North Vietnam begins, and ground troops leave for Vietnam. Cesar Chavez, agricultural trade union leader, announces a boycott of California grapes.

1966

The National Organization of Women (NOW) is formed, with Betty Friedan as its first president. The Black Panthers is founded in Oakland, California.

1967

The Six-Day War begins in Israel on June 5, as Israel is attacked by several Arab states. The Human "Be-In" in San Francisco and the "Summer of Love" mark the high point of the hippie movement. In October enormous antiwar protests mount, with tens of thousands of people demonstrating in Washington, D.C.

1968

On January 30 the North Vietnamese launch a mass attack on the South referred to as the Tet Offensive. On March 16, in the My Lai Massacre, American troops massacre a village of Vietnamese women and children. In late March, President Johnson withdraws from the upcoming presidential race. On April 4 pacifist civil rights leader Martin Luther King Jr. is assassinated by a white racist in Memphis, Tennessee, where King had gone to lend support to a sanitation workers' strike. The Columbia University campus erupts in violence in April as students strike and institute a sit-in and are dragged out by police as reporters televise the events. Robert Kennedy is assassinated in Los Angeles, California, in June 1968. The Nuclear Non-Proliferation Treaty is signed on July 1. The August Democratic Convention in Chicago is the site of mass conflict between student activists and police. In September feminists protest the Miss America competition. Richard Nixon defeats Hubert Humphrey in the November presidential election.

1969

On July 20, Neil Armstrong lands on the moon. In June gay men resist police attempts to arrest them in a bar in New York's East Village, and the resulting Stonewall Riots mark the beginning of the gay rights movement. In July, Nixon announces his doctrine holding that in the future, Asian countries must defend themselves rather than rely on U.S. protection. He had already begun withdrawing U.S. troops from Vietnam and beginning the "Vietnamization" of the war. The first Chicano National Conference is held in Denver to lobby for civil rights and promote cultural separatism from white America. In November, discussions toward the Strategic Arms Limitation Talks (SALT) begin.

1970

On April 22 Earth Day is celebrated by over 20 million Americans. The Environmental Protection Agency (EPA) is established. On April 30, Nixon announces the expansion of the Vietnam War to Cambodia. In early May, National Guardsmen kill four students at Kent State and injure nine others during a nonviolent protest of Nixon's decision to invade Cambodia. A few days later, amid racial tensions, police kill two African American students at Jackson State University after firing into a women's dormitory.

1971

On July 15, Nixon announces plans for a historic visit to the People's Republic of China. In August, China joins the United Nations. The *Pentagon Papers* are published, detailing the government's covert involvement in Vietnam.

1972

In February, Nixon visits China. On May 26, Nixon and Soviet premier Aleksei Kosygin sign SALT I. On June 17 a break-in occurs at the Democratic Party headquarters at the Watergate Hotel in Washington, D.C. On November 7, Nixon defeats George McGovern in the presidential election. In late

December the heavy "Christmas" bombing of North Vietnam begins.

1973

In January the Watergate burglars are convicted by U.S. district judge John Sirica and receive stiff sentences in the hope that they will provide information about the break-in. On January 27 a peace agreement is signed with North Vietnam. The war continues, but American troops are steadily withdrawn. The Watergate Committee begins televised hearings on the affair on May 17. Both East and West Germany enter the United Nations in June. A group of Arab countries launches a surprise attack on Israel on October 6, the Yom Kippur fast day. Despite initial heavy losses, with strong American support Israel succeeds in defeating its attackers. The United States signs a truce with North Vietnam, and attempts are made to conclude the war. An Arab oil embargo is instituted, resulting in acute energy shortages. The Supreme Court decides in *Roe v. Wade* that abortion is legal during the first trimester and is permissible during the second trimester for medical reasons. The American Psychiatric Association renounces their position that homosexuality is deviant behavior. Vice President Spiro Agnew is forced to resign, and Gerald Ford takes his place.

1974

On August 9, President Richard Nixon is forced to resign from office after he realizes that his impeachment and conviction are imminent due to his involvement in the Watergate affair. Ford takes over as president, with Nelson Rockefeller as his vice president.

1975

In April Cambodia falls under the control of the pro-Chinese Khmer Rouge, and large-scale genocide ensues. The last U.S. troops leave Vietnam. North Vietnam captures South Vietnam. On April 30 the North captures Saigon, and the country is unified under Communist control.

1976

Mao Zedong dies in September. In the November presidential election, Georgia governor and Democrat Jimmy Carter defeats Ford.

1977

Carter announces his focus on human rights as a fundamental international relations issue. In November, Egyptian president Anwar Sadat makes a historic visit to Israel.

1978

In April the United States agrees to return the Panama Canal to Panama. At Camp David, during the weeks of September 5–17, Carter brokers a peace treaty between Israel's Menachem Begin and Egypt's Sadat. In October, Begin and Sadat share the Nobel Peace Prize. In December, Vietnam invades Cambodia.

1979

The United States and China establish diplomatic relations. In January the Shah of Iran, Mohammad Reza Pahlavi is overthrown by Shi'ite fundamentalists headed by the Ayatollah Khomeini. Another oil crisis ensues. In February, China invades Vietnam in retaliation for Vietnam's invasion of Cambodia. On March 28 rods overheat at the nuclear energy plant at Three Mile Island, Pennsylvania, and a major nuclear disaster is narrowly averted. At the Vienna summit in June, Carter and Soviet premier Brezhnev sign SALT II, an arms limitation treaty. On November 4 sixty-six Americans are taken hostage at the American embassy in Iran by Islamic fundamentalists. Thirteen of the hostages are quickly released, but the remaining fifty-three are held for fourteen months. On December 27 the Soviets invade Afghanistan and install a new president.

1980

In January, Carter shelves SALT II in response to the Soviet takeover of Afghanistan. The Carter Doctrine is announced in late January, stating that the United States will use force to protect its oil interests in the Persian Gulf region. On April 24 a U.S. attempt to rescue the hostages from Iran fails, and eight American soldiers are killed. In July the United States and forty other nations boycott the Moscow Olympic Games. In November, California governor Ronald Reagan defeats Carter and is elected president.

1981

The hostages being held in Tehran are freed after 444 days on January 20. In April the United States withdraws its funding of the Nicaraguan Contras. On October 6, Egypt's President Sadat is assassinated.

1982

In June a massive antinuclear demonstration takes place in New York. Soviet premier Leonid Brezhnev dies on November 10 and is succeeded by Yuri Andropov.

1983

Reagan announces to the nation his plans for the Strategic Defense Initiative (SDI) in a televised address on March 23. Arab terrorists bomb the U.S. embassy in Beirut, Lebanon, killing sixty-three people. The Soviets shoot down Korean Air flight 007 after it wanders off course and into Soviet airspace. The Soviets believe it to be a disguised spy plane. On October 23, 241 American soldiers are killed when a suicide bomber drives into their barracks in Beirut. U.S. forces invade Grenada on October 25, and depose its Marxist regime.

1984

Soviet leader Yuri Andropov dies on February 9 and is replaced by Constantin Chernenko, who is also old and sick. In April the human immunodeficiency virus (HIV) is determined to cause AIDS. In June the U.S. Senate cuts off all U.S. aid to the Contras in Nicaragua. In July the Soviets and their satellites boycott the Los Angeles Olympic Games. Reagan is reelected in November, defeating Walter Mondale.

1985

On March 11, Mikhail Gorbachev becomes general secretary of the Communist Party and premier of the USSR. In late November, Gorbachev and Reagan meet in Geneva.

1986

In January the space shuttle *Challenger* explodes, killing the crew of seven. In February, Gorbachev calls for reforms in the USSR. On April 26 a reactor at the Chernobyl nuclear power plant in Ukraine, USSR, explodes, killing thirty-one and forcing massive evacuations. In October, Reagan and Gorbachev meet in Reykjavik, Iceland, and discuss arms reductions, but no agreement is reached. In November the press reveals details of the Iran-Contra affair.

1987

The Iran-Contra hearings begin on May 5. In December, Reagan and Gorbachev agree to massive reductions in nuclear missiles.

1988

Gorbachev announces in February that Soviet troops will withdraw from Afghanistan. In May, Reagan visits Moscow. George Bush is elected president in November, defeating Michael Dukakis.

1989

In February the Soviets withdraw from Afghanistan. In March the *Exxon Valdez* oil tanker spills millions of barrels of oil into Alaska's Prince William Sound. On March 26 the USSR allows non-Communists and former dissidents to run for office in the Congress of People's Deputies. In May, Lieutenant Colonel Oliver North is convicted for his leading role in the Iran-Contra affair. On June 3 and 4, troops kill and injure thousands of prodemocracy protesters in Tiananmen Square, Beijing, China. In June, Poland holds free elections, voting out the Communist Party. In July, Gorbachev announces that the countries of Eastern Europe can hold elections. Within the next few months, Czechoslovakia and Romania become independent from the USSR. In October huge demonstrations occur throughout East Germany. On November 9 the Berlin Wall falls, as East Germany opens its borders in a last-ditch effort to survive. The hated wall is immediately destroyed by jubilant crowds. In December, Panamanian dictator Manuel Noriega is captured by U.S. forces. On December 25, Romanian dictator Nicolai Ceausescu and his wife, Elena, are executed.

1990

On February 11, Nelson Mandela, the leader of the African National Congress, is released from prison on Robben Island after nearly thirty years of captivity. In March, Lithuania declares its independence. In August the United States sends troops to the Middle East after Iraq invades Kuwait. On October 3, Germany is united. In mid-October, Gorbachev receives the Nobel Peace Prize. At a large summit meeting of world leaders between November 18 and 21, UN military forces are reduced and the Charter of Paris is signed, officially terminating the cold war.

1991

In January and February the United States wages war on Iraq in order to force Iraq's withdrawal from Kuwait. On July 1 the Warsaw Pact, which binds the Soviet satellites to Moscow, is dissolved. In August a group of hard-line Communists attempt—and fail—to take over the Soviet government. Boris Yeltsin, a high-level former Communist Party member comes to power, and the Communist Party is officially jettisoned. On December 25, Gorbachev resigns. On December 31 the Union of Soviet Socialist Republics is ended, and the country splinters into fifteen small republics.

FOR FURTHER RESEARCH

COLD WAR HISTORY

S.J. Ball, *The Cold War: An International History, 1947–1991*. London: Arnold, 1998.

A.W. DePorte, *Europe Between the Superpowers: The Enduring Balance*. New Haven, CT: Yale University Press, 1979.

Melvyn Dubofsky, *Imperial Democracy: America Since 1945*. Englewood Cliffs, NJ: Prentice-Hall, 1983.

John Gaddis, *Strategies of Containment*. Oxford, UK: Oxford University Press, 1982.

————, *We Now Know: Rethinking Cold War History*. Oxford, UK: Oxford University Press, 1997.

Gabriel Kolko, *Main Currents in Modern American History*. New York: Harper and Row, 1976.

Michael Kort, *The Columbia Guide to the Cold War*. New York: Columbia University Press, 1998.

GENERAL AMERICAN HISTORY SINCE 1945

Hugh Brogan, *Longman History of the United States of America*. New York: Longman, 1985.

William H. Chafe, *The Unfinished Journey*. New York: Oxford University Press, 1986.

Gary Gerstle, *American Crucible: Race and Nation in the Twentieth Century*. Princeton, NJ: Princeton University Press, 2001.

Philip Jenkins, *A History of the United States*. New York: St. Martin's Press, 1997.

Paul Johnson, *A History of the American People*. New York: HarperCollins, 1997.

Arthur S. Link and William A. Link, *The Twentieth Century: An American History*. Arlington Heights, IL: Harlan Davidson, 1983.

Walter T.K. Nugent, *Modern America*. Boston: Houghton Mifflin, 1973.

Thomas C. Reeves, *Twentieth-Century America: A Brief History*. New York: Oxford University Press, 2000.

Norman L. Rosenberg and Emily S. Rosenberg, *In Our Times: America Since World War II*. Englewood Cliffs, NJ: Prentice-Hall, 1987.

Frederick F. Siegel, *Troubled Journey: From Pearl Harbor to Ronald Reagan*. New York: Hill and Wang, 1984.

Joseph M. Siracusa, *The Changing of America: 1945 to the Present*. Arlington Heights, IL: Forum Press, 1986.

Lawrence S. Wittner, *Cold War America: From Hiroshima to Watergate*. New York: Praeger, 1974.

Allen Yarnell, ed., *The Postwar Epoch: Perspectives on American History Since 1945*. New York: Harper and Row, 1972.

THE SOVIET UNION

Jonathan Eisen, *The Glasnost Reader*. New York: Penguin, 1990.

John Gaddis, *Russia, the Soviet Union, and the United States*. New York: McGraw-Hill, 1990.

Michael J. Sodaro, *Moscow, Germany, and the West from Khrushchev to Gorbachev*. Ithaca, NY: Cornell University Press, 1990.

Robert Strayer, *Why Did the Soviet Union Collapse?* Armonk, NY: M.E. Sharpe, 1998.

Joseph L. Wieczynski, *The Gorbachev Encyclopedia*. Salt Lake City: Charles Schlacks, 1993.

THE POSTWAR PERIOD AND THE 1950S

Griffin Fariello, *Red Scare: Memories of the American Inquisition: An Oral History*. New York: W.W. Norton, 1995.

Alonzo L. Hamby, *Beyond the New Deal: Harry S. Truman and American Liberalism*. New York: Columbia University Press, 1973.

Allen J. Matusow, *Joseph R. McCarthy*. Englewood Cliffs, NJ: Prentice-Hall, 1970.

Douglas T. Miller and Marion Novak, *The Fifties: The Way We Really Were*. New York: Doubleday, 1975.

THE 1960S

Alexander Bloom and Wini Breines, eds., *"Takin' It to the Streets": A Sixties Reader*. New York: Oxford University Press, 1995.

David Farber, *The Age of Great Dreams*. New York: Hill and Wang, 1994.

David Farber and Beth Bailey, *The Columbia Guide to America in the 1960s*. New York: Columbia University Press, 2001.

Edward P. Morgan, *The 60's Experience: Hard Lessons About Modern America*. Philadelphia: Temple University Press, 1991.

James A. Nathan, ed., *The Cuban Missile Crisis Revisited*. New York: St. Martin's Press, 1992.

THE 1970S

Stephen E. Ambrose, *Nixon*. New York: Simon and Schuster, 1989.

Allen J. Matusow, *Nixon's Economy: Booms, Busts, Dollars, and Cents*. Lawrence: University of Kansas Press, 1998.

Stephen Paul Miller, *The Seventies Now: Culture as Surveillance*. Durham, NC: Duke University Press, 1999.

William Appleton Williams et al., eds., *America in Vietnam*. Garden City, NY: Anchor Press/Doubleday, 1985.

THE 1980S AND THE END OF THE COLD WAR

Larry Berman, ed., *Looking Back on the Reagan Presidency*. Baltimore: Johns Hopkins University Press, 1990.

David Boaz, ed., *Assessing the Reagan Years*. Washington, DC: Cato Institute, 1988.

Peter Duignan and Alvin Rabushka, eds., *The United States in the 1980s*. Stanford, CA: Hoover Institution on War, Revolution, and Peace, 1980.

Sean M. Lynn-Jones and Steven E. Miller, eds., *The Cold War and After: Prospects for Peace*. Cambridge, MA: MIT Press, 1993.

INDEX